# CHRIST ACROSS THE GANGES

# CHRIST ACROSS THE GANGES

## Hindu Responses to Jesus

## Sandy Bharat

BOOKS

Winchester, UK
Washington, USA

First published by O Books, 2007
O Books is an imprint of John Hunt Publishing Ltd., The Bothy, Deershot Lodge, Park
Lane, Ropley, Hants, SO24 0BE, UK
office1@o-books.net
www.o-books.net

Distribution in:

UK and Europe
Orca Book Services
orders@orcabookservices.co.uk
Tel: 01202 665432 Fax: 01202 666219 Int. code (44)

USA and Canada
NBN
custserv@nbnbooks.com
Tel: 1 800 462 6420 Fax: 1 800 338 4550

Australia and New Zealand
Brumby Books
sales@brumbybooks.com.au
Tel: 61 3 9761 5535 Fax: 61 3 9761 7095

Far East (offices in Singapore, Thailand, Hong Kong, Taiwan)
Pansing Distribution Pte Ltd
kemal@pansing.com
Tel: 65 6319 9939 Fax: 65 6462 5761

South Africa
Alternative Books
altbook@peterhyde.co.za
Tel: 021 447 5300 Fax: 021 447 1430

Text copyright Sandy Bharat 2007

Design: Sandy and Jael Bharat. Cover: Detail from the ceiling of the Shri Jalaram
Mandir (Hindu temple) in Leicester, UK, depicting founders and important figures of
the major world faiths.

ISBN-13: 978 1 84694 000 2
ISBN-10: 1 84694 000 1

A CIP catalogue record for this book is available from the British Library.

Printed by Maple Veil Press.

'All things are possible, O Mother, through Thy grace;
Obstacles mountains high Thou makest to melt away.
Thou home of Bliss! To all Thou givest peace and joy.'
*Song from The Gospel of Sri Ramakrishna*

This book is dedicated to Swami Dayatmananda
Of the Ramakrishna Vedanta Centre UK
For all his support and encouragement
When the project first began.
Thank you Swamiji.

# Contents

*Devotions in the sacred Ganga (river Ganges)*

# PREFACE

For readers new to Hinduism, these two brief but succinct introductions might be helpful. The first is from Sarvapelli Radhakrishnan, a great writer, thinker and former President of India.

> While fixed intellectual beliefs mark off one religion from another, Hinduism sets itself no such limits. Intellect is subordinated to intuition, dogma to experience, outer expression to inward realization. Religion is not the acceptance of academic abstractions or the celebration of ceremonies, but a kind of life or experience. It is insight into the nature of reality (*darshana*), or experience of reality (*anubhava*). This experience is not an emotional thrill, or a subjective fancy, but is the response of the whole personality, the integrated self to the central reality.[1]

K L Seshagiri Rao, chief editor of the Encyclopedia of Hinduism, soon realized in his university teaching career that "students had to be taught first what *Hinduism is not*, before teaching them what *Hinduism is*."

> Hinduism is not a founded religion. There is no single person whose life and ministry started Hinduism; there are many seers and sages who have contributed to the tradition, but none of them is regarded as its founder. It has no beginning in history; no single historical event marks its birth. Actually, Hindus hold that Truth has no beginning and no end; that is why it is called *sanatana dharma*, eternal religion. Hinduism is not a 'creedal' religion. There is no creed that regulates Hindu beliefs.... Hinduism is not a missionary religion; proselytization has no place in Hinduism....Nor is it a dogmatic religion. It is a religion based on experience and realization....Hinduism is not an ecclesiastical religion. Hindus have never been an organized church body. Although there is a place in the tradition for congregational worship practices, the Hindu community, as a whole, does not belong to any church nor does it accept any ecclesiastical head as the sole spokes-person for the whole community....The aim of Hindu sages has been to illumine faith in its various forms and consolidate values, and not to condemn or destroy any particular form of faith or worship. Hinduism has practiced an

---

[1] S Radhakrishnan, *The Hindu View of Life*, Unwin, London, 1988, p 13. All Radhakrishnan quotes in the Preface are from this book, made up of the Upton Lectures, delivered in 1926 at what is now Harris Manchester College, Oxford, and originally published in 1927.

approach of harmony *(samanvaya)* and reconciliation *(samadhana)* towards different sects within and outside the tradition. Truth is one, paths are many.[2]

In this book, the designation 'Christ' is used far more than the name Jesus because Hindus have generally responded to Christ rather than Jesus, with some significant exceptions. The historical Jesus of the Christian quest is almost entirely missing from and irrelevant to Hindu reflections so 'Christ' seems better to represent this absence also. For Hindus, the historical quest seems immaterial. As Radhakrishnan wrote, " It is no more necessary to dissect Hinduism than to open a tree to see whether the sap still runs."

What is the difference between Jesus and Christ? Jesus was the historical prophet who lived at a certain time, in a certain place, touched the lives of many and whose teachings are recorded in a variety of documents. A Church that gradually developed as his earthly representative has officially sanctioned some of these. The title Christ - meaning 'anointed one' - may include Jesus but is much more. Compare it with the title Buddha or 'enlightened one.' There is certainly more than one Buddha, even if the title is most popularly associated with the historical person, Gautama. Even if there was no Jesus of history, the teachings reveal a high wisdom, 'come down to earth.' They exist. It is through them and through direct spiritual experience that some Hindus love the Christ incarnation, one among many that they know and love. As one Hindu Yogi, Paramahansa Yogananda, explained:

> There is a difference of meaning between Jesus and Christ. Jesus is the name of a little human body in which the vast Christ Consciousness was born. Although the Christ Consciousness manifested in the body of Jesus, it cannot be limited to one human form. It would be a metaphysical error to say that the omnipresent Christ Consciousness is circumscribed by the body of any one human being.[3]

Some of the most significant contributions to this book can be found in the Appendices, in responses to recent questions and to a Questionnaire devised in 1994. Do read them – they are only at the back of the book due to their size. You will find them valuable resources, addressing the theme with insight, diversity and depth.

The most readable form of transliteration for Sanskrit words is used without any diacriticals etc. In some instances, explanations of Sanskrit words and certain theological terms are given in the text. They are also italicized the first time they are used. This means they are in the Glossary. The definitions of

---

[2] K L Seshagiri Rao, 'Hindus in America and the Emerging World Culture,' paper presented to Symposium 'Hindus in America and the Emerging World Culture,' organized by the Sri Venkatesvara Temple, Pittsburgh, and sent to author, August 2005.
[3] Paramahansa Yogananda, *Autobiography of a Yogi*, Self-Realization Fellowship, Los Angeles, USA. P 144

words in the Glossary are generally not precise dictionary versions but my own understandings. This may often be more 'popular' than 'classical.' Quite often, due to transliteration, the same word may be spelt in various ways, for example, Sanatan, Sanatanan, Sanatana Dharma. The meaning remains the same.

Naturally, in a book this size, only an introduction is possible to the many Hindus who have reflected on Jesus and Christ. The Bibliography and Resources should be helpful in following up any particular interest.

There are many quotes in this book. I prefer to let the wise souls included speak for themselves as much as possible, though this has not precluded some occasional comment by the author!

# Acknowledgements

I first began this work, many years ago, but was unable then to complete it. I finish it now, in a different way, grateful to all who supported me along the way.

I start with thanks to my friend and fellow student 'back then,' Dr Helen Fry. She dreamed with me how to continue our studies after we completed our Theology degrees at Exeter University and has become an accomplished editor, author and active participant in Jewish-Christian dialogue and localized Jewish history.

The staff at Exeter University were also very special – our inspiring Prof, David Catchpole, our lively and lovable supervisor, Ian Markham, and our kindly and linguistically talented tutor, Alastair Logan. The departmental secretary, Sally O'Shea, cannot be omitted. She provided a space in the Theology corridor where she not only battled through her heavy workload but helped years of students with their battles. She once remarked that Helen and I had become part of the departmental furniture!

My family – Glen, Sarah and Steven - were very supportive and gave me the space needed when I needed it. My mother helped too, looking after the children and letting me stay with her when necessary, close to the university.

The Spalding Trust made getting started at all possible with grants for fees and books, many now in the Exeter University Library. Other trusts gave help too, for which I was and am grateful.

Brijmohan Thapar in India gave me access to books that I would not otherwise have known. My thanks to him for opening and sustaining that source. I retain a fond memory of his arrival in Oxford once with a suitcase almost heavier than himself, full of books!

Someone who must be remembered is Swami Dayatmananda. The love and support from Swamiji and the whole sangha at the UK Ramakrishna Vedanta Centre in Bourne End is one of the principal reasons why I now finish what was so long ago begun. This book is dedicated to Swami.

My appreciation includes Marcus Braybrooke and Karan Singh for their contribution of Forewords to this book. Both are eminent interfaith activists and people of deep faith, examples for us all.

Pranams to all who responded to questions and requests: Sita Ram Goel, Swami Dayatmananda, Bibhuti Yadav, Mathoor Krishnamurti, Seshagiri Rao, Arun Gandhi, Ravi Ravindra, Anantanand Rambachan, K R Sundararajan, Keshav Sharma, Shaunaka Rishi Das, Jay and Seetha Lakhani, Kalyansri Dasgupta, Dena Merriam, Rob Sidon, Manoj Das Gupta, Swami Vimalananda, Hiten Bhagtani, Atreyee Day, Vikram Seth, Ramola Sundram, Marianne Marstrand, Basana Ranja Halder, Asaf Hussain, Vijay, Vinod Sreedhar and Gwyneth Little. Beautiful people.

Ravi, Arun, Mathoor, Shaunaka, Seshagiri, Jay, Dena, Swamiji, and Atreyee – with thirteen others – have also contributed reflections on special spiritual inspirations in their lives to Sandy and Jael Bharat (Eds), *Touched by Truth: A Contemporary Hindu Anthology* (Sessions of York, 2006). Others are included in the one hundred and five contributors to Sandy and Jael Bharat, *A Global Guide to Interfaith: Reflections from around the world* (O-Books, 2007).

My grateful thanks to all organizations and publishers that so generously and sweetly gave permission to quote from their publications and websites. Every effort has been made to ensure that no one has been omitted and that specific instructions have been followed.

Gwyneth Little deserves a second mention for coming up with the photo for the cover! My gratitude to Swami Prabuddhananda of the Vedanta Center of Northern California for use of the Yogi Christ image on the page facing the Introduction. Carol Jordan supplied the beautiful picture from Self-Realization Fellowship gardens on P133. The Ganges photos (opposite the Copyright page and P210) are from Steve Evan's impressive collection at www.flickr.com. Suniti Kumar Basu supplied the photo of Swami Dayatmanada. The lotus clip art came from www.wisegorilla.com. Most Oms are from the Himalayan Academy collection – although the one below is Jael's own creation! Thanks to everyone mentioned for these enhancing images.

John Hunt, the publisher, is a wonder! So are those who endorsed the book and gave me feedback, especially Ramesh Kallidai and Bob Traer.

To my Gurudev, Paramahansa Yogananda, I am forever indebted. Jai Guru.

Finally, to all un-named friends and colleagues who directly or indirectly have made this book possible, thank you.

Oh yes, one special person remains to be mentioned. Thanks Jael, for everything.

*www.spiritualityfordailylife.com*

# FOREWORD BY KARAN SINGH

One of the major problems that humanity faces as it moves into the future astride the irreversible arrow of time is the continuing conflict and confrontation that is still taking place in the name of religion. Our earlier assumption that religious fanaticism would gradually subside and disappear with the growth of globalization and economic development has been belied. Indeed over the last few decades the growth of fundamentalist activities, accompanied by wanton acts of violence and terrorism, constitute a major challenge to thinking men and women around the world, regardless of their religious affiliations.

In this context the interfaith movement, with which I have been associated now for several decades, assumes special significance. This movement, which could be said to have begun with the First Parliament of the World's Religions in Chicago in 1893, has over the last eleven decades been striving to bring together people of different religious persuasions in a creative dialogue set in a harmonious background. While several such global meetings and parliaments have been held, I often get the feeling that they tend to preach to the converted and that the message of interfaith harmony is not spreading around the world as effectively as it should.

In this background, a creative dialogue between various religions is of the essence. India has a unique tradition of multiple religious pluralism. Four of the world's great religions – Hinduism, Jainism, Buddhism and Sikhism – were born in India, and five others – Christianity, Zoroastrianism, Judaism, Islam and the Bahai Faith – have come to us from the West and have flourished here for many centuries. The interaction between these religions and Hinduism has not always been peaceful. With Christianity, for example, the Inquisition in Goa was not a happy chapter. Nonetheless, there have been benign interactions also which have produced such remarkable Christian scholars as Father Bede Griffiths and my good friend Raimundo Panikkar. After the advent of the British there was a lively interaction between Christianity and the Hindu social reform movement, which substantially impacted each other.

In her well-researched book, Sandy Bharat has studied in depth some of the Hindu encounters with Christ. Jesus represents a powerful spiritual focus, and I never miss the opportunity to visit Saint Peter's Cathedral whenever I happen to be in Rome, the latest occasion being a few months ago. This flows from my belief in the Vedantic tradition based upon the Rig Veda dictum – *Ekam sat viprah bahudha vadanti* – The Truth is one, the wise call it by many names.

This book is part of the growing literature on the interfaith movement, and will be of value to students both of Hinduism and Christianity. One can only hope and pray that despite the negative factors, the process of dialogue and the attempt to genuinely understand the foundations of the world's religions will continue to grow, so that even though each one of us will continue to follow our own religious tradition we will be able to approach the others with a positive mindset.

Delhi, September 2005

---

DR KARAN SINGH was born heir-apparent to the Maharaja of Jammu and Kashmir. In 1949, at the age of eighteen, he was appointed Regent and was Head of State thereafter for eighteen years as Regent, elected Sadar-i-Riyasat and as Governor. In 1967, he was inducted into the Union Cabinet by Shrimati Indira Gandhi. He held important Cabinet portfolios of Tourism and Civil Aviation, Health and Family Planning, and Education and Culture. His appointment as India's Ambassador to the United States was warmly welcomed by both countries.

He was awarded a Ph.D. by the University of Delhi for his thesis on the Political Thought of Sri Aurobindo. He has been Chancellor of Jammu and Kashmir University and Benaras Hindu University, President of the Authors' Guild of India, the Commonwealth Society of India, and the People's Commission on Environment and Development; Chairman of the Temple of Understanding, a global interfaith organization; Member of the Club of Rome, the Club of Budapest, and the Green Cross International. He was a four-time Member of the Lok Sabha and a Member of the Rajya Sabha since 1996. He is Chairman, Ethics Committee of the Upper House of Parliament, Chairman, Governing Board of the Auroville Foundation, Chancellor of the prestigious Jawaharlal Nehru University, and President of the Indian Council for Cultural Relations, having rank equal to Central Cabinet Minister.

Karan Singh has written many books and has lectured on political science, philosophy, education, religion and culture, in India and abroad. He is recognized as one of India's outstanding thinkers and leaders.

# FOREWORD BY MARCUS BRAYBROOKE

Hindu responses to Jesus Christ have been summarized by a number of Christian writers, but it is valuable to have an account that is written from a Hindu perspective. Sandy Bharat, with her wide reading and personal contacts, allows us to hear what Hindu thinkers have actually said and she puts their remarks in context. She includes a wide range of Hindu teachers from the eighteenth century right up to the present day.

Despite often strong criticism of those Christian missionaries who denounced Hinduism and continuing resentment of efforts to convert Hindus, most of the Hindu spiritual teachers discussed in the book have shown a reverence for Christ. Few have been interested in the Western quest for the historical Jesus, but most have been attracted by Jesus' teaching, especially the Sermon on the Mount, and by his example of forgiveness. Swami Vivekananda said, "I pity the Hindu who does not see the beauty in Jesus Christ's character." Christian talk of 'atonement' has usually seemed incomprehensible to Hindus, who have also rejected claims for the uniqueness of Jesus. Usually, Hindu spiritual leaders – especially if they were appealing to Western audiences - have recruited Christ to support their own message, arguing that his true teaching, which has been distorted by the Church, was essentially the same, in Swami Sivananda's words, "as the Voice of the Vedas and the Upanishads." Hindu spiritual leaders, therefore, have fitted Christ into their existing way of thinking. Only a few professors of religious studies, who are Hindus, have really tried to appreciate what Christians themselves believe about Jesus.

This raises the question whether a person of one faith can ever really enter into and appreciate another faith, which Sandy Bharat, who has deep experience of interfaith dialogue, discusses. My own view is that just as some people are bi-lingual, so some scholars can gain a deep appreciation of another religion while others will draw on aspects of another faith to enrich their personal pilgrimage.

Some Christians resent what they consider Hindu distortions of Christian belief – just as some Hindus have been critical of Christians, such as Fr Bede Griffiths, who at his Christian ashram adopted some of the language and rituals of Hinduism. But the great spiritual teachers are a gift to the whole of humanity not the possession of their followers. Just as many Christians have been deeply inspired by Mahatma Gandhi, a Hindu, so many Hindus have found divine wisdom in the teaching and example of Jesus Christ.

There is much to learn from Sandy Bharat's important book. I hope it will encourage many Christians and Hindus to enter into a deeper dialogue with each other. This will surely bring them spiritual enrichment and be a sign of hope in a divided world.

Oxford, September 2005

REVD DR MARCUS BRAYBROOKE is a retired Anglican parish priest, living near Oxford, England. He has been involved in interfaith work for over forty years, especially through the World Congress of Faiths, of which he is now President. He is a Co-Founder of the Three Faiths Forum, Patron of the International Interfaith Centre at Oxford and a Peace Councillor.

In September 2004, he was awarded a Lambeth Doctorate of Divinity by the Archbishop of Canterbury in recognition of his contribution to the development of inter-religious co-operation and understanding throughout the world.

His many books include *A Heart for the World: the Interfaith Alternative, Pilgrimage of Hope, Faith and Interfaith in a Global Age, Time to Meet, How to Understand Judaism, What We Can Learn from Hinduism,* and *Christian-Jewish Dialogue: The Next Steps.* He has also written *Learn to Pray* and *365 Meditations for a Peaceful Heart and a Peaceful World* and has edited several anthologies of prayers and meditations, including *1,000 World Prayers* and *Life Lines.*

Marcus is married to Mary, a social worker and a magistrate. They have a son and a daughter and six granddaughters.

(JESUS CHRIST IN HIS YOGA POSTURE.)

'HE WAS THERE IN THE WILDERNESS....
AND WAS WITH THE WILD BEASTS.' S.MARK I 13.

*Jesus through Hindu eyes*

# INTRODUCTION

Why are Hindus interested in Jesus Christ? Is Jesus or Christ the focus of Hindu interest? Has Hindu interest changed Christology for Christianity or Christians in any meaningful way? What is an *avatar*? How did the Jewish Jesus, the Jesus Christ of Christianity, become a Hindu avatar? Did he really make this transition or was it just historical expediency in the face of colonialism? How are contemporary Hindu 'avatars' relating to Jesus? These are some of the questions explored in this book.

As the most popular Hindu understanding of Jesus has been as an avatar, it might be helpful to begin with some illustrations on the nature of avatars. Like all religions, Hinduism is a living family of beliefs and practices, adjusting itself to each generation in order to stay fresh and relevant. Underpinning all is the *Sanatan Dharma*, the eternal religion or unchanging Truth, the term Hindus prefer for their faith, rather than the western label of 'Hinduism.' Contemporary Hinduism is a mix of both Sanatan Dharma and historically evolving religion. This mix has influenced recent use of the term 'avatar.'

Traditionally there have been ten historical avatars – though more are given in the *Puranas* - with one still to come, the *Kalki* avatar, described by Professor Seshagiri Rao as one who "has to deal, among other things, with the conflict of religions, and give a constructive direction to the forces of history in the interfaith realm."[1] An interfaith avatar, an avatar for all faiths!

In Hindu spiritual circles, of recent centuries at least, there are far more avatars than those traditionally (or scripturally) recognized: many *gurus* are claimed by their followers to be avatars. When the Kalki avatar comes it will be a challenge not only to all faiths but even to Hindus to accept 'the' one. Maybe there will be a better understanding then of the Christian *problem*![2]

So what is an avatar? Briefly it is God who has descended, who 'comes down' into human form for a human lifetime. R K Pandey reveals a little more:

> The prophet descends in history very much a mortal human being. But it would be a mistake to think that he is just an ordinary man. By virtue of

---

[1] Seshagiri Rao, Letter to author, 7 April 1994.
[2] Christian exclusivist claims that Jesus is the ONLY saviour certainly causes problems for those of other faiths - and for quite a few Christians as well!

the charismatic power, the Kala, vested in him, he occupies an extra-
ordinary place in history…he is the inaugurator of the historical process.
As such he is himself outside history. History has not made him what he
is. On the contrary, it is the avatar that makes history. In the Hindu
myths the divine incarnations have always been considered a-historical
and eternal. But, in so far as his birth is a descent, a coming-down
process, he has to assume the human or animal form.[3]

And why does such a one descend to our world? The *Bhagavad Gita* gives a
well-known reason why. Lord *Krishna* says: "In every age I come back, to
deliver the holy, to destroy the sin of the sinner, to establish righteousness."[4]
Paramahansa Yogananda comments:

> This earth is a stage whereon a divine drama is being evolved.
> Whenever the majority of human actors misuse their God-given
> freedom, and by the creation of evil bring suffering and upset the divine
> plans concerning their fellow beings and their own destiny (plans
> intended to be carried out by man's proper use of free choice), then
> God, the Cosmic Director, appears on the stage in a human form (an
> avatar) to instruct the amateur thespians in the proper art of living. God
> thus teaches man, made in His image, how to evolve by using free will,
> manifesting the divine nature inherent in the human nature.[5]

Avatars can be full or partial manifestations of Divine Reality, depending on
their accomplishments and level of realization. A full or *purna* avatar has been
described as having the following special *kalas* or divine qualities: omni-
presence, omnipotence, omniscience, and the powers – past, present and future
- to create, preserve, dissolve, dispense *anugraha* (grace) and have knowledge
of all previous existences.[6] This may help you decide who fits where! Perhaps
the fruits of each incarnation are the best indicators.

Sometimes this aspect of 'primary' and 'secondary' can open up a competitive
streak! Some devotees can create problems, cause mischief, through their
attachment to one particular manifestation and their translation of this into
'better than' all others, a clearly destructive and divisive process completely
against the holistic vision of every true avatar. When I first realized myself as
a Hindu in this life, this process was one of the biggest disappointments to me.
A few of the Hindus I met were aggressively ambitious about the superior
nature of their own teacher or Guru. This seems to be a troublesome tendency
in religiously inclined people, whatever their persuasion.

[3] R K Pandey, *The Concept of Avatars*, BR Pub Corp, Delhi, 1979, pp 45-6.
[4] Swami Prabhavananda and Christopher Isherwood, trans, *Bhagavad-Gita: Song of God*, Chapter IV,
Phoenix House Ltd, London, 1947.
[5] Paramahansa Yogananda, *God Talks With Arjuna: The Bhagavad Gita: Royal Science of Self-Realization*,
Self-Realization Fellowship, Los Angeles, U.S.A. P 439.
[6] Helen Cuerdon, *Sai Baba - A Christian's Story*, Global Services Publishing, India, 2001, pp 165-6.

Avatars come to give us the right example, to set us back on the right paths to realize our own divinity, to lift us up to where they have come from: the Godhead, the Real, the Source and meaning of all. There is often the suggestion that avatars are not the products of spiritual evolution but direct manifestations of God, direct from God. However, there does seem to be an evolutionary process in the lives of many of those (non-mythical) personalities considered to be avatars. They grow in realization, or at least remembering, through the latest life, and also often recall previous lives. Whatever the classical understandings of avatar, it might, for many of us, be most helpful and therefore legitimate, to think of them as Self-realized beings that have evolved to full divinity. By their example they offer us a model for our own growth or at least reveal to us that it is possible, if we make the effort.

Avatars come to help by reminding us who we are. They do not come to mediate between God and us. They come to make us free, not only from our bad habits and ignorance, but also from the need for avatars, religion and all dependencies. As previously indicated, perhaps one of the greatest mistakes we can make about avatars is to become attached to and focused on their historical personalities, to think of them as this Jesus or that Buddha, Krishna or *Rama*. Better to focus on the life-changing soul attributes they reveal to us and which we must personally imbibe. Then their missions can be fulfilled and our lives reveal their full significance.

Following chapters will reveal more Hindu thought on avatars and how Hindus have included Jesus in that category. Some Hindus are uncomfortable with this (for example Goel and Yadav) while, for others, it is as natural as thinking of Krishna or Rama in this way.[7] It may provide some Christians, uneasy with the exclusive Christ of their church, with a more satisfying way of thinking about Jesus, significant but not superior. Some devotees (Christian and Hindu) have thought of Jesus as guru or yogi. An avatar can be both or either of these. As very little is known about the historical Jesus, the transcendental aspect of his nature must dominate almost any category of thought about him. Whether Jesus existed or not and, if he did, how he thought about himself – rabbi, healer, revolutionary, messiah, Son of God – is not certain but the naming of him as a spiritual influence cannot be denied as the passing centuries have shown. 'Avatar' encapsulates this experience, whatever outward form is then taken.

Major Hindu individuals and organizations active in the west will be studied to see if Jesus now plays any role in Hindu life and faith. The Indian context will also be examined to understand the history and extract the current thinking on

---

[7] For responses from Sita Ram Goel and Bibhuti Yadav, see Chapters 6 and 7 respectively and Appendix 1B.

avatars and Jesus. Finally, Hindu reflections on Christ will be assessed to see if they have any significance for others.

The study as a whole concentrates only on Hindu attitudes to Jesus and the relationship Hindus form with him within a Hindu spirituality. For much of the text I am only an editor, preferring to use the language of those included as much as possible. Of course, only a sample of Hindu responses to Christ can be included here. If you are interested, there is much more to discover. Here, we begin the story of Jesus through Hindu eyes with the first encounters between Hindus and Christians in India.

CHAPTER I

# THE COLONIAL CHRIST

*Even an enemy must be offered appropriate hospitality, if he comes to your home.*
*A tree does not deny its shade to the one who comes to cut it down.*
*- Mahabharata, XII, 374*

INTRODUCTION

This chapter focuses on the first known meetings between Hindus and Christians in India and the gradual development of exchanges between them up to the end of the 19th century CE.[1] Our primary Hindu guide for the first part of this exploration is Sita Ram Goel. As far as I am aware, he is one of very few Hindu writers to have studied the available texts and to have proffered Hindu perspectives on these initial contacts.[2] His reflections are not for the Christian faint-hearted!

Christian mission was then, as now, often targeted at poor and illiterate villagers and accompanied by inducements of material and educational advancement, rarely delivered. Aggressive tactics were also employed – the destruction of Hindu shrines, denigration of Hindu practices – to help persuade the doubters. The missionaries of this period were not concerned with the Jewish-ness of Jesus. Theirs was the confident Christ of Christendom, a colonial Christ, a reflection of their own racial and cultural superiority. There was no real dialogue, only a series of encounters.

During the 18th century records begin to show an evolution, from encounter to dialogue, not yet between equals with authentic listening but primarily for self-interest: Christians wanting more conversions and realizing that a better understanding of Hinduism would assist this aim; Hindus becoming more confident of their own traditions and their ability to resist the lures of conversion. There seems to be no clear impression that these early dialogues transformed their participants into greater respect and comprehension of each other's beliefs.

Gradually the position shifted, from Christian dominance, backed up by all the resources of an Empire, to renewed Hindu self-esteem. This was stimulated by

---

[1] CE stands for Common Era (Jewish and Christian). It is used instead of the solely Christian AD.
[2] Sita Ram Goel, *History of Hindu-Christian Encounters*, Voice of India, Delhi, 1989. Sita Ram Goel was one of the first Hindus to study the history of Hindu-Christian encounter and dialogue in India. He offers a defined Hindu perspective, highly polemical of the motives and methods of Christian missionaries. For Goel, Christian soldiers for Christ continued the *dawah* (proselytization) of Islamic colonisers.

re-examination and re-emphasis of Hindu resources in the light of criticism; the *inculturation* of Jesus into a Hindu framework; and a growing nationalist confidence that led inexorably towards independence.

We can now look in some greater detail at this process, starting with the arrival of Christians on Indian soil.[3]

THE EARLIEST ENCOUNTERS (TO THE 18TH CENTURY)

The first meeting between Hindus and Christians on Indian soil might be traced back to 52CE and the purported arrival of the Apostle Thomas in Malabar. There is a strong Christian faction in Southern India but its origins are shrouded in myth and conjecture and there is no certainty about Thomas' arrival in India. Radhakrishnan and others, both Hindu and Christian, have detailed such evidence as there is which is, however, beyond the scope of this book.[4]

Early Christian travelers in India seem to have had an extremely negative response to the Hinduism they encountered, unable to see beyond its outer symbols, which were anathema to them. They left testimonies to the horrors they found: monstrous and devilish idols worshipped by the indigenous people. However, it was not a completely one-sided situation as revealed by Gonçalo Fernandes, a Portuguese high official in the sixteenth century. Witnessing Christian missionaries active in India he wrote:

> I do not know where else can be found such a vile clergy and friars as come here. I say this on account of the wicked deeds which they commit, their ignorance of their duties, their knavery in the confessional, and the contaminated beastly, filthy and dissolute life of many of them…which is scandal alike to the faithful, catechumens and non-Christians.[5]

In 1542 Frances Xavier arrived in India with fellow missionaries. Goel describes the written records of this period as "the most painful reading in the

---

[3] Short extracts, in modified form, from chapters 1, 2, 3, and 4 were published in *Dialogue and Alliance*, Fall / Winter 1998, Vol.12 – No.2.

[4] See S Radhakrishnan, *Eastern Religions and Western Thought*, Clarendon Press, Oxford, 1939; Ian Davie, *Jesus Purusha*, Lindisfarne Press, USA, 1985; P J Marshall, Ed, *The British Discovery of Hinduism in the 18th Century*, CUP, 1970; Ram Swarup, *On Hinduism: Reviews and Reflections*, Voice of India, Delhi, 2000, Chp 8. It is a well-established Hindu belief that Jesus was in India during the 'missing' years not recorded in the Christian Testament; that it was here that he learnt the yogic practices that he later employed to survive the crucifixion, returning to India after his 'resurrection;' that he is now buried in Kashmir where his shrine is attended by Hindus and Sufis. In 1945, Paramahansa Yogananda said, "The parallelisms of Christ's teachings with Yoga-Vedanta doctrine strongly supports the records known to exist in India which state that Jesus lived and studied there during fifteen of the unaccounted-for years of his life." See Paramahansa Yogananda, *Man's Eternal Quest*, Self-Realization Fellowship, Los Angeles, U.S.A. P 285.

[5] Letter of 1510 quoted in A M Mundaran, *History of Christianity in India*, Vol. 1, Church History Association of India, Bangalore, 1984, p 514.

history of Christianity in India."[6] Xavier is classed as the pioneer of mass forced conversions, the destroyer of Hindu temples and religious practice, progenitor of serious abuse of Hindu peoples to persuade them of the one true faith. The Christian historian, T R de Souza, lists the various ways in which Xavier and his fellow Christians put across their message of salvation in Christ: Hindu priests were banished, Hindu rites banned, temples were destroyed, idols smashed, certain employment was denied to Hindus, Hindu orphans were brought up by the Christian state, and Hindus had to periodically attend church to listen to refutation of their religion.[7]

Thekkedath also provides material for this period, exposing Christian mission as flawed. He describes how the residents of Kanniyakumari, a fishing village in southern India (now famous for Vivekananda's Rock), asked the Portuguese for baptism, primarily to gain their protection. Xavier baptized them, giving only a brief explanation of the Christian faith. However, if the villagers later "failed" as Christians, pressure was exerted on them by confiscation of their boats, refusal of permission to fish etc. Also, after mass baptisms of this kind, the village temple was usually destroyed and its 'idols' smashed.[8]

Whilst convert numbers soon swelled, the accompanying commitment to Christianity was not forthcoming so that, in 1606, Robert Di Nobili, a Jesuit, put on ochre robes and presented himself as a Brahmin. Goel does not regard this as authentic or acceptable, whether practiced by Di Nobili or later adherents - thinking perhaps of Bede Griffiths or Henri le Saux - despite the high respect often accorded them by Christians.[9] There would surely be uproar, even now, if a Hindu swami arrived in Rome, changed his ochre cloth for the white robes of a Benedictine monk, set up a monastery, attracted followers, and then offered up the daily mass to the Lord - Lord Krishna! With regard to Di Nobili, Goel has no doubt – "a truly ethical criterion would dismiss him as a plain and simple crook."[10]

Similar accounts illustrate Christian mission policy at this time. There was no dialogue. Force was used where persuasion failed. Even when a new and startling admission emerged in 1651, in a book by a Dutch missionary,

---

[6] Sita Ram Goel, *History of Hindu-Christian Encounters*, Voice of India, Delhi, 1989, pp 6 -7.
[7] Sita Ram Goel, *History of Hindu-Christian Encounters*, pp 10 -14. T R de Souza quoted in M D David, Ed, *Western Colonialism in Asia and Christianity*, Himalaya Publishing House, Bombay, 1988, p 18.
[8] J Thekkedath, *History of Christianity in India*, Vol. 2, Church History Association of India, Bangalore, 1982, p185.
[9] See especially the lively exchange between Bede Griffiths and Swami Devananda Saraswati in the *Indian Express* during 1987, partially chronicled in 'Sannyasins or Swindlers?', Sita Ram Goel, *History of Hindu-Christian Encounters*, revised and enlarged edition, 1996, p 386f. Also featured in Goel, *Catholic Ashrams*, see 10 below. The Christian, Bettina Baumer, wonders if such adoption is honest or if it could be seen as a kind of "spiritual theft." See Tosh Aria and W Ariarajah, *Spirituality in Interfaith Dialogue*, World Council of Churches, Geneva, 1986, p 37.
[10] Sita Ram Goel, *History of Hindu-Christian Encounters*, Voice of India, Delhi, 1989, p 14. The "masquerade" of Robert de Nobili is described in detail in Sita Ram Goel, *Catholic Ashrams*, Voice of India, Delhi, 1988.

Abraham Rogerius, that some Hindus actually did have some concept of a Supreme Being and so did evidence a suggestion of natural theology, there was no consolation as, of course, this was brought into focus only by the revelation of Christ.[11] Was this an embryonic kind of what is now known as 'anonymous' Christianity? This is a fairly recent theology, Catholic in origin, claiming that other faiths do have some saving graces but only through the unseen blessings of Jesus Christ. For those not Christian, this seems the most disgraceful theological position possible, denuding all other religions of their own unique spiritual insights, revelations and saviors.

However, the purpose of this chapter is not to assess the theological rights or wrongs of the situation but to present events, as far as possible, from a Hindu perspective and to keep in mind how these early negative Christian responses to Hinduism have influenced some Hindu responses to Christianity.

THE BEGINNING OF HINDU-CHRISTIAN DIALOGUE (18TH AND 19TH CENTURIES)

Tentative dialogue between Hindus and Christians began to appear in written records in the 18th century. These indicate a movement away from encounter between non-equals towards a deepening Christian interest in Hinduism, often in order to facilitate meaningful and lasting conversion. They also show evolving Hindu responses to Christianity as something that can be competed with and countered, part of a renewed sense of nationalism and pride in indigenous Indian traditions.

The German Lutheran missionary, Bartholomaeus Ziegenbalg, active in India from 1696, wrote letters to various Hindu *Brahmins* inviting their responses to a number of questions. He sent a booklet, *Abominable Heathenism*, with these letters describing Hinduism as a state of ignorance with five primary sins: idolatry, fornication, fraud, quarrel, witchcraft and laziness.[12] Despite this unattractive invitation, Hindus did respond to Ziegenbalg. From 1715 onwards some of these returns were published whilst others were suppressed. The transcripts appear to show a first serious attempt, whatever the motives, to gain some insight into the beliefs held by Brahmins. However, even though these Brahmins issued proscriptions against killing any living creature, abuse of the senses, lies and fraud, as well as positive injunctions to develop pure worship, care for the poor and oppressed, they were, for Ziegenbalg, still "the greatest imposters in the world...there is not, perhaps, a more wicked race of men."

---

[11] Sita Ram Goel, *History of Hindu-Christian Encounters*, p18. Rogerius' book, *The Open Door to Secret Heathenism*, was published posthumously in 1651.

[12] Sita Ram Goel, *History of Hindu-Christian Encounters*, pp 21-2. B Ziegenbalg, *Thirty Four Conferences between the Danish Missionaries and Malabarian Brahmans (or Heathen Priests) in the East Indies*, trans. I B Phillips, London, 1719, p iii-iv. See also H Grafe, 'Hindu Apologetics at the Beginning of the Protestant Mission Era in India' in *Indian Church History Review*, June 1972, p 64.

The Brahmins' responses reveal this was not just a one-way polemic. They found much of the Christianity they received unacceptable, confused and illogical, inferior to the principles expressed in Hindu philosophy. Christians led unclean lives, were debauched and proud, engrossed in internal squabbles so that Indians did not know which group represented true Christianity. Christian doctrine also seemed illogical. Jesus' *ontological* stature did not appear consistent with his earthly life. Original sin and salvation through belief alone did not make sense alongside Hindu *karma* and *dharma* co-inherence. Eternal damnation for unbelievers was repugnant to those believing in the eventual *moksha* or spiritual emancipation of all.

By the early 19th century, India was a British colony and pressure was being exerted from England to open the country up to concentrated Christian mission. Parliament was won over and the gates to India were officially opened. In June 1813, William Wilberforce declared that, "Our religion is sublime, pure and beneficent. Theirs is mean, licentious and cruel."[13] Lord Hastings, writing in his diary on his arrival in India as Governor General, also in 1813, concluded, "The Hindoo appears a being nearly limited to mere animal functions…with no higher intellect than a dog or an elephant or a monkey might be supposed capable of attaining."[14] Similar depictions sprung effortlessly from official British lips at this time, arising from the sure conviction of the one true faith and its association with a superior nation and culture. There was, as yet, still no development of real dialogue, no sense of vulnerability before the other, no hesitation in pre-conceived certainty. Hindus, when asked, were responding to the primitive yet orthodox Christianity preached by most of the missionaries at this time. Missionaries were still armed with literalist interpretations of Christian belief.

Sanskrit soon became a new missionary tool, instigated by William Carey who, according to Goel, "wanted to train a group of Christian Pandits who would probe 'these mysterious sacred nothings' (ie. Sanskrit texts) and expose them as worthless." Although impressed with the language itself, Carey thought the texts "filled with nothing but pebbles and trash." These needed to be replaced by the "riches beyond all price" of Christian doctrine.[15] The naive belief seemed to be that it was the language and not what it expressed that attracted Indian hearts and minds.

Between 1839 and 1845, John Muir, a civil servant, also studied Sanskrit as a means to discredit Hinduism. He set out to "combat hydra-headed paganism" through his tract *Matapariksha*, a dialogue between a teacher and disciple.

---

[13] *Hansard* XXXVI, June 1813, 831-72.
[14] Diary of Lord Hastings, 2 October 1813. Sita Ram Goel, *History of Hindu-Christian Encounters*, p 33.
[15] Sita Ram Goel, *History of Hindu-Christian Encounters*, p 49. From Richard Fox Young, *Resistant Hinduism: Sanskrit Sources on Anti-Christian Apologetics in Early Nineteenth-Century India*, De Nobili Research Library, Indological Institute, University of Vienna, Vienna, 1981, p 34.

This lay down the criteria for true scripture which, unsurprisingly, Christianity alone fulfilled and by which Hindu sacred texts were proved false.[16] Subsequently he engaged, through written encounter, with three Hindu pandits: Somanatha, Goreh and Tarkapanchanana.

Somanatha was a pseudonym for a scholar named Subaji Bapu, who, through his work with an English orientalist, Lancelot Wilkinson, had come to know something of Christianity. He argued against Jesus' miracles as the grounds for being 'special' - miracles are elsewhere and by others attested. Christian universality he dismissed as uniformity unsuited to a plurality of races, cultures and personalities. Mission he found repugnant, as a religion could be more successful when praised as the best one for its own particular adherents. He believed that God had incarnated as the avatar Christ in order to deliver the theistic scripture needed at a particular time by a particular people.[17]

Takaparchanana, a Bengali Brahmin about whom nothing is known, brought out a short treatise against Muir that was also strongly against mission as Indians had experienced it. Force rather than free will was seen as the prod to conversion. Takaparchanana urged Christians to take up the tenets of Sanatan Dharma and so begin the march to *moksha* (spiritual liberation).[18] The fierce Christian reaction against this text is described by Goel as a "classical case of seeing the mote in the other man's eye while missing the beam in one's own."[19]

The third respondent, Goreh, was also stirred by distaste for the Christian mission of this time. He expounded a series of doubts about Christianity which, summarized, reject salvation through Christ alone when so many have not known him; question the justice of *atonement* theories; quibble over the sole validity of Jesus' miracles; express amazement at a just God who created evil; condemn Christianity's understanding of Hinduism as idolatrous; and sees great injustice in a one-life syndrome. He wondered how God could have created so many nations, innumerable generations, condemned by not knowing Christ, even though God had provided the remedy to save them. He wondered why Christians deny miracles affirmed by Hindus whilst Hindus accept the miracles of Jesus. He considered the denial of *transmigration*, the affirmation of atonement, and the hellish destinations so relished for non-Christians, unjust

---

[16] Sita Ram Goel, *History of Hindu-Christian Encounters*, p 51. Richard Fox Young, *Resistant Hinduism: Sanskrit Sources on Anti-Christian Apologetics in Early Nineteenth-Century India*, p 72.

[17] Somanatha, *Mataparikshasiksha*, 1839, 2.29-30.32. Quoted in Richard Fox Young, *Resistant Hinduism: Sanskrit Sources on Anti-Christian Apologetics in Early Nineteenth-Century India*, p 92.

[18] Harachandra Takaparchanana, *Mataparikshottara*. See Sita Ram Goel, *History of Hindu-Christian Encounters*, p 53; Richard Fox Young, *Resistant Hinduism: Sanskrit Sources on Anti-Christian Apologetics in Early Nineteenth-Century India*, p 93.

[19] Richard Fox Young, *Resistant Hinduism: Sanskrit Sources on Anti-Christian Apologetics in Early Nineteenth-Century India*, p 55.

and merciless. Further he found unreasonable a God who, through Christ, healed while incarnate but no longer does so despite the faith of believers.[20]

Jesus was not a central figure of these particular dialogues and encounters. He was not here hinduized in any way but received notions of him were rejected as both extreme and unlikely and just part of an illogical religion. Responses were based more on a negative response to Christian mission than a positive inclusion of Jesus. There is still, at this stage, more reactionary encounter and polemic than true dialogue, conditioned by the type of Christian theology asserted in India at this time and the limited awareness of those involved in the exchanges.

Muir himself became increasingly affected by his reading of Hindu scriptures through his further study of Sanskrit so that, gradually, he moved from evangelical certainty to a view that "Christian virtues are neither superior to others nor sui generis."[21] In 1879 he published a book attempting to combine Indian, Biblical and Greek literature, concluding that, "These sentiments and observations are the natural expression of the feelings and experiences of Universal humanity; and the higher and nobler portion of them cannot be regarded as peculiarly Christian."[22]

Some think these early encounters and dialogues gave birth to a Hindu renaissance as Hindus considered the Christian challenge to them. Of course, the idea of there being a renaissance or the need for one is highly contestable and belongs mainly to western ideas that there was something out-of-touch or even missing in Hinduism as revealed through encounter with Christianity. Whilst all religions evolve and develop through inter-action with others, it might be more appropriate to see, even as Muir began to realize, that the encounter with Hinduism led to a Christian renaissance!

In the south of India during this same period, the mid-nineteenth century, a variety of denominational missionaries were moving into the area intent on conversions. Regarding Hinduism, one Methodist missionary wrote home how he "never had so plain demonstration of depravity heathenism binds upon its votaries in the shape of religion....The principal pagoda abounds with the most obscene and polluting representations, and decidedly proves, if proof be necessary, how greatly this people need the hallowing light of Christianity."

[20] Goreh, *Shastratattvavinimaya*, 1844, 1.14-18. See Richard Fox Young, *Resistant Hinduism: Sanskrit Sources on Anti-Christian Apologetics in Early Nineteenth-Century India*, p 111.

[21] Sita Ram Goel, *History of Hindu-Christian Encounters*, p 63.

[22] Sita Ram Goel, *History of Hindu-Christian Encounters*, p 63; Richard Fox Young, *Resistant Hinduism: Sanskrit Sources on Anti-Christian Apologetics in Early Nineteenth-Century India*, pp 168-9. From John Muir, *Metrical Translations for Sanskrit Writers*, 1879.

Such people should receive the "tenderist pity" and missionaries should exert "all their means to rescue them from impending destruction."[23] Louis Rousslet, traveling in India in 1876, observed something of this 'tenderness.' He viewed the spectacle of a Protestant missionary projecting religious insults at his audience of respectful and attentive Hindus. Rousslet commented:

> Perhaps we should be disposed to admire the courage of the missionary if the well-known toleration of the Hindoos did not defraud him of all his merit; and it is this tolerance that most disheartens the missionary, one of whom said to me, our labours are in vain; you can never convert a man who has sufficient conviction in his own religion to listen, without moving a muscle, to all the attacks you can make against it.[24]

If your faith is strong, there is no fear in listening and every advantage if something new can be learnt that will enhance current knowledge or inspire devotion. Rousslet seemed to recognize the strong faith of the Hindus he saw that enabled them to withstand Christian attack and the weak faith of Christian missionaries who had to resort to denigration to make claims about their God of love!

DIALOGUE WITH THE BRAHMO SAMAJ

In 1828, some years before Rousslet's experience, Raja Rammohun Roy had founded the Brahmo Samaj. The organization is still active today, describing itself as a community of people who worship the one true God or *Brahma* in a spiritual rather than "idolatrous" way.[25] The fundamental principles of the Brahmo Samaj are:

> The unity of God, the inadequacy of worship through images, the centrality of reason in understanding God, the importance of service to others as the authentification of true religion, the primacy of direct experience of God, and the tolerance of true worshippers who recognised that all views of God were but partial.[26]

The Samaj eventually split into two parts, the original or Adi Brahmo Samaj of Rammohun, and the Brahmo Samaj that came to be led by Keshub Chunder Sen. Both Rammohun and Keshub had an engaged dialogue with Christianity so the focus here is on them.

---

[23] Sita Ram Goel, *History of Hindu-Christian Encounters*, p 72. Quote from S Manickam, 'Hindu Reaction to Missionary Activities in the Negapatam and Trichinopoly Districts of the Methodists, 1870-1920' in *Indian Church History Review*, December 1981, pp 84 and 82.

[24] Sita Ram Goel, *History of Hindu-Christian Encounters*, p 79. Louis Rousslet, *India and its Native Princes*, 1876, cited by Marie Louise Burke, *Swami Vivekananda in America*, Advaita Ashrama, Calcutta, 1958, p 145.

[25] For further information: www.thebrahmosamaj.org

[26] J N Pankratz, 'The Response of the Brahmo Samaj,' in Harold G Coward, Ed, *Modern Indian Responses to Religious Pluralism*, State University of New York Press, Albany, 1987, p 22.

*Rammohun Roy, 1772-1833*

Roy was born into an orthodox Brahmin family in 1772 in Bengal and has been described as the father of modern India. Rabindranath Tagore spoke of him as belonging to "the lineage of India's great seers, who age after age have appeared in the arena of our history with the message of Eternal Man."[27] He was one of the most influential Hindu figures of this era. His link with western Unitarians gave him access to a modern and liberal version of Christianity. Many of his perspectives were unknown to evangelical Christian missionaries then in India. Evangelicals, such as Joshua Marshman, were "greatly discomfited, being out of contact with developments in contemporary biblical criticism."[28]

Roy was a keen reformist. Although he was partly influenced by Unitarians, unlike them, he worked with two religious traditions - Christianity and Hinduism - comparing, reconciling them so that, eventually, some leading western Unitarians were disappointed at his distinctly Hindu orientation. In 1829, William Adam, a close associate of Roy's and a Unitarian missionary, wrote:

> There has been formed a Hindu Unitarian association, the object of which is, however, strictly Hindu and not Christian ie. to teach and practice the worship of the One Only God on the basis of divine authority of the Ved and not the Christian Scriptures. This is the basis of which I have distinctly informed Rammohan and my other native friends that I cannot approve.[29]

Jesus attracted Roy primarily as a moral teacher and his *Precepts of Jesus*, published in 1820, was a compilation of Jesus' moral teaching taken from the four gospels, omitting all references to his divinity, atoning death, miracles or prophecies. One reviewer, the "discomfited" Marshman, described Roy as "an intelligent heathen whose mind is as yet completely opposed to the grand design of the Saviour's becoming incarnate."[30]

Christian atonement theories puzzled Roy. How could those 'saved' be "equally with others liable to the evil effects of the sins already remitted by the

---

[27] 'Rammohun Roy, the path maker and luminous star in our hour of decadence,' Address delivered by Rabindranath Tagore as President of the Preliminary Meeting of the Rammohun Roy Centenary held at the Senate House, Calcutta, 18 February 1933.

[28] Richard Fox Young, *Resistant Hinduism: Sanskrit Sources on Anti-Christian Apologetics in Early Nineteenth-Century India*, p 64.

[29] Sophia Dobson Collet, *The Life and Letters of Raja Rammohun Roy*, Sadharan Brahmo Samaj, Calcutta, 1962, p 222.

[30] Sita Ram Goel, *History of Hindu-Christian Encounters*, p 35. Quote from introduction by Joshua Marshman, editor, to a review by Deocar Schmit of Roy's *The Precepts of Jesus* in *Friend of India*, a missionary magazine.

vicarious sacrifice of Jesus?"[31] Hinduism seemed on much more certain ground here. As for Jesus' miracles, if they were to be taken seriously (not Roy's position), then they could only be equated with similar acts attested in other scriptures and similarly verified by contemporary or near-contemporary witnesses. Some Christians regarded this as a perversion of the truth and an Englishman, once a friend of Roy, demanded a suitable reaction from his compatriots:

> Are you so degraded by Asiatic effeminacy as to behold with indifference your holy and immaculate religion thus degraded by having it planted in an equality with Hinduism, with rank idolatry, with disgraceful ignorance and shameful superstition? [32]

Neither could Roy accept Trinitarian theology. In correspondence with the missionary, Marshman, he questioned "whether it's consistent with any rational idea of the nature of deity that God should be appointed by God to act the part of a mediator by laying aside his glory and taking upon himself the form of a servant."

> Is [it] not most foreign to the nature of the most immutable God that circumstances could produce such a change in the condition of the Deity and that he should not only have been divested of his glory for more than thirty years but even subjected to servitude? [33]

Roy's reservations were not reserved for Christianity alone. At a time when Sanskrit texts were beyond the reach of most Indians and when their content, distribution and interpretation were the preserve of Brahmins, Roy began translating selections to counter the ignorance of his own people about their own scriptures, counter Christian missionaries' condemnation of Hinduism as false and of low moral content, and claim Jesus' moral concepts as essentially Hindu.

Rammohun, sympathetic to Jesus and many things British, finally proved allergic to much Christian theology. Perhaps, the best hope Christians had of infiltrating Hindu circles and securing a significant conversion was lost with the final defection of Roy from Christianity back to his Hindu roots. He was not one who could be confined within narrow theological borders. Whilst his defense of Hinduism endeared him to many of the people of India, Christians increasingly rejected him, feeling he had failed their expectations. He died in

---

[31] Rammohun Roy, *Padri Sisya Sambad*, 1823. Quoted in Richard Fox Young, *Resistant Hinduism: Sanskrit Sources on Anti-Christian Apologetics in Early Nineteenth-Century India*, pp 116-117n.
[32] Sita Ram Goel, *History of Hindu-Christian Encounters*, p 41, Sisir Kumar Das, *Shadow of the Cross: Christianity and Hinduism in a Colonial Situation*, Munshiram Manoharlal Pubs, Delhi, 1974.
[33] Sita Ram Goel, *History of Hindu-Christian Encounters*, p 41; Sisir Kumar Das, *Shadow of the Cross: Christianity and Hinduism in a Colonial Situation*, p 29.

Bristol and is buried there, having become ill during a visit to England as a guest of Unitarians.

*Keshub Chunder Sen, 1838-1884*

Sen was born in 1838 into a pious *Vaishnava* family. He joined the Brahmo Samaj in 1857, became joint secretary in 1859, and from 1860-1861 published tracts that attracted many young Bengalis to the society. Thereafter he formed a small group meeting at his house where western philosophy and religion were discussed, some of this group subsequently becoming Brahmo missionaries. Sen became an ordained Brahmo minister in 1862 but his reforms against orthodox Hinduism in 1866 caused a Samaj split. In the same year, his lecture, *Jesus Christ, Asia and Europe*, awakened fears that he might be about to convert to Christianity.

Sen recognized Jesus as an Asiatic and so best understood by Asians. In *Asia's Message to Europe*, 1883, he wrote, "The great religions are mine, saith Asia, and their founders are all my children."[34] This should foster brotherhood, not hostility, between Europeans and Asians.

> Behold he comes to us an Asiatic in race, as a Hindu in faith, as a kinsman and brother, and he demands your heart's affection....
> He will come to you as self-surrender, as the life of God in man, as obedient and humble sonship.[35]

Sen claimed that the doctrine of divine humanity was Hindu and that Christ's life and character exemplified the ideal Hindu life. Christ was the 'way' for every person, a means not an end. In Jesus "we see human nature perfected by true affiliation to the divine nature," the goal of all.[36]

> The Holy Ghost drags Christ-life into the hearts and souls of all men breathing and annihilating the sins of all ages, and making all mankind partakers of Divine life. And thus man after man is carried Christ-like into the father's home in heaven; and heaven is the grand and final purpose of creation filled.

Like Roy, Sen saw moral greatness in Jesus. This was grounded in the cross as a symbol of self-sacrifice, a supreme example which all must follow. In *India Asks: Who is Christ*, Sen explained that Jesus' total self-abnegation - 'I and my father are one' - reveals the end of Jesus' 'I.' He had become completely God-conscious, filled by divinity, and so revealed the spirit of God at work to

---

[34] K C Sen, 'Asia's Message to Europe.' See *Selected Writings of Brahmananda Keshav*, 150th Birth Anniversary Committee, Calcutta, 1990, p 65. See also, *Keshub Speaks*, Navavidhan Chittabinodini Trust, Bombay, 1975, p 12.

[35] K C Sen, *India Asks -Who is Christ?*, Indian Mirror Press, Calcutta, 1879. Lecture given in Calcutta Town Hall, April 1879.

[36] K C Sen, 'That Marvellous Mystery the Trinity,' Lecture, 21 January 1882.

others. "Christ wants complete self-sacrifice, a casting away of the old man and a new growth in the heart. The crucified Christ does not belong to him who is not prepared to crucify himself."

Jesus' commission from God is not one of Sonship but as a teacher of sonship to the rest of humanity. "I go to my Christ to learn what a son ought to be." The true sonship revealed by Jesus is made possible by the ongoing work of the Holy Spirit. "Thus God sends down his divinity into the world through the Son, that Divinity reproduced in millions is carried by the Holy Spirit back into its source in heaven."[37]

Sen resented Christian sectarianism, which he saw as both aggressive and against God's will. Christ was for all in a unity not uniformity. Christians should reconcile themselves to each other and to followers of Christ every-where in the true spirit of love. He argued against presenting Jesus as another avatar as this would swallow him up in Hindu 'superstition.' Regarding Hindu disciples of Christ, he argued, "Whether particular bodies of Christians would admit us into fellowship or not is problematical, but that Jesus, the Prince of Peace, includes us all in spite of our errors and transgressions, and Hindus though we are, in his vast scheme of reconciliation, even the most orthodox Christians cannot deny."[38]

He became increasingly syncretistic. In 1881 he replaced the bread and wine of the Christian Eucharist with rice and water, calling on Jesus to recognize this Hindu form of the sacrament. He also blended many symbols in other ceremonies, such as baptism and *Vedic* rituals. Sen moved towards a new universal religion with himself as its prophet, forming the Church of the New Dispensation. "Jesus claimed to be the King of the Jews, so am I ambitious of being crowned as king of the Indians - of the Bengalis at any rate."[39] In his tract, *We Apostles of the New Dispensation*, he expounded the purpose of the New Dispensation:

> It gives to history a meaning, to the action of Providence a consistency, to quarrelling churches a common bond, and to successive dispensations a continuity....Before the flag of the New Dispensation, bow ye nations and proclaim the Fatherhood of God and the Brotherhood of all men. In blessed eucharist let us eat and assimilate all the saints and prophets of the world....The Lord Jesus is my will, Socrates my head, Chaitanya my heart, the Hindu rishi my soul.[40]

---

[37] K C Sen, 'That Marvellous Mystery the Trinity.'

[38] K C Sen, 'Asia's Message To Europe.'

[39] K C Sen, Lecture, 'We Apostles of the New Dispensation,' Calcutta Town Hall, 1881 in David Kopf, *The Brahmo Samaj and the Shaping of the Modern Indian Mind*, Archives Publishers PVT, Delhi, 1988, p 274.

[40] K C Sen, 'We Apostles of the New Dispensation.' See also Sivanath Sastri, *History of the Brahmo Samaj*, Sadharan Brahmo Samaj, Calcutta, 1974, p 227f.

Sen passed away in 1884 after suffering from diabetes. Some years after his passing but still filled with the vivid memory of his visit to England in 1870, J Eslin Carpenter said of him: "Here was a voice of rare power, eloquence and charm. His dignified presence, the glow of faith in his face, his courage, his passionate sincerity, his conviction of the reality of the presence of God, all made a deep impression." Carpenter concluded, "When he bade England farewell he left behind in many hearts a clearer vision of the supporting power of the Everlasting Love."[41]

*The Brahmo Samaj Today*

I asked Dr Kalyansri Dasgupta, author and Samaj Minister, about the organization's relationship now with the ideas of Roy and Sen.[42] He replied:

> The Brahmo Samaj today, by and large, agrees with Roy, and does not believe in the infallibility of scriptures, the Trinity, the divinity of Jesus, or his power of working miracles. Keshub Sen, on the other hand, was far more influenced by Christ, and constantly referred to him in his preaching from the pulpit. But today, even the members of the Nababidhan Samaj, which he founded, do not relate to Christianity the way he did, and are more inclined to accept Rammohun Roy's views.

It has been some decades since the Samaj experienced difficulties from Christian mission so was the Samaj today primarily a Hindu Reform organization? Sri Dasgupta responded:

> All the seeds of universalism existed all along in Hinduism, especially in the Vedas and the Upanishads. They had, however, been eclipsed by mythology and the vested interests of the hierarchical priesthood. What Rammohun Roy did was to separate the wheat from the chaff, and remind India of the tremendous spiritual wealth that is contained in classical Hinduism. The Brahmo religion is, therefore, not reformed Hinduism, but 'reborn' Hinduism.

What are the primary spiritual legacies of Roy and Sen? Kalyan thought that Keshub Sen showed us "how to listen to God in one's own conscience, and how to worship Him with deep religious fervour" whereas "Roy was truly a universal man, and founded the first *universalist* church in India." Duncan Howlett's description of universalism is the best Kalyan has ever heard: "A process of testing, questing, and never resting." Today the universalist Samaj offers the world this relevant message, that "religion can never be static. It has

---

[41] Foreword, *Keshub Chunder Sen in England: Diaries, Sermons, Addresses, Epistles*, Writers Workshop Greybird Book, Calcutta, 1980, p v.

[42] All Kalyansri Dasgupta quotes from e-mail to author on 11 August 2005.

to constantly evolve, as it has done in the past. Otherwise we will become bigots."

THE ARYA SAMAJ AND CHRISTIANITY

In 1875, Swami Dayananda Saraswati founded the Arya Samaj in Mumbai as a Hindu reform organization based on the truth of the Vedas, against which all else was tested. The Ten Principles of the Arya Samaj state:

> God is the primary cause of all true science and of all that can be known through it.
> God is Existent, Intelligent and Blissful. He is Formless, Almighty, Just, Merciful, Unborn, Infinite, Unchallengeable, Beginningless, Incomparable, the Support and Lord of all, Omniscient, Imperishable, Immortal, Fearless, Eternal, Holy and the Maker of the universe. To Him alone worship is due.
> The Vedas are scriptures of true knowledge. It is the duty of all Aryas to read them, hear them being read and recite them to others.
> All persons should be ready to accept the truth and give up untruth.
> All action should be performed in conformity with Dharma, that is, after due consideration of the right and wrong.
> The primary aim of the Arya Samaj is to do good for all, that is, promote physical, spiritual and social well-being.
> All people should be treated with love, fairness and due regard for their merit.
> One should aim at dispelling ignorance and promoting knowledge.
> One should not only be content with one's own welfare, but should look for it in the welfare of others also.
> One should regard oneself under restriction to follow altruistic rulings of society, while all should be free in following the rules of individual welfare.

*Swami Dayananda Saraswati, 1824-1883*

Dayananda Saraswati was born into an affluent Brahmin family and became a fierce reformer for the emancipation of women and the abolition of caste systems. He became a renunciant when twenty four years old and practiced austerities before finding them deficient. "The conviction grew within him that his mission in life was to help others."[43]

Having founded the Arya Samaj, he applied the Vedic truth test to Hindu sects as well as to Christianity and Islam. He fiercely opposed the Brahmo Samaj for its pro-British stance, for its neglect of Hindu prophets while honoring Christian and Islamic ones, and for its denial of the truths from its own Indian

---

[43] 'Dayananda's Arya Samaj' in *Hinduism Today*, March / April 2001.

inheritance. Dayananda wrote of his own belief: "That alone I hold to be acceptable which is worthy of being believed by all men in all times." For him *Brahma* or the Most High was the Great God and the four Vedas were the Word of God.[44] On principle, he tried to read original sources when in debate with Christian missionaries and others. This only served to strengthen his belief in the eternal, universal truth of the Vedas, and even stimulated his use of *shuddhi*, ritual purification, to enable converts to return to the Hindu fold.

Dayananda's most famous book, *The Light of Truth*, is a comprehensive study ranging from "child-rearing, marriage and the science of government to the Vedic meaning of emancipation to detailed studies of other religions."[45] Chapter 13 of Swami's uncompromising book is reserved for Christianity.[46] Having studied Christianity, he found it totally flawed. As the Bible was not the Word of God it was not revelation, so Christianity, based on the Bible, was not a true religion.[47]

He found Jesus lacking in many respects, neglecting his parents and asking others to follow suit, against the Jewish commandment to honor father and mother. Jesus' call to mission and the family division entailed further high-lighted this flaw. His disciples were also found wanting through their lack of loyalty, and the usual claim against the injustice of Christian *soteriology* was maintained. Goel paraphrases Dayananda's shock that, "We are told that Jesus was the only Son of God and that nobody can reach God except by his recommendation. God is thus reduced to the status of a servant of Jesus."[48]

Dayananda taught that salvation was possible through social service and that working for this was a 'noble' cause. Arya Samaj means the Society of Noble People. Although he passed away in 1883, poisoned by someone unable to stand his sharp observations, his work continues through the many branches of the Arya Samaj around the world.[49] As one commentator remarked, suggesting high honor: "Dayananda is the only person that Vivekananda has described as 'great.'"[50]

---

[44] Dayananda Saraswati, 'Extracts from The Light of Truth' in Paul J Griffiths, *Christianity Through Non-Christian Eyes*, Orbis, New York, 1990, pp 202-203.
[45] 'Dayananda's Arya Samaj' in *Hinduism Today*, March / April 2001.
[46] Swami Dayanand on Christianity in *Light of Truth*: www.aryasamajjamnagar.org/chapterthirteen.htm
[47] J T F Jordens, *Dayananda Saraswati: His Life and Ideas*, OUP, Delhi, 1978, p 267. See also H G Coward, 'The Response of the Arya Samaj' in Harold G Coward, Ed, *Modern Indian Responses to Religious Pluralism*, State University of New York Press, 1987.
[48] Sita Ram Goel, *History of Hindu-Christian Encounters*, p 66. Translated and summarised from Dayananda Saraswati, *Satyarthaprakasha*, Delhi, 1975, pp 330-335. See also 46 above, English version of this work.
[49] For more information about the Arya Samaj, see www.aryasamaj.org
[50] Quoted by Rohit Arya: www.indiayogi.com/content/indsaints/dayanand.asp

## Swami Agnivesh and the Arya Samaj Today

The fierce reforming mission of Dayananda has been continued by one of the Samaj leaders today, Swami Agnivesh. He is passionate in the struggle against bonded labor in India and in the fight to free children from slavery and to create an equal society. He is as critical as the Samaj founder about aspects of Hinduism – ritualism and nationalism – and also about members of the Samaj who use shuddi in a way that perpetuates rather than helps abolish the caste system. For Agnivesh, "The caste-based system in Hindu society today is the worst thing that any society could have. This is the main reason for the downfall of our Hindu society. This is why Hindus are converting to Islam and Christianity."

Agnivesh's response to Christianity is more moderate than that of Dayananda. Indeed he is an active player in the global inter-religious arena. Many an interfaith meeting is lit up by his bright orange glow! Although he accepts "Swami Dayananda Saraswati, his life, mission and teachings, as guiding principles" he admits to broader influences, including "Jesus Christ, Mohammed, Buddha, Vivekananda, Gandhiji and Karl Marx."[51] Indeed Christians helped prompt his reforming zeal. When he taught at Saint Xaviers College in Calcutta from 1963 to 1968, he was impressed by the "dedication, simplicity of living and lifestyle of the staff, whether they were teachers or missionaries going out into the slums and helping the poor." Seeing this was one "real great motivation" in his becoming a swami. Now Agnivesh's reforming agenda includes justice for Christians in India. In an interview, he said, "To fight injustice whether it is against women, lower castes, or members of the Muslim and Christian minorities is to come closer to God….If God is truth and compassion, how can you not fight injustice?" He even recruits Christians to help him in his efforts to reform Hindu society.[52]

For Swami Agnivesh, the Vedas - the words of God, "books of knowledge for all humanity," eternal principles for all times and all places - are still at the heart of the Samaj. Reading them is dharma. "It is high time we stop things that divide human society in the name of religion. The dharma for one has to be the dharma for all." There has to be a paradigm shift away from religion, with all its vested interests, to spirituality. "One of the foremost needs in the Indian context today is to reform the very idea of religion. Our tragedy is that we have too much of religion and too little of spirituality. Religion without spirituality, especially in its social dimension, tends to be a system of oppression and exploitation." Although those wanting prestige and power can monopolize religion, spirituality belongs to everyone. In the final analysis, "He who gives a glass of water to quench the thirst of another is spiritually

---

[51] Interview in *Hinduism Today*, March / April 2001.
[52] Interview with Swami Agnivesh by Edward Luce, Financial Times, 10 July 2004.

more evolved than those who chant their scriptures with their eyes closed on the giant agony of our world."[53]

HINDU-CHRISTIANS

Some Hindus attracted by Christ's life and teachings during this seminal period did convert to Christianity. Two are briefly mentioned here. Most also still called themselves Hindu. Perhaps they were ahead of their time. Today it is quite religiously trendy to engage in bi-tradition spirituality! Most dual-religion participants now seem to be predominantly Christians who have brought a specific type of meditation technique or devotional practice from another religion into their existing religious framework and have done so to such a meaningful extent that both traditions have to be acknowledged. This may create theological conundrums for some but does not seem to impede the experience itself, though for the early pioneers mentioned here it was certainly a choice that carried with it serious social implications and intense spiritual challenges.[54]

*Pratap Chandra Mozoomdar, 1840-1905*

Mozoomdar was one of the participants at the first Parliament of the World's Religions in Chicago in 1893 and author of *The Oriental Christ*.[55] He believed that a Hindu Church of Christ avoided all Christian sectarianism and that Jesus, separated from Christianity, could work naturally with Hindus. He depicted Jesus as unbounded love and grace, not theology, formalism and force. There is constant contrast between the Christ of Mozoomdar's vision and that received by him from Christian missionaries in India. He felt that the western Christ was an "elaborately learned man, versed in all the principles of theology."

> His doctrine is historical, exclusive, arbitrary, opposed to the ordinary instincts and natural commonsense of mankind....He continually talks of blood and fire and hell. He considers innocent babes as the progeny of deadly sin. He hurls invectives at other men's faith, however truly and consciously held. No sacred notions are sacred to him, unless he has taught them....Wherever he goes men learn to beware of him.

---

[53] Swami Agnivesh, 'Social spirituality.' http://www.swamiagnivesh.com/social.htm.

[54] Bi-tradition spirituality is not always, if ever, easy. I remember the anguish of the Benedictine monk, Henri Le Saux later known as Swami Abishiktananda, as shown in the beautiful documentary video, *Swamiji*, when, during one period of his life, he realised he could no longer be just the Catholic he once was and yet would also never be fully accepted as a Hindu sannyasi. At that moment, he just wanted to die. He also spoke of the problem of wanting to 'name' the divine experience instead of just being it.

[55] Sita Ram Goel, *History of Hindu-Christian Encounters*, pp 95-96. Goel depicts Mozoomdar in a purely negative contrast to Vivekananda, also a participant at the first Parliament of World Religions. He relates an incident at the Parliament when the missionary, J Murray Mitchell, having selected Mozoomdar as the "real representative" of "advanced and intelligent Hindus" was disappointed that he did not "draw the applause he deserved because of his admiration for Christianity."

However, the eastern Christ was "simple, natural…a stranger to the learning of books."

> His sentiments are the visions of a heaven in which all…are united in love. His doctrines are the simple utterances about a fatherhood which embraces all the children of men, and a brotherhood which makes all the races of the world one great family. His every word is a revelation.[56]

## Brahma Bandhab Upadhyaya, 1861-1907

Upadhyaya was a convert to Christianity who yet remained a Hindu and he published a journal, *Sophia*, to establish reconciliation. He was a key player in the movement for India's independence and died whilst in prison on charges of sedition. During his life, he was influenced by many contemporary figures, including Keshub Sen and Swami Vivekananda. This is how he described his religious identity:

> By birth we are Hindus and shall remain Hindu till death. But as Dviji (second born) by virtue of our sacramental rebirth, we are Catholic, we are members of an indefinable communion embracing all ages and climes….In short we are Hindus so far as our physical and mental constitution is concerned, but in regard to our immortal souls we are Catholics. We are Hindu Catholics.[57]

Rabindranath Tagore described Upadhyaya as a "Roman Catholic ascetic yet a Vedantin - spirited, fearless, self-denying, learned and uncommonly in-fluential." Julius Lipner adds to the praise by referring to him as "Christian and Hindu, holy man and savant, prophet and revolutionary." He believes that Upadhyaya's life leaves us with many questions, still relevant today: "How narrow must our religious labels be? How open to hyphenated religious identities should we become? What is the scope for religious dialogue in a religio-culturally divisive world?"[58]

SUMMARY

Early Hindu inculturation of Jesus seems to have been primarily a response to aggressive Christian mission and anti-Hindu polemic. As Hindus were already used to Islamic colonial 'persuasion' they were also able to adapt to the new combination of British colonial rule and Christian mission. A unique strategy was used, one that has enabled Hinduism to survive all conditions: Jesus was absorbed into Hinduism - hinduized and removed from his Christian context.

---

[56] Sisir Kumar Das, *Shadow of the Cross: Christianity and Hinduism in a Colonial Situation*, p 141. Quotes from P C Mozoomdar, *The Oriental Christ*, George H Ellis, Boston, 1883, pp 42-46.
[57] Hans Staffner, *The Significance of Jesus Christ in Asia*, Gujarat Sahitya Prakash Anand, India, 1984, p101
[58] Julius J Lipner, *Brahmabandhab Upadhyay: The Life and Thought of a Revolutionary*, OUP, Delhi, 1999, p 385.

During this period, Hindus began to relate themselves to Christian challenges, causing internal splits as well as creative reformation. Christian challenges were more than just religious as they were accompanied by a colonial power, threatening the very fabric of Hindu society. Hindus increasingly became aware of the clear link between perceived western religious and racial supremacy, and between Christianity and imperialist power, important factors in early Hindu responses to Jesus. "The Hindu intellectual slowly realised that Christianity was linked up with European civilisation - it was linked up with the power that ruled India."[59]

By the end of the nineteenth century, it had become clear that many factions of Hindu society in India were awakened to a need, understood variously, to counter the kind of Christianity being experienced and epitomized in this statement:

> A people agonisingly conscious of long political subservience dread the possibility of coming under the religious dominance of the West. Yet it would appear that in their inmost consciousness they are aware of the supremacy of the claims of Christ. In resisting it they are compelled to be on the defensive and cling to the untenable argument that Hinduism should be sufficient for the Hindu.[60]

This Hindu awakening resulted in an emerging patriotism and religious resurgence. Defensive days were coming to an end and major new figures were filling the horizons to prove indeed that Hinduism was sufficient for the Hindu - and perhaps also for many of those whom it was soon to meet on western soil.

Christians too became more appreciative of what a real dialogue could offer them. Stanley Jones, a Christian missionary from this period, refers to growing Indian self-confidence and increasing Christian sensitivity on Indian soil.[61] He was positive about the ways some Hindus inculturated Jesus, separating him from Christianity and British imperialism, and he saw in it new life for the Christian community. This "may mean that at this period of our racial history the most potentially spiritual race of the world may accept Christ as Christianity…may restore the lost radiance of the early days when he was the centre, and may give us a new burst of spiritual power."

The old methods of mission had proved counter-effective, had shown up the flaws in received Christianity, had led to a resurgence of Hindu identity and even nationalism. Jones quotes Tagore, stating that, "When missionaries bring

---

[59] Sita Ram Goel, *History of Hindu-Christian Encounters*, p 41; Sisir Kumar Das, *Shadow of the Cross: Christianity and Hinduism in a Colonial Situation*, p 29.
[60] G V Job, P Chenchiah et al, *Rethinking Christianity in India*, A N Sundarisanam, Madras, 1938.
[61] Stanley Jones, *The Christ of the Indian Road*, Hodder and Stoughton, London, 1955.

their truth to a strange land, unless they bring it in the form of homage, it is not accepted and should not be." He demonstrates his willingness to de-culturise the westernized Christ to reveal the Christ of the Indian Road. He gives an example of how Indians were already doing this for themselves, re-interpreting Christ in the light of their own spiritual insights:

> Nine years ago in the National Congress at Poona a Hindu gentleman in addressing the Congress used the name of Christ. There was such an uproar and confusion that he had to sit down unable to finish his speech. That name of Christ stood for all that India hated, for he was identified with empire and the foreign rulers. He had not yet become naturalised upon the Indian Road.

But in the meantime:

> A disassociation of Jesus from the West had been made, so that nine years later when that same National Congress met, the Hindu president in giving his presidential address quoted great passages from the New Testament...there were some seventy references to Christ in that Congress.

From this book's perspective, the most globally significant figure of this period, to the end of the 19th century CE, was Sri Ramakrishna Paramahansa. It is probably true to say that he, with his disciple, Swami Vivekananda, influenced western perceptions of Hinduism in such a way, with such potency, that the whole Hindu-Christian encounter might have been radically different, depleted, without them. Because of their significance the whole of the third chapter is dedicated to Sri Ramakrishna and the development of the Ramakrishna Mission. Together they have contributed more reflections on Jesus as Christ the avatar than any other Indian spiritual movement.

With the advent of Sri Ramakrishna came the genesis of a new Hindu-Christian interaction in India. From this evolved a changed and developed response to Jesus from within some parts of the Hindu community.

In the next chapter, Hindu contributions to this new exchange will be explored. We look at eminent Hindu figures whose thinking on Jesus perhaps influenced as many Christians as Hindus. With these great teachers there is no hint of convertibility, though with one of them, Gandhi, maybe there was, for a while, some Christian hope of it!

CHAPTER II

# THE INCULTURATED CHRIST

Where the mind is led forward by thee into ever-widening thought and action
Into that heaven of freedom, my Father, let my country awake.

*- Rabindranath Tagore*

INTRODUCTION

The focus of this chapter shifts to some significant figures of the early to mid 20th century. Each of them contributed to western perceptions of modern Hinduism and each had some influence on Hindu conceptualizations of Jesus, primarily as a Christ figure. All wrote about or experienced this Christ in an including way without diminishing or apologizing for the Hindu context into which he was received. Each of them spoke with authority. They are Sri Aurobindo Ghose, Mohandas Gandhi, Sarvapelli Radhakrishnan, and Swami Sivananda.

AUROBINDO GHOSE, 1872-1950

Rabindranath Tagore, great Indian poet, philosopher, and Nobel Prize winner, introduces us to Sri Aurobindo in this way:

> At the very first sight I could realize he had been seeking for the Soul and had gained it, and through this long process of realization had accumulated within him a silent power of inspiration. His face was radiant with an inner light....I felt the utterance of the ancient Hindu Rishis spoke from him of that equanimity which gives the human Soul its freedom of entrance into the All. I said to him, 'You have the word and we are waiting to accept it from you. India will speak through your voice to the world....O Aurobindo, accept the salutations from Rabindranath.'

Sri Aurobindo Ghose was born in West Bengal in 1872. He was educated partly in England and on returning to India became a civil servant. As he began to study Indian culture, he was drawn into the political struggle for India's independence. In 1908 he was arrested on a charge of sedition. During his imprisonment he had several spiritual experiences that changed him so that, on his release, he began a life devoted to spiritual writing and living.

One afternoon as I was thinking streams of thought began to flow
endlessly and then suddenly these grew so uncontrolled and incoherent
that I could feel that the mind's regulating power was about to cease....
I called upon God with eagerness and intensity and prayed to Him to
prevent my loss of intelligence. That very moment there spread over my
being such a gentle and cooling breeze, the heated brain became
relaxed, easy and supremely blissful such as in all my life I had never
known before. Just as a child sleeps, secure and without fear, on the lap
of his mother, so I remained on the lap of the World-Mother.

It was during his imprisonment that he was visited and inspired by Swami
Vivekananda. The visit was a spiritual one as Vivekananda had already passed
away. Sri Aurobindo told how the Swami taught him matters previously unknown to him and which, from the life accounts of Vivekananda, Swami had
also not necessarily known during his lifetime. "Vivekananda came and gave
me the knowledge of the intuitive mentality. I had not the last idea about it at
that time. He too did not have it when he was in the body. He gave me detailed
knowledge illustrating each point. The contact lasted about three weeks and
then he withdrew."[1] When asked if this kind of teaching transmission was
usual, Sri Aurobindo replied, "Why not? That is traditional experience from
ancient times. Any number of Gurus give initiation after their death. But I had
another direct experience of Vivekananda's presence when I was practicing
Hathayoga. I felt this presence standing behind and watching over me. That
exerted a great influence afterwards in my life."[2]

Sri Aurobindo is, perhaps, best known for his system of integral yoga, a
synthetic philosophy influenced by Vedanta but incorporating eastern and
western thought, that seeks a total transformation and "reconciliation of matter
and mind, mind and spirit, finite and infinite, God and Man."[3] He passed away
in 1950 leaving Mirra Alfassa, a French woman known as the Mother, in
charge of his community and philosophical transmission.

Sri Aurobindo's legacy includes not only volumes of profound writings on
diverse topics, now gathered together as the Sri Aurobindo Birth Centenary
Library and the Collected Works of Sri Aurobindo, but also many institutions:

> The Sri Aurobindo Ashram in Pondicherry is a spiritual community in
> which about 1500 disciples of Sri Aurobindo and the Mother live and
> work and practice the Yoga. There is the Sri Aurobindo Society, an
> independent organization for devotees of Sri Aurobindo and the

---

[1] Remark in a talk, 10th July 1926, recorded in 'Pondicherry 1910-1926' in A B Purani, *The Life of Sri Aurobindo*, Sri Aurobindo Ashram, Pondicherry, 1978, p 209.
[2] Quote from Sri Aurobindo made on 10 January 1939 in Nirodbaran, *Talks with Sri Aurobindo*, Vol 1, Sri Aurobindo Society, Calcutta, 1985, pp 161-162. For an excellent online resource of Sri Aurobindo's writings, see www.intyoga.online.fr
[3] Glyn Richards, Ed, *A Source Book of Modern Hinduism*, Curzon Press, London, 1985, p 171.

Mother, with its headquarters in Pondicherry and hundreds of branches in India and abroad. And there is Auroville, located ten kilometers north of Pondicherry, the township set up by the Mother and based on the ideals of Sri Aurobindo and the Mother.[4]

As Sri Aurobindo's writings cover such vast territory only samples can be given here, those that most directly address our theme of Hindu encounters with Christ.

*On Religion*

For Sri Aurobindo, every religion has helped humanity in some way. For example, Paganism increased in us "the light of beauty, the largeness and height" of our lives, our "aim at a many-sided perfection." Christianity gave us "some vision of divine love and charity." Buddhism has shown us "a noble way to be wiser, gentler, purer." Judaism and Islam reveal to us "how to be religiously faithful in action and zealously devoted to God." Hinduism has opened to us "the largest and profoundest spiritual possibilities." The ideal would be "if all these God-visions could embrace and cast themselves into each other; but intellectual dogma and cult egoism stand in the way."[5]

> All fanaticism is false, because it is a contradiction of the very nature of God and of Truth. Truth cannot be shut up in a single book, Bible or Veda or Koran, or in a single religion. The Divine Being is eternal and universal and infinite and cannot be the sole property of the Mussulmans or of the Semitic religions only....Hindus and Confucians and Taoists and all others have as much right to enter into relation with God and find the Truth in their own way. All religions have some truth in them, but none has the whole truth; all are created in time and finally decline and perish....God and Truth outlast these religions and manifest themselves anew in whatever way or form the Divine Wisdom chooses.[6]

One of the problems with some religions is their historical inclination to look outwards rather than inwards. "A mere intellectual, ethical and aesthetic culture does not go back to the inmost truth of the spirit; it is still an Ignorance, an incomplete, outward and superficial knowledge." This leads to "a spiritual exclusiveness which revolts from the outward existence rather than seeks to transform it."

> A spirituality of this intolerant high-pointed kind, to whatever elevation it may rise, however it may help to purify life or lead to a certain kind of

---

[4] Manoj Das Gupta, Managing Trustee of the Sri Aurobindo Ashram Trust. All his quotes from e-mails to author between 18 and 26 August 2005.
[5] Sri Aurobindo, 'Essays in Philosophy and Yoga,' *Complete Works of Sri Aurobindo*, Vol 13, Sri Aurobindo Ashram, Pondicherry, 1998, p 211.
[6] Sri Aurobindo, *On Himself*, Sri Aurobindo Ashram Trust, Pondicherry, 1976, p 483.

individual salvation, cannot be a complete thing. For its exclusiveness imposes on it a certain impotence to deal effectively with the problems of human existence; it cannot lead it to its integral perfection or combine its highest heights with its broadest broadness....It must have a wider outlook, a more embracing range of applicability and, even, a more aspiring and ambitious aim of its endeavor. Its aim must be not only to raise to inaccessible heights the few elect, but to draw all men and all life and the whole human being upward, to spiritualize life and in the end to divinize human nature.[7]

## On Avatars

For Sri Aurobindo, the description of avatars given in Hindu scriptures clearly depicts an evolution, parallel to the one we all undertake.

> Avatarhood would have little meaning if it were not connected with the evolution. The Hindu procession of the ten Avatars is itself, as it were, a parable of evolution. First the Fish Avatar, then the amphibious animal between land and water, then the land animal, then the Man-Lion Avatar, bridging man and animal, then man as dwarf, small and un-developed and physical but containing in himself the godhead and taking possession of existence, then the rajasic, sattwic, nirguna Avatars, leading the human development from the vital rajasic to the sattwic mental man and again the overmental superman. Krishna, Buddha and Kalki depict the last three stages, the stages of the spiritual development - Krishna opens the possibility of overmind, Buddha tries to shoot beyond to the supreme liberation but that liberation is still negative, not returning upon earth to complete positively the evolution; Kalki is to correct this by bringing the Kingdom of the Divine upon earth, destroying the opposing *Asura* forces. The progression is striking and unmistakable.[8]

Sri Aurobindo has written extensively on avatars in *Essays on the Gita*.[9] For him, "It is the inner Christ, Krishna or Buddha that matters." Here are some references to Jesus, or Christ:

"Such controversies as the one that raged in Europe over the historicity of Christ would seem to a spiritually-minded Indian largely a waste of time; he would concede to it a considerable historic, but hardly any religious, importance; for what does it matter in the end whether a Jesus son of the carpenter Joseph was actually born in Nazareth or Bethlehem, lived and taught

---

[7] Sri Aurobindo, 'Indian Spirituality and Life –2' in *Arya*, September 1919, Sri Aurobindo Birth Centenary Library (SABCL), Volume 14, Sri Aurobindo Ashram, Pondicherry, pp 156-171.
[8] Sri Aurobindo, 'The Purpose of Avatarhood' in *Letters on Yoga*, SABCL, Vol 22, pp 401-430.
[9] Unless indicated, all avatar quotes from Sri Aurobindo Ghose, *Essays on the Gita*, Arya Pub House, Calcutta, 1926, p 19; pp 215-252.

and was done to death on a real or trumped-up charge of sedition, so long as we can know by spiritual experience the inner Christ, live uplifted in the light of his teaching and escape from the yoke of the natural law by that atonement of men with God of which the crucifixion is the symbol? If the Christ, God made man, lives within our spiritual being, it would seem to matter little whether or not a son of Mary physically lived and suffered and died in Jerusalem. So too the Krishna who matters to us is the eternal incarnation of the Divine not the historical teacher and leader of men."

"The Avatar comes as the manifestation of the divine nature in the human nature, the apocalypse of its Christhood, Krishnahood, Buddhahood, in order that the human nature may by moulding its principle, thought, feeling, action, being on the lines of that Christhood, Krishnahood, Buddhahood transfigure itself into the divine. The law, the dharma which the Avatar establishes, is given for that purpose chiefly; the Christ, Krishna, Buddha stands in its centre as the gate, he makes through himself the way men shall follow. That is why each Incarnation holds before men his own example and declares of himself that he is the way and the gate; he declares too the oneness of his humanity with the divine being, declares that the Son of Man and the Father above from whom he has descended are one."

"The divine manifestation of a Christ, Krishna, Buddha, in external humanity has for its inner truth the same manifestation of the eternal Avatar within our inner humanity. That which has been done in the outer human life of earth may be repeated in the inner life of all human beings."

"The Avatar does not come as a thaumaturgic magician, but as the divine leader of humanity and the exemplar of a divine humanity. Even human sorrow and physical suffering he must assume and use so as to show, first, how that suffering may be a means of redemption, - as did Christ, - secondly, to show how, having been assumed by the divine soul in the human nature, it can also be overcome in the same nature, - as did Buddha. The rationalist who would have cried to Christ, 'If thou art the Son of God, come down from the cross,' …has missed the root of the whole matter. Even the Avatar of sorrow and suffering must come before there can be the Avatar of divine joy; the human limitation must be assumed in order to show how it can be overcome; and the way and the extent of the overcoming, whether internal only or external also, depends upon the stage of the human advance; it must not be done by an nonhuman miracle."

"The Avatar may descend as a great spiritual teacher and savior, the Christ, the Buddha, but always his work leads, after he has finished his earthly man-ifestation, to a profound and powerful change not only in the ethical, but in the social and outward life and ideals of the race."

"An Avatar always has three companions in his work: dharma, sangha, and himself as Avatar, soul of the dharma and sangha. So in Christianity we have the law of Christian living, the Church and the Christ."

It is clear that for Sri Aurobindo, the inner Christ is primary and the historical Jesus of little significance. He is one of many divine incarnations bringing a new or renewed dharma or law into the world that has to be assimilated into the lives of every responding individual. Such beings reveal the way to trans-formation, individual and social, by the examples of their lives. However, as "Christ realized himself as the Son who is one with the Father - he must there-fore be an amshâvatâra, a partial incarnation." Sri Ramakrishna "was certainly quite as much an Avatar as Christ."[10]

Although very important for this study, Manoj Das Gupta, Managing Trustee of the Sri Aurobindo Ashram Trust, told me that "understanding avatars plays no direct role in the Society or Auroville" at this time. However, the thoughts of Sri Aurobindo on religion and leading the ideal life are pivotal. Manoj feels that Sri Aurobindo's primary spiritual message for the modern world is best summed up in this aphorism from the great sage:

> The changes we see in the world today are intellectual, moral, physical in their ideal and intention: the spiritual revolution waits for its hour and throws up meanwhile its waves here and there. Until it comes the sense of the others cannot be understood and till then all interpretations of present happenings and forecast of man's future are vain things. For its nature, power, event are that which will determine the next cycle of our humanity.[11]

Rhoda LeCocq describes how she felt at the last living darshan given by Sri Aurobindo. As she stood before him:

> All thought ceased, I was perfectly aware of where I was; it was not 'hypnotism' as one Stanford friend later suggested. It was simply that during those few minutes, my mind became utterly still. It seemed that I stood there a very long, an uncounted time, for there was no time. Only many years later did I describe this experience as my having experienced the Timeless in Time.[12]

She goes on to describe what happened, following the Master's mahasamadhi. His body did not decay as would be usual in the heat of South India and darshan was given to all who could come to see him. Rhoda felt the same energy field around the deceased body as she had felt close to the living one.

---

[10] Sri Aurobindo, 'The Purpose of Avatarhood,' *Letters on Yoga*, SABCL, Vol 22, pp 401-430.
[11] Sri Aurobindo, 'Thoughts and Glimpses,' *The Supramental Manifestation and Other Writings*, SABCL, Volume 16, p 394.
[12] Rhoda P LeCocq, *The Radical Thinkers*, Sri Aurobindo Ashram Press, Pondicherry, 1969, pp 198-202.

The body of Sri Aurobindo was finally buried on 9<sup>th</sup> December, nearly five whole days after his passing away. For Rhoda, it is because of great spiritual beings like Sri Aurobindo that "life continues to have hope and meaning."

## MOHANDAS KARAMCHAND GANDHI, 1869-1948

Gandhi was born in Gujarat in 1869 into a Vaishnava family and married when he was 13. He studied law in England and spent some years in South Africa where he began to form his ideas of *satyagraha*[13] and *ahimsa*.[14] Arun Gandhi, one of the Mahatma's grandsons and founder of the M K Gandhi Institute for Non-Violence, feels that it was there that the great inspiration for Gandhi's work for non-violence began.

> In South Africa he became a victim of prejudice and was beaten up several times. Before that he had been aware of hate but had not become a victim of it. He realized this was wrong and that society needed to be changed. As a lawyer he was also aware that the judicial system was not conducive to changing people since it focused more on punishment. Punishing or killing people because they did wrong does not help change society. It comes from the western family of religions that tends to divide the world between the good and the bad and the simplistic notion that get rid of the bad and you have a better world. People are not born bad, they are made bad by circumstances and unless society addresses those circumstances a society cannot change. These were some of the important revelations that led grandfather to non-violence.[15]

I asked Arun if he felt that Hinduism had a special attribute that helped develop non-violence in people and society. He felt this was not the case.

> At the core of every religion is the message of love, respect, understanding, compassion and so on. These are positive attributes that lead to non-violence and understanding of our relationships and our responsibilities in society. However, the Culture of Non-violence as practiced by grandfather does not permit a capitalist/materialist life style which is so heavily based on the principles of selfishness and self-interests, greed and so on. It is to foster this greedy attitude that

---

[13] "Gandhiji has explained Satyagraha as soul-force or spiritual force, or the force which accrues to one out of a living faith in God. This last he regards as indispensable for the success of non-violence." R R Diwakar, *Satyagraha: The Power of Truth*, Henry Regnery, Illinois, 1948, pvii.

[14] Ahimsa means "non-injury, harmlessness; abstaining from evil towards others in deed, word and thought. Propagated by radical early renouncers outside the Vedic tradition, it became a part of the ethics and practice of Jainism, Buddhism and classical Yoga (as the first *yama* of Patanjali's ashtanga yoga) and later influenced a large part of Hinduism, leading to wide-spread adoption of vegetarianism and virtual abandonment of animal sacrifices." Karel Werner, *A Popular Dictionary of Hinduism*, Curzon Press, Richmond, 1994, pp 25-6.

[15] All Arun Gandhi quotes from e-mail to author, 28 July 2005.

religions of the world have been misinterpreted and a culture of violence introduced.

Paramahansa Yogananda, visiting Gandhi in August 1935, tells an amusing anecdote illustrating the Mahatma's awareness of the difficulties of living a non-violent life. As Yogananda wished Gandhi goodnight, the Mahatma laughingly handed him a bottle of citronella oil, remarking, "The Wardha mosquitoes don't know a thing about ahimsa, Swamiji!"[16] Yogananda later created the Gandhi World Peace Memorial at the Self-Realization Fellowship Lake Shrine, an outdoor shrine where an authentic one thousand year-old Chinese stone sarcophagus holds some of the Mahatma's ashes.

Returning to India from South Africa, Gandhi practiced satyagraha in civil disputes against the British government and in the national *swaraj* (self-rule) independence movement. Swaraj meant more for Gandhi than just freedom for India from British rule. Built into the word is the idea of self-restraint and he used it to mean freedom for all in India, whatever the caste or religion, from every form of oppression. Not everyone understood this. In 1948, a young Hindu, angered by Gandhi's support for Muslims, assassinated him.

*Gandhi and Christianity*

Gandhiji had considerable contact with Christians and various forms of Christianity. There were occasions when his Christian friends felt sure of his conversion. Certainly he was impressed by some of whom he met and what he read, and particularly moved and influenced by the Sermon on the Mount. Gandhi finally disappointed Christian hopes for he found within the Hindu faith all the spiritual nourishment he required, believing it also gave him the freedom to believe in the teachings of Jesus and to follow his example. Arun Gandhi unpacks how the Mahatma thought about this:

> Grandfather once said to someone: I believe in Jesus, but not in Christ. What he was trying to say is that we human beings are quick to take the easy way out. Jesus was a great person, with outstanding achievements and most importantly a very significant message, but instead of following him we choose to worship him. Toward the end of his life grandfather said poignantly about Indian people: 'They will follow me in life, worship me in death but not make my cause their cause.' These words could be uttered by Jesus or by any of the religious giants that we worship. It is so easy to elevate them to sainthood or even Godhood and worship them but not make their cause our cause. This unfortunately is the weakness of all religions of the world, not just Christianity.

---

[16] Paramahansa Yogananda, *Autobiography of a Yogi*, Self-Realization Fellowship, Los Angeles, U.S.A. P 495.

Gandhiji was not interested in the historicity of Jesus. For him the Sermon on the Mount remained true whatever its source. He urged Hindus to study the teachings of Jesus, recognizing their influence on his own life. However, he differed from most of the Christians he met in that he could not believe Jesus was the only son of God. Only God is perfect and, metaphorically, we are all the children of God. Western Christianity had lost the plot and Gandhi did not think Jesus would approve of it. He argued that quoting a biblical text did not make you a true follower of Christ and that many who did not know of him at all lived his teachings better than many of those who professed their faith in him only verbally. God did not die 2,000 years ago but must live today in each one of us. We must become like Christ and be true satyagrahis: "He was the most active resister known perhaps to history. His was non-violence par excellence."[17]

K L Seshagiri Rao feels that Gandhi has brought fresh insights to Christian texts and teachings, revealing "aspects of Jesus' life and character which the west had not so clearly perceived." He gives an example, relating to the symbology of the cross and crucifixion, and quotes a missionary to show that Gandhi's insights have proved meaningful to sensitive Christians.

> [Gandhi] demonstrated how the soul force fights and overcomes evil only with the weapons of Truth and love. Although satyagraha was used by Gandhi, a Hindu, against governments run by Christians (whether in South Africa or Britain), many Christians all over the world recognized that his movements were in truth Christian, a reviving and reinterpretation of the cross. Dr. Stanley Jones, the well-known American missionary (in his *Gandhi: An Interpretation.* P. 105) observes: 'Never in human history has so much light been shed through this one man, and that man not even called Christian. Had not our Christianity been vitiated and overlain by our identification with unchristian attitudes and policies in public and private life, we would have seen at once the kinship between Gandhi's method and the cross.'[18]

Has anything changed? When we look at current global situations it seems very difficult (as indeed it is) for western political leaders, who profess themselves Christian, to follow Christ's ahimsic command to 'turn the other cheek.' There is no real grasp of its deep meaning and potency. By contrast, Gandhi's life revealed a profound understanding of and commitment to Christ's message.

---

[17] Most of Gandhi's thoughts on Christianity are compiled in Robert Ellsberg, Ed, *Gandhi on Christianity*, Orbis, NY, 1991.

[18] K L Seshagiri Rao, 'Hindu-Christian Dialogue: A Hindu Perspective' in *Journal of Hindu-Christian Studies*, Vol 14, 2001.

For Gandhi, Hinduism proved primary. It was the most tolerant of religions. Its freedom from dogma gave the greatest scope for self-expression. Its lack of *exclusivism* allowed its adherents to respect and make good spiritual use of the best of other religious traditions. Non-violence found its highest expression in Hinduism.[19] Hindus believe in the oneness of all beings, all life, and this is the foundation for unity and co-existence.[20]

For Gandhi, the primary factors were not belief only but action and belief together. Believing in someone else's goodness but not becoming good ourselves will not change situations for the better. "Salvation" was a "life of compassionate service, sacrifice and satisfaction" that each of us has to live.[21] It cannot be done on, our behalf, by another. We cannot live *vicariously*.

I asked Arun Gandhi if Christian mission / evangelism had caused problems for his work today, sustaining and developing his grandfather's legacy. He replied: "By and large we are accepted and our work appreciated."

Arun feels "convinced that at the very root of the spiritual problems we face today is the intense competitiveness which we have injected into each religion." These pressures and their consequences reveal themselves through-out the world, including India, the homeland of ahimsa and satyahgraha. Religion is used for destructive purposes in increasingly violent ways. For Mahatma Gandhi, "It was during his youth in England and then in South Africa that he came to the conclusion that the ills of the world were the result of the Culture of Violence that dominates all aspects of human life, including religion."

> What appalled him was the competitiveness that was, and is, the main theme of all religions. It was the difference between 'possessing' the Truth and 'Pursuing' the Truth. He studied all the religions of the world with an open mind and realized that none were as open and accepting as Hinduism, largely because it is not really a religion. It is not organized and has no strict rules like baptism or allegiance to a particular temple and such. One of the important aspects of Hinduism is the belief that no one really knows the true image of God because no one has ever seen him/her. So, while Hindus believe there is only one God, that God has many different images. Thus it recognizes all the different images as being equally valid. It was this freedom of belief and worship that Gandhi admired because he wanted to change the Culture of Violence to

---

[19] Non-violence includes all actions and respect to all beings, not just humans. Vegetarianism is a key ingredient of many Hindu lives.
[20] M K Gandhi, 'Why I am a Hindu' in *Young India*, 21 October 1927, quoted in B R Nanda, *Gandhi and Religion*, Gandhi Smriti and Darshan Samiti, New Delhi, 1990, p 12.
[21] M K Gandhi, 'Why I am a Hindu.'

a Culture of Non-violence by impressing on people the need to respect all the different religions of the world.

For Arun, his grandfather's most potent spiritual message for the world is contained in this quotation: "A friendly study of all the scriptures is the sacred duty of every individual." Gandhiji "made the friendly study and absorbed the good from all the religions and that gave him the strength to respect all the religions with the same sense of devotion that he showed towards Hinduism."

Karan Singh, interfaith activist and member of the Upper House of India's Parliament, feels that Gandhi's message is right on target for us today.

> [He] speaks to us across the decades, across the ages as if from another planet, cutting across barriers of race and religion, caste and creed, nationality and language, sex and social status. He preaches the inner gospel of inner striving and outer commitment, of social concerns and interfaith harmony. And he echoes in his words, the ancient prayer that has come down through the long and tortuous corridors of time – May all beings enjoy happiness, may all be without disease, may all witness an auspicious life, may none have to bear of suffering.[22]

Honoring the Mahatma on his 70th birthday in 1939, Sarvapelli Radhakrishnan said: "The greatness of Gandhi is more in his holy living than in his heroic struggles, in his insistence on the creative power of the soul and its life-giving quality at a time when the destructive forces seem to be in the ascendant."

For Seshagiri Rao, Gandhi's contribution to life is only just beginning to have its full impact.

> Gandhi was thought to be old-fashioned, and it was considered that his ideas would turn the clock of progress back. Then came the environmentalists with their focus on global pollution of the elements (water, air, earth, etc) that industrialization had caused. Now Gandhi's 'simple living' is making sense. He is becoming more relevant today than during his own lifetime. His definition of modernity as the development of the whole person and all persons is making sense. People have started saying that Gandhi was ahead of his time. His emphasis on the 'quality of life' has much to offer to human happiness and peace.[23]

Paramahansa Yogananda wrote, "Mahatma Gandhi has left a richer world today, a world in which the practical power of these spiritual truths of love

---

[22] Downloaded on 27 July 2005 from http://www.karansingh.com/hindu/gandhi01.htm
[23] K L Seshagiri Rao, 'Hinduism in America,' paper presented at the Symposium on *Hinduism: Past, Present, and Future* organized by the Sri Venkatesvara Temple, Pittsburgh.

and understanding, which was laughed at before, has been effectively demon-strated before the mouths of cannons."[24]

In the final analysis, as Gandhi told one prominent Indian Christian, Kali Charan Banerjee, it was Hinduism that proved his greatest sustenance:

> I must tell you in all humility that Hinduism, as I know it, entirely satisfies my soul, fills my whole being, and I find solace in the Bhagavad Gita and the Upanishads that I miss even in the Sermon on the Mount....I must confess to you that when doubts haunt me, when disappointments stare me in the face, and when I see not one ray of light on the horizon I turn to the Bhagavad Gita, and find a verse to comfort me; and I immediately begin to smile in the midst of overwhelming sorrow. My life has been full of external tragedies and if they have not left any visible and indelible effect on me, I owe it to the teachings of the Bhagavad Gita.[25]

Gandhi ended his life with the name of Ram on his lips. Loyal to the spirit of Jesus that he found in the Sermon of the Mount, he had moved far from the Christianity he experienced in the India of his time. Like many Hindus, he found the primary significance of Jesus' life in the model it provided for others to follow. From Christian perspectives, he was, perhaps, the most significant of all Hindus engaging in dialogue with them in this period. It is with the advent of Gandhi that Goel perceives the end of serious Christian challenge to Hinduism in India. With Hinduism and the movement towards independence in such safe and effective hands, other concerns begin to dominate Hindu minds and hearts.

SARVAPELLI RADHAKRISHNAN, 1888-1975

Radhakrishnan was born in South India in 1888 where he received a mainly Christian education. He studied Hindu philosophy as a means to counter Christian criticisms of it, becoming a leading philosopher, statesman and President of India. In his writings he sought not only to expound the highest Hindu philosophical insights but also to connect them with the best of western thought for the common good.

> That the Hindu solution of the problem of the conflict of religions is likely to be accepted in the future seems to me to be fairly certain. The spirit of democracy with its immense faith in the freedom to choose one's ends and direct one's course in the effort to realize them makes

---

[24] Paramahansa Yogananda, *Journey to Self-Realization: Discovering the Gifts of the Soul*, Self-Realization Fellowship, Los Angeles, U.S.A. PP 193-194.
[25] M K Gandhi, *The Collected Works*, Volume 27, Publications Division, Indian Government, New Delhi, 1968, p 434-435; and D P Singhal, *India and World Civilizations*, Pan Macmillan Limited, London, 1993, p 258.

for it. Nothing is good which is not self-determination. The different religions are slowly learning to hold out hands of friendship to each other in every part of the world....The study of comparative religion is developing a fairer attitude to other religions....We are learning to think clearly about the inter-relations of religions. The more religious we grow, the more tolerant we will become of diversity.[26]

Glyn Richards, Head of Religious Studies at Stirling University, comments:

Radhakrishnan recognizes the significance of learning about the basic principles of the great religions of the world and sees it as essential to the promotion of international understanding. Where interreligious rivalries prevail there is no possibility of establishing a world community with a world culture. Interreligious activity involves also the abandonment of missionary activity and proselytizing which presupposes the belief that one religion is superior to another.[27]

However, for Radhakrishnan, thus far in history, differences remain between Hindu and Christian philosophical interpretations. Unlike Christianity, Hindu philosophy has an experiential base as "wide as human nature itself." Hindus are, therefore, interested in all points of view, enrich their thought and life with all uplifting ideas, whatever their source, realizing that all comes from God. "Every view of God, from the primitive worship of nature up to the Father-love of a St Francis and the Mother-love of a Ramakrishna represents some aspect or other of the relation of the human to the divine."[28] In contrast to this, "Christian theology...takes its stand on the immediate certitude of Jesus as one whose absolute authority over conscience is self-certifying and whose ability and willingness to save the soul it is impossible not to trust."

Christian theology becomes relevant only for those who share or accept a particular kind of spiritual experience, and these are tempted to dismiss other experiences as illusory and other scriptures as imperfect.[29]

*Radhakrishnan and Christ*

Radhakrishnan, like many of his compatriots, felt unable to fully equate the Jesus of Christian theology with the Jesus of the Gospels. "If He [Jesus] had returned to Europe in the Middle Ages, He would certainly have been burnt alive for denying the dogmas about His own nature!"[30] The disconnection between Jesus as he was and the Jesus portrayed by the Church is further emphasized: "The interpretation of God's will at the Council of Clermont (AD

---

[26] S Radhakrishnan, *The Hindu View of Life*, Unwin, London, 1988, p 43.
[27] Glyn Richards, Ed, *A Source-Book of Modern Hinduism*, Curzon Press, London, 1985, p 186.
[28] S Radhakrishnan, *The Hindu View of Life*, pp 22-23.
[29] S Radhakirshnan, *The Hindu View of Life*, pp 16-17.
[30] S Radhakrishnan, *Eastern Religions and Western Thought*, OUP, Oxford, 1939, p 276.

1095) as a behest to go forth and slaughter the Saracens marks the victory of the European West over the crucified Jesus."[31]

Radhakrishnan thought of Jesus as an avatar, a man become God-realized, example for all to imitate, one who reveals what all must become, the inaugurator of a new dharma. Absolute claims for Jesus have to be refuted as he was working in the sphere of relativity where absolutes cannot prevail. All should become Christ-like for "we are all partakers of God's nature and can incarnate God's love even as Jesus did."[32]

Radhakrishnan argued that what counts is "conduct and not belief." Thus Christ's life has to be lived out in one's own life. This, in turn, leads to right conduct and understanding. Mere belief about another can lead to mis-understanding and wrong conduct. Living the life of a Christ oneself corrects this.

> Religion is not correct belief but righteous living....Jesus did not tell the Jewish people among whom he found himself, 'It is wicked to be Jews. Become Christians.' He did his best to rid the Jewish religion of its impurities. He would have done the same with Hinduism had he been born a Hindu. The true reformer purifies and enlarges the heritage of mankind and does not belittle, still less deny it.[33]

On the dangers of sectarianism, Radhakrishnan remarked, "Those who love their sects more than truth end by loving themselves more than their sects."

> We start by claiming that Christianity is the only true religion and then affirm that Protestantism is the only true sect of Christianity, Episcopalianism the only true Protestant Christian religion, and our particular standpoint the only true representation of the High Church view.[34]

The point is emphasized further by a story he retold of an event experienced by a *Vishnu* worshipper antagonistic to a *Siva* worshipper.

> As he bowed before the image of Vishnu, the face of the image divided in half and Siva appeared on one side and Vishnu on the other, and the two smiling as one face on the bigoted worshipper told him that Vishnu and Siva were one.[35]

Hindus are free to respond to God as the *ishtadevata* (favorite form of God) that will best ignite each one's spiritual longing and understanding. This will

---

[31] S Radhakrishnan, *Eastern Religions and Western Thought*, p 272.
[32] Quoted in *Religion and Society*, Vol XI No 3, Sept 1964, p 45.
[33] Radhakrishnan, *The Hindu View of Life*, p 37.
[34] Radhakrishnan, *The Hindu View of Life*, p 3 & pp 7-8.
[35] Radhakrishnan, *The Hindu View of Life*, p 28.

be true also for Christians coming to a Hindu preceptor for spiritual guidance. Such a teacher "would not ask his Christian pupil to discard his allegiance to Christ but would tell him that his idea of Christ was not adequate, and would lead him to a knowledge of the real Christ, the incorporate Supreme."[36]

On the moral influence of Jesus, so important to Roy, Sen and other Hindu leaders, Radhakrishnan remarked that, "It is interesting to know that the moral teaching of Jesus with its ascetic and other-worldly emphasis has been anticipated several hundred years by the Upanishads and Buddha."[37] In *Eastern Religions and Western Thought*, Radhakrishnan spent some time connecting Christianity and Buddhism, a link that leads back directly to Hinduism. Buddhist monks could be seen in Palestine at the time of Jesus' incarnation and Radhakrishnan was keen to trace their formative influence on the milieu to which Jesus belonged and the religious grounding of his ministry. He gives many examples of parallels between Christ and Buddha. Whilst beyond the scope of this book, it might be reasonable to wonder about the origins of the monasticism or asceticism Jesus demanded of himself and his disciples, for the mission of his disciples that he sent out in twos wearing sandals, for his detachment from current moral norms such as his injunction to let the dead bury the dead. None of this is easily identifiable in the family oriented Judaism of past and present times. Radhakrishnan is clear: "Two centuries before the Christian era, Buddhism closed in on Palestine. The Essenes, the Mandeans, and the Nazarite sects are filled with its spirit."[38]

Parallels with Krishna are also introduced: a special light accompanying the births of both Christ and Krishna; universal gladness of nature at their births; the threat of death to both infants; the mocking of Herod and Kamsa, the potential killers; the massacre of infants in the search for the babies; the paying of tribute and taxes by the parents; flights out of the country to protect the children.[39]

Radhakrishnan once told a missionary friend, "You Christians seem to us Hindus rather ordinary people making extra-ordinary claims." He continued, "If your Christ has not succeeded in making you better men and women, have we any reason to suppose that he would do more for us, if we became

---

[36] S Radhakrishnan, *The Hindu View of Life*, p 34.
[37] S Radhakrishnan, *Eastern Religions and Western Thought*, p 173f. Radhakrishnan also refers to other, western books, which have explored such possibilities. See also f/n 2 in Chapter 1, this book. Sri Aurobindo also refers to India's global influence: "She expands too outside her borders; her ships cross the ocean and the fine superfluity of her wealth brims over to Judaea and Egypt and Rome; her colonies spread her arts and epics and creeds in the Archipelago; her traces are found in the sands of Mesopotamia; her religions conquer China and Japan and spread westward as far as Palestine and Alexandria, and the figures of the Upanishads and the sayings of the Buddhists are re-echoed on the lips of Christ." See Sri Aurobindo, 'The Renaissance in India' in *Arya*, Aug-Nov 1918, SABCL, Vol 14, Sri Aurobindo Ashram, Pondicherry, pp 397-433.
[38] S Radhakrishnan, *Eastern Religions and Western Thought*, p 158.
[39] S Radhakrishnan, *Eastern Religions and Western Thought*, p 182.

Christians?"[40] His question might lead to a lot more profound silence in our world if indeed we all refrained from trying to change others before first changing ourselves!

## SWAMI SIVANANDA, 1887-1963

Swamiji was born in India in 1887, became a doctor and moved to Malaysia to practice there. He was very successful but soon began to be interested in the spiritual life, meeting a monk who instructed him in yoga and Vedanta. He returned to India, met his guru, and took *sannyas* (monastic vows). After many years of intense sadhana he established a centre in Rishikesh, remaining there, apart from two tours in India, until his mahasamadhi in 1963. Paramahansa Yogananda paid this tribute to him: "The life of the great Rishi, Swami Sivananda, serves as a perfect example of selfless activity. He blesses India and the world by his presence."[41]

Sivanandaji founded the Divine Life Society in 1936 with the aim to revive spirituality, worldwide. He taught Yoga of Synthesis, developing the head, heart and hand for perfect spiritual balance. Many Yoga Centers around the world are inspired by the life and teachings of Swami Sivananda. His injunction "do good, be good" is written all over the Divine Life Society's walls in Rishikesh. He was fondly known as 'Give-ananda'![42] One disciple described a meeting between Sivananda and a Christian missionary to illustrate his nature:

> One so humble, the Master never discussed his own spiritual attainments. A Christian evangelist from America, Rev. Stanley Jones, visited the Ashram in 1956. At a small round-table discussion on the morning of March 14, the Master, Rev. Jones and others narrated their 'experiences.' When it came to the Master's turn, he simply said, 'Seek, find, enter and rest. I sing this formula. I live this formula. I try to be good. I try to live in God. I cultivate virtues. This is my experience.'[43]

### The Life and Mission of Jesus

For Sivanandaji, Jesus descended to earth for the same reasons as Krishna and other avatars:

> The Law governing the Lord's descent upon earth is the same at all times, everywhere. When unrighteousness grows and righteousness is

---

[40] Sarvapelli Gopal Radhakrishnan, *Radhakrishnan: A Biography*, OUP, 1989, p 195; quoted in Sita Ram Goel, *History of Hindu-Christian Encounters*, revised edition, Voice of India, Delhi, 1996, p xi.
[41] Quoted on www.sivananda.dls.org.za Downloaded on 5 September 2005. For more about Paramahansa Yogananda and Self-Realization Fellowship, see Chapter 4.
[42] Interview with Swami Krishnananda, *Hinduism Today*, Hawaii, December 1999, p 41.
[43] N Ananthanarayanan, 'Personality of the Master.' Published by Yoga and Inner Peace, an affiliated yoga center with the Sivananda Yoga Vedanta Centers. www.yogapeace.com/personality_of_sivananda.htm

waning, when the forces undivine seem to be stronger than the divine forces, when the Word of God or commandments of His Messengers are forgotten or disobeyed, when religious fanaticism follows the letter of the scriptures killing the spirit, it is then that the Lord incarnates Himself on earth, to save Man, to save righteousness. That is why we find so much in common between the birth of Lord Jesus and the Avatara of Lord Sri Krishna.[44]

Who was Jesus? Jesus was a world teacher, prophet and Messiah. "Jesus was an incarnation of the Hebrew God Jehovah."[45] His Sermon on the Mount is "nothing but the practice of Sadachara or right conduct. It corresponds to the practice of Yama-Niyama of Raja-Yoga, the Eightfold Path of Lord Buddha. It is marvelous, inspiring and soul-stirring."[46] Like Radhakrishnan and many other Hindus, Sivananda believed Jesus lived in India during the 'missing years' alluded to in the Gospels. "Between his 18th and 32nd years of age, Jesus spent his life in India and lived like a Hindu or Buddhist monk. He had burning Vairagya (dispassion) and spirit of renunciation. In India he assimilated Hindu ideals and principles."[47] Although this cannot be proved, "there is nothing untenable in this view, and its acceptance would only strengthen the bonds of love between the East and the West, and promote good will between the two hemispheres, which is the Mission of the Lord."

For Sivananda, Jesus was a visible expression of the highest truth, a living witness to Supreme Reality indwelling in humanity, ahimsa incarnate. He integrated head, heart and hand, the balance taught also by the Divine Life Society. Jesus lived the divine life, ever in samadhi, aware of Oneness, yet also a true Karma Yogi. Through resistance to temptations in the desert and at the time of his trial, and by the way he lived his whole life, Jesus proved a model for others to follow.

> In Jesus the Man, the aspirant or the *Sadhaka* finds two traits to be faithfully emulated, namely, an admirable moral courage in being Witness to Truth. His life displays a silent yet supreme heroism in the face of the most determined opposition, persecution and mis-understanding. And He has set an example how a true seeker repulses the temptations on the spiritual path….Manifest the same Living Reality, the Spotless Purity and the lofty Divine Compassion. Divinise thy life. Lead the Divine Life.

---

[44] Swami Sivananda, *Life and Teachings of Lord Jesus*, Divine Life Society, 1959. WWW pdf edition 1998, Chapter 1, p 1. Downloaded on 22 June 2005 from http://www.rsl.ukans.edu/~pkanagar/divine/
[45] Swami Sivananda, 'Lord Jesus,' published at http://www.dlshq.org/saints/jesus.htm#india
[46] Swami Sivananda, *Lives of Saints*, Divine Life Society, 1941. www.dlshq.org/saints/jesus.htm
[47] Swami Sivananda, 'Christianity.' www.dlshq.org/religions/christianity.htm#jesus. See also, 'Jesus in India.' www.dlshq.org/saints/jesus.htm#india

All special anniversaries and occasions, like Christmas, carry a special purpose and meaning, reminding us too of the one who inspired them.[48]

> The Call of Christmas is the Call to a new Birth in the Spirit. Its message is the lofty one of the Divine Life, the Christ-Life of Compassion, Truth and Purity. That moment is the real joyous Christmas to you when the Divine Consciousness that shone through Jesus blossoms and lights up the inner chambers of thy heart. Christmas is to you that day you start to lead the divine life of *Satya*, Ahimsa and *Brahmacharya* that the great Vedanti of the West lived.

Historical details are not important – the teachings prevail. Jesus' teaching was way ahead of its time: revolutionary, spiritual socialism. His religion was of the heart. He led the same life, gives the same message as Krishna, Buddha and Mohammad, the message that leads all to Heaven's Gate. "Love your neighbor as yourself" is the highest Vedanta, a teaching for people of all faiths, a call for self-transformation and purification. Yet, Sivananda muses, if Jesus wanted to come again now, into the West, it is unlikely he would get a visa or be recognized by any Church Synod!

For Swamiji, real adoration of Christ, the real meaning of being Christian, is the awakening of the Christ spirit within each believer. This new birth is Yoga, the path to Self-realization, an inner transformation. It will overcome gross materialism with spirituality; there will be more harmony and peace, more community and individual happiness. The second coming is the birth of Christ in his followers. "From then onward light begins to shine where darkness was before. Ignorance gives place to the beginning of wisdom. Impurity is replaced by purity. Hatred ceases and love begins to blossom forth." The message of Christ is not different from that in all the great sacred scriptures of the world.

> The Voice of Jesus is verily the Voice of the Eternal Being. Through Him is expressed the call of the Infinite to the finite, the Cosmic Being to the individual, the call of God to man. His Divine Voice is the same, therefore, as the Voice of the Vedas and the Upanishads, the Voice of the Koran, the Guru Granth Saheb, the Zend Avesta, the Dhammapada, and all such sacred scriptures of the great religions of the world.

All point not to beliefs but to praxis, not to salvation by grace alone but to real spiritual effort by everyone. Supremely, Jesus' prayer from the cross, for forgiveness of those who murdered him, reveals the full glory of living a Christ-like life. "What a large and forgiving heart he had! Jesus was an embodiment of forgiveness or *Kshama*. That is the reason why he still lives in

---

[48] All quotes from Swami Sivananda, 'Christmas Messages,' 1945-1956. For some of these see also *World Parliament of Religions: Commemoration Volume*, Sivanandanagar, The Yoga-Vedanta Forest University, Rishikesh, 1956.

our hearts and why millions of people now worship him."[49] However, the history of Christianity does not show this example personified in the lives of Jesus' followers. It is not too late for Christians to re-incarnate Christ in their hearts.

When Rajagopala Iyer asked Sivananda about proselytizing missions, he replied:

> What is in this? A Christian comes, gives you a Bible and converts you into Christianity: a Mohamadan gives you a copy of the Quran and changes you into a Mohamadan: a Hindu has his Gita for the same purpose. Truth is one: all the scriptures expound this Truth though in different words. What purpose can ever be served by these proselytizers? They only change man's external cloak, a few of his habits. Can they ever go near the Atman, the Eternal Sakshi? Only dull-witted people engage themselves in such missions. Wise men will only seek to strengthen the individual's faith in his own religion.[50]

Sri Sivananda's admonition to Christians, and so, indirectly, to everyone, can be summed up in this plea:

> Study the Sermon on the Mount again and again. Meditate upon it. Choose the Lord's instructions one after the other, month after month, and endeavour diligently to put them into practice. Thus will you grow into a worthy child of Lord Jesus. Thus will you reincarnate Lord Jesus in your own heart. There are many today who truly and sincerely follow the teachings of the Saviour. In their hearts has Jesus reincarnated, to guide you, to lead you to the Kingdom of God, where he has his supreme seat. May you all be living embodiments of the Sermon on the Mount! May you realize the Kingdom of God within you here and now! [51]

## Divine Life Society

The disciples of Sivananda have continued to preach about Jesus, particularly the Divine Life President, Sri Swami Chidananda (1916-), and the previous General Secretary (a "horrible" title), Sri Swami Krishnananda (1912-2001).[52]

Chidananda, named Hindu of the Year in 1999, explains that this is partly because many of those who listen to the preaching are from Christian

---

[49] Swami Sivananda, *Lives of Saints*.
[50] 'All Religions Are One,' Inspiring Talks of Swami Sivananda, 21st September 1948. Published at: www.divinelifesociety.org/html/misc/ITGS/september.shtm
[51] Swami Sivananda, 'Jesus and the Modern Man,' www.dlshq.org/religions/christianity.htm#man
[52] Interview, *Hinduism Today*, December 1999, p 41.

backgrounds, even if no longer practicing Christians. Yoga is the bridge. How is Yoga different from Christianity?

> It differs in its refusing to accept the doctrine of 'original sin.' It does not call man a sinner. It may call man a fool but it doesn't call him a sinner. Man is God playing the fool, or, man is God who has lost his way home, wandered away, stumbling and running about in circles. It clears up the path, puts light and puts man on the path again and says, 'go ahead now, go straight to your home.' So it doesn't want you to consider yourself a sinner. And the other thing is this: Much of Christianity, unfortunately, in certain of its areas, becomes wholly a preoccupation with avoiding hell, trying to avoid hell, and somehow or other slip past the doors of heaven; somehow or other, even if you are not fully qualified for it. Yoga says: 'This is a little childish, you have got something more glorious. Why do you play this game of heaven and hell?' Yoga rejects hell, and Yoga rejects heaven also. Go to the Creator of heaven, the Master of heaven. Why heaven? Heaven is also a petty desire. You don't want it. 'I want God. I want to experience God, the Supreme Being, the Master of heaven.' Yoga concerns itself with God, not heaven or hell. You can say these are some of the differences, the way that Yoga differs from Christianity.[53]

Swamiji teaches that, where a religion declines or seems meaningless in changing contexts, Yoga can restore the "most precious part of religion."[54] Yoga is scientific, universal, transcends religion, is timeless, the heritage of humanity, the path of God-realization. Through serious and sustained Yogic practice all can find Christ and Christ-consciousness.

Krishnanandaji, like Sri Sivananda, addressed the problems of understanding the role of religions in our world.

> Many religions, rightly or wrongly, knowingly or unknowingly, have given the impression that they are teaching an otherworldly gospel which has roused the wrath of many socially-oriented thinkers who do not feel that the world of nature is an unreality to the extent that it demands a religious abnegation. I do not think that the prophets of religion, whether it is a Krishna or a Christ or a Mohammed, were responsible for creating this difficulty in our religious thinking. Most followers, whether of the gospel of Krishna or Christ or Mohammed or any other prophet, seem to be expressing the weakness characteristic of

---

[53] Swami Chidananda, 'Yoga and Christianity,' published at www.dlshq.org/religions/yogachristian.htm
[54] Swami Chidananda, *Guidelines to Illumination*, Divine Life Society, 1976. Web pdf edition, 1999, p 85. Downloaded on 22 June 2005 from http://www.rsl.ukans.edu/~pkanagar/divine/

human nature and demonstrating that they cannot be up to the mark or the level of the prophet.[55]

As religion is an "outlook of consciousness…an *attitude* of what we are, and not an expression necessarily of what we do in our outward lives," the only way to change the world is to change our selves, to be true to our own Self, to put aside all else but God. "It is high time that we are honest to the *true* God. When our deepest spirit, the basic being of ours is en rapport with the Being of the cosmos, perhaps the millennium, *Rama Rajya* or the Golden Age of *Kritayuga* descends. God reigning the world is not an impossibility. This is my humble conviction."

The current General Secretary of the Divine Life Society sent me this message to sum up this section and give us a timely reminder that much of what we read is best described as the Sanatanan Dharma and not Hinduism.

> Sri Swami Sivananda was a mighty Saint. The nomenclature Hindu – Hindu Religion etc - are the terms used by the western and oriental scholars and academicians to distinguish the way of life in India from other faiths like Christianity etc. In India the Saints and Seers follow 'Sanatanan Dharma' meaning, they follow 'Eternal Truth.' Swami Sivananda has spoken about all Great Ones like Christ, Mahavir of Jainism, Gurunanakh of Sikhism, Lord Buddha of Buddhism etc for the Sanatanan Dharma is universal and it beholds that the Indwelling Reality in everything is the Supreme Lord or the Supreme Reality. This great truth is traditionally handed down by the Masters to their students over these years in this country and is eternally relevant to all Saints and Seers who go by 'Sanatana Dharma.' The essence of Divine Life Society teaching is that God Realization is the Goal of life and all living beings are That Supreme Reality, 'Thou art That,' or otherwise the world is God. The Spiritual insight and the message the Divine Life Society wants to live and convey is 'Thou art Divine,' unfold and be aware of this ever-present Divinity.[56]

SUMMARY

This chapter has focused on some Hindus who contributed strong Hindu interpretations of Jesus as Christ, superseding what they had heard from Christians. They reinforced positive images of Hinduism, integrating Jesus into established patterns, not creating newly denuded versions of Hinduism to accommodate him. They did not consider Hinduism inadequate in any way but proudly posited its values as worthy of western and Christian adherence. Jesus

---

[55] Swami Krishnananda, 'To Thine Own Self Be True' in *Spiritual Import of Religious Festivals*, Appendix 3, The Divine Life Society Sivananda Ashram, Rishikesh. www.swamikrishnananda.org/fest/fest_apx3.html
[56] E-mail to author on 1 September 2005.

becomes ever more a Hindu and further and more severely detached from the Christian theology known at that time. And, even as Christian scholars increasingly demythologized the Jesus story, Hindus kept him firmly placed on a transcendental altar. Then, as now, the primary focus for interested Hindus is the Christ of faith rather than the Jesus of history. Even the Jesus of dynamic social change, also of interest to some Hindus, is not primarily based on an authentically historical figure but on the moral teachings received and the corresponding inner experience and change they induce, whatever their actual source.

Some of the Hindus here were very involved in the struggle for India's independence. With the advent of an independent India, interest in Jesus waned. The necessity for accommodating him diminished. Only certain strands of Hinduism retained their exposure to the encounter with Christianity on Indian soil. Orthodox Hinduism seemed little impacted, if at all.

As this chapter closes, Hindus no longer consider Jesus or Christianity or colonial powers a threat. Jesus becomes a feature of some strands of Hinduism and even a tool of some Hindu mission, an attraction to western devotees, dis-affected from their Christian backgrounds, who then re-encounter a more 'authentic' Jesus. He is offered back by preceptors themselves considered his equal, giving him a renewed authoritative status. He is returned as more spiritually and ethically profound than anything heard about from Christian quarters. The missionised become the missionaries!

The next three chapters focus on three pivotal organizations whose under-standings of Jesus arise from the spiritual experience and teachings of their founders, Hindus themselves considered Christs. This consolidation of Hindu reflection on Jesus parallels a new era of Christian thinking about Jesus, perhaps as theologically incompatible as earlier models but for very different reasons. As Christians awakened to the significance of the human and Jewish Jesus, Hindus, moving westward, were placing Jesus within an increasingly a-historical setting, part of their own richly significant mythology and spiritual heritage.

Chapter III

# THE RAMAKRISHNA MISSION

*As a large and powerful steamer moves swiftly over the water, towing rafts and barges in its wake, so when a saviour comes, he easily carries thousands to the haven of safety across the ocean of Maya.*

*- Sayings of Sri Ramakrishna, 722.*

## INTRDODUCTION

In this chapter we begin the exploration of important responses to Christ and Christianity from organizations active in the West as well as in India. We start with the Ramakrishna Mission founded by disciples of Sri Ramakrishna Paramahansa. His encounter with Christ proved an incipient factor in the genesis of enduring Hindu inculturations of Christ.

## SRI RAMAKRISHNA PARAMAHANSA, 1833-1886

Sri Ramakrishna was an immensely significant figure of this period and for this topic. Through his meeting with Keshub Sen in 1875 he heard about Jesus and famously practiced some form of Christianity resulting in his personal experience of Christ. He spoke about Christ with authority. His allegiance to Hinduism was never questioned. As he was and is widely considered to be an avatar, his was an inclusion by a spiritual equal, an outcome of realization not faith.

Ramakrishna was born a Brahmin in rural Bengal in 1836. As a young man he became a priest at the Kali temple in Dakshineswar where he soon began a life of spiritual intensity and training, engaging in many variant forms of *sadhana* (spiritual practice). In 1859 he was married to Saradamani Devi, a young girl who later became known by Ramakrishna devotees as the Holy Mother and who was worshipped by her husband as a manifestation of the Divine Mother. Soon many disciples were attracted to him by his spiritual magnetism. These included Narendranath Datta who became Swami Vivekananda. On 16 August 1886 the Master left his body after suffering for one year from throat cancer. He was the prototype global theologian, discovering in all his various sadhanas an essential underlying unity leading to the same divine destination.

Before turning to his insights on Jesus, it could be helpful to review ways in which Sri Ramakrishna himself was described and understood, both by fellow

Indians and by westerners. These testify to his significance and authority, and are a prelude to his own teachings on avatars and Jesus.

*As Others Saw Him*

Swami Premananda described Sri Ramakrishna as the incarnation who had come to end the arguing amongst devotees of earlier incarnations. "He has verified all the religions by his living, and bound them together by their common aim: realization of God."[1]

Vivekananda identifies Ramakrishna as a Buddha or a Christ in contra-distinction to social reformers like Keshub Sen. Their influence is greater than any other, they are the real "world-movers....They are all principle, no personality, free from ego and its constraints."[2]

Rt Rev John Sadiq emphasized, "The very advent of...spiritual giants is a miracle. The birth of Jesus was such an event, as was Sri Ramakrishna's."[3]

Swami Abhedananda wrote, "His mission was to establish harmony between religious sects and creeds...and to show by his own example that true spirit-uality can be transmitted and that salvation can be obtained through the grace of a Divine Incarnation."[4]

Sir Francis Younghusband, founder of the World Congress of Faiths, re-marked, "In a way, we Christians were able to understand our own religion better by the way in which he [Ramakrishna] had entered into it."[5]

The French writer, Nobel Prize winner, and life-long pacifist, Romain Rolland, in his biography of Sri Ramakrishna, concludes that, "Allowing for differences of country and of time, Ramakrishna is the younger brother of our Christ."[6]

Sri Aurobindo gave Sri Ramakrishna high praise and avatar status. He wrote that Sri Ramakrishna was the last and greatest avatar because he experienced God's unity in multiple ways, renewing and uniting all previous spiritual experiences. He offered the world a new vision, a new communion, for all peoples.[7]

[1] Swami Sridurgananda, 'Sri Premananda's Incarnation: A Study,' *Prabuddha Bharata*, Vol. 101 August 1996, p 196.
[2] Swami Vivekananda, *Inspired Talks*, Ramakrishna Math, Mylapore, 1969, p 58.
[3] *Studies on Sri Ramakrishna*, Ramakrishna Mission Institute of Culture, Calcutta, 1988, p 107.
[4] *Studies on Sri Ramakrishna*, p 11.
[5] *Studies on Sri Ramakrishna*, p 22.
[6] Romain Rolland, *The Life of Ramakrishna*, Advaita Ashrama, Almora, 1954, p 12.
[7] Swami Lokeswarananda, Ed, *World Thinkers on Ramakrishna-Vivekananda*, Ramakrishna Mission, Calcutta, 1983, pp 16-18.

*Sri Ramakrishna and Avatars*

How do these understandings of Sri Ramakrishna's life compare to his own teachings on divine incarnations? A summary of these insights taken from the *Sayings of Sri Ramakrishna* follows as a preliminary to Sri Ramakrishna's experience and interpretation of Jesus.[8] For him avatars are historical human messengers of God sent to guard virtue and to foster its growth. They can be interpreted allegorically and are to *Brahman* (Undivided Ultimate Reality) as waves are to an ocean. They are "always one and the same."

"Having plunged into the ocean of life, the one God rises up at one point and is known as Krishna, and when after another plunge, He rises up at another point, He is known as Christ….On the tree of *Sachidananda* (Absolute Existence-Knowledge-Bliss ie. Brahman) there hang innumerable bunches of Ramas, Krishnas, Buddhas, Christs etc. Out of these, one or two now and then come down into this world and produce mighty changes and revolutions."

Avatars are born with Divine powers and qualities. God is always visible in them through their lack of ego. They are "hard to comprehend. It is the play of the Infinite on the finite." They are only recognized by a few and best appreciated from a distance, like seeds carried by the wind and rooted elsewhere. They are God's love manifest in human form and they incarnate to teach true *Jnana* (wisdom, discrimination) and *Bhakti* (devotion).

"The Avatara is like a great engineer who sinks a new well in a place where there was no water before." He is "the son of Divine Knowledge whose Light dispels the accumulated ignorance of ages." Avatars save all through Grace and carry others across the ocean of *Maya* (delusion). They are willingly reborn to "teach and lead struggling humanity to its goal." They willingly deny themselves Nirvana for this purpose. They come for the "sake of those pure souls who love the Lord." They bring with them, as helpers, free souls or those in their last incarnation.

For Ramakrishna, the concept of competitiveness or superiority among avatars was foolish. All were complete revelations of the Divine and not subject to human notions about them. Avatars come of their own free attunement to the Divine Will at those *kairos* (pivotal) moments in human history when there is both the need and potential for the incarnation of new or fresh spiritual vision. Sri Ramakrishna himself can be seen as such an initiator and innovator in recent Hindu history. He awoke many in his lifetime and since to the effectiveness of spiritual sadhana, the search for God or Reality, and to the nature of that Reality as expressed in the human form of Sri Ramakrishna.

---

[8] *Sayings of Sri Ramakrishna*, Sri Ramakrishna Math, Madras, 1960, pp 215-222.

## Jesus and Sri Ramakrishna

Ramakrishna's encounter with or vision of Jesus and his practice of some form of Christianity are well recorded. This account captures the moment in 1874 when Ramakrishna, visiting the home of Jadunath Mallick, saw there a painting of the Madonna and Child. This picture seemed to come alive and "rays of light coming from the Mother and Child entered his heart and began to change radically the ideas stored there."

> Hindu conceptions were being chased into hiding and new thoughts were displacing them. In vain he struggled within himself and prayed, 'Mother, what strange changes are you bringing in me?' His devotion to the gods and goddesses were eclipsed for the time being and replaced by a great love for Christ, while pictures of Christian priests and devotees performing worship filled his mind. Although Sri Ramakrishna returned to his room at Dakshineswar, he remained absorbed in the new mood which had swept over him. He did not visit the Kali Temple on the morrow, nor the next day, nor the next: the Divine Mother was forgotten. Near the end of the third day, as he was walking in the Panchavati, he saw, evidently with open eyes, a Godman of fair complexion coming toward him with a steadfast look. Recognising him as a foreigner, he saw that his eyes and face were beautiful.... Sri Ramakrishna wondered who this was. The answer came from his heart, but in words loud enough that he described them as 'ringing': 'Lord Jesus Christ, the Master-Yogi, eternally one with God, who shed his heart's blood for the deliverance of man! It is He!' The figure embraced the Master and disappeared into his body, leaving the latter in *bhavasamadhi* (devotional ecstasy).[9]

As a result of these experiences, Ramakrishna held a "lifelong conviction of the divinity of Christ."[10] When asked why he so revered Christ, Ramakrishna replied "Why, I look upon Him as an Incarnation of God...like Rama or Krishna."[11]

Francis Clooney, a Jesuit, claims that the "foreignness" of Jesus, even as he and Ramakrishna merge, leaves Jesus situated in a Christian environment. He sees this experience within Ramakrishna's own context and without denigration of Christianity. "Because and not despite the fact that he remained thoroughly Hindu and not Christian, Ramakrishna crossed the religious boundary in a non-threatening, non-violent fashion: he made his claim without questioning the possibility of other, different experiences."[12]

---

[9] Swami Yogeshananda, *The Vision of Sri Ramakrishna*, Sri Ramakrishna Math, Madras, undated, pp 75-77.
[10] Swami Yogeshananda, *The Vision of Sri Ramakrishna*, p 77.
[11] *Teachings of Sri Ramakrishna*, Advaita Ashram, Calcutta, 1981, pp 44-5.
[12] *Studies on Sri Ramakrishna*, pp 90-92.

Clooney raises some interesting theological questions. Can an experience such as Ramakrishna's of Christ have integrity or validity for others? Can the subject of a vision really be separated from the context of the envisioner? Perhaps reflecting on the first experiences of Jesus' Jewish disciples might be helpful. When did 'Christian' visions of Jesus begin? Who decides on the authenticity of any such vision?

Sri Ramakrishna's experience of Jesus was one in a whole series of such encounters and cannot be isolated from the total picture of this period of his life. The encounters formed part of the meaning of his mission in so far as others have since described it - the establishment of harmony between religious sects. In this sense, Jesus, even though experienced from a context alien to Ramakrishna, was plunged into a Hindu pluralism by the connection then made between him and other divine manifestations and by the very fact of Ramakrishna's non-conversion. The integrity of Sri Ramakrishna's experience cannot be seriously doubted as there are broad resources, both Christian and other, testifying to his God-intoxicated state and significance. From a Hindu perspective, this indicates that a Hindu experience and understanding of Jesus has a valid place in any Christian contemplation of him.

Even so, Christopher Isherwood, a western writer who worked with Swami Prabhavananda of the California Ramakrishna Mission on many important translations of Hindu texts, told how his book, *My Guru and His Disciple*, got a hostile reception from some Christians. His impression was that many of the reviewers were offended by the suggestion that Ramakrishna was an avatar, thus denying the uniqueness of Jesus. In reviews of the book, Ramakrishna's life and experiences were decried as "not so much unbelievable as purposeless." His ecstasy was "without ethics, mere escapism." His loss of consciousness during *Samadhi* (spiritual ecstasy, union with God), were signs of "weakness, not strength."[13]

Ramakrishna himself, in instructions to friends and devotees, did not distinguish in terms of superiority among avatars but urged his listeners to "place your devotion whole-heartedly at the service of the ideal most natural to your being, but know with unwavering certainty that all spiritual ideals are expressions of the same supreme Presence."

> Do not allow the slightest trace of malice to enter your mind toward any manifestation of God or toward any practitioner who attempts to live in harmony with that Divine Manifestation. Kali, Krishna, Buddha, Christ, Allah - these are all full expressions of the same indivisible Consciousness and Bliss. These are revelatory initiatives of Divine Reality, not man-made notions....The ecstatic lover has burning faith in

---

[13] Christopher Isherwood, *My Guru and His Disciple*, Eyre Methuen, London, 1980, p 288.

every Divine Manifestation - as formless Radiance, as various Forms or Attributes, as Divine Incarnations like Rama and Krishna and as the Goddess of Wisdom, who is beyond form and formlessness, containing both in Her mystic womb.[14]

Sri Ramakrishna suggests that awareness of individual divine incarnations dissolves in the depth of a devotee's realization. God as many dissolves into One Absolute Reality as the devotee's insight and intuition develops. The mission of avatars is to stimulate this movement back to the recognition of the Formless Oneness just behind the veil of each incarnation, cloaked by maya to appear as separate and different manifestations. He refers to Krishna showing his disciple *Arjuna* a tree that, close-up, reveals its fruit. These are not berries but dark blue Krishnas, growing in clusters. The closer we approach God the fewer attributes we see. At last, in the presence of the Divine Reality, all becomes One, without attributes.[15]

SWAMI VIVEKANANDA AND THE RAMAKRISHNA MISSION

After the death of Sri Ramakrishna, nine of his disciples gathered together and took formal vows of renunciation. They later discovered this night to have been Christmas Eve. Swami Vivekananda, as he then became, asked them "to become Christs themselves - to pledge themselves to aid in the redemption of the world, and to deny themselves as Jesus had done."[16] From this time, *puja* (worship) was celebrated by the monks every Christmas. For one Swami, Prabhavananda, such an occasion, in 1914, was "the first time I realized that Christ was as much our own as Krishna, Buddha, and other great illumined teachers whom we revered." According to Swami Mridananda, the Rama-krishna Samnyasi Sangha or Order of Monks was set up using a Roman Catholic monastic model.[17] Now there are more than one hundred and thirty branches worldwide and over one thousand monks. In 1998 it was awarded the Gandhi Peace Prize for its service to India.

Some Christians in India in the early days of the Mission's foundation saw it as anti-Christian. Others saw it as a westernized and modernized movement. For example, J N Farquhar thought, "It led the average educated Hindu to believe the doctrine that everything Indian is pure, spiritual, and lofty, and that everything western is materialistic, sensual, devilish."[18] As we have already seen, this kind of polemic between Christians and Hindus was fairly character-istic of these times but here shown in reversal!

---

[14] Lex Hixon, *Great Swan. Meetings with Ramakrishna*, Shambala Press Publications, London, 1992, p viii.
[15] M, *The Gospel of Sri Ramakrishna*, Ramakrishna-Vivekananda Center, New York, 1973, p 853. Trans: Swami Nikhilananda.
[16] Swami Prabhavananda, *The Sermon on the Mount According to Vedanta*, Vedanta Press, Hollywood, 1963, pp 14-16.
[17] Paper on *Samnyasa,* in my keeping, unknown origin.
[18] J N Farquhar, *Modern Religious Movements in India*, Macmillan, New York, 1915, p 357f.

Today, the accusations from modern India against the Ramakrishna Mission are more likely to stress an anti-Hindu attitude. Indeed there is a lively debate within the movement whether or not it should be classified as Hindu or only as Vedantic. In 1980 the Mission went to the Calcutta High Court to plead that it was not a Hindu organization but "a collection of individuals classed together as the followers of Shri Ramakrishna" so that, under Article 30 of the Indian Constitution, they were a "religious minority."[19] According to Ram Swarup, the reasons for this application were based on the trade and economical advantages to be gained as a religious minority. The truth or otherwise of this, the ethics of such action, and any implications for Hinduism, are beyond the scope of this study. I only know that one Ramakrishna Mission swami that I spoke with some years ago was genuinely engaged with the Mission's relationship to Hinduism, whether or not it should take on all the difficulties of the latter or go its own way. I have met many Christians with this dilemma too, trying to decide whether to work for reform within the Church or to have the freedom of being outside it.

The Ramakrishna Mission has published a great deal of comment on the nature of avatars, Jesus' inclusion amongst them. No other Hindu organization has contributed so much to this topic. The reasons for this might be manifold: the original formative context in an India just recovering from some aggressive Christian mission linked to political imperialism; the considered avataric equality of Sri Ramakrishna with Jesus and his experience of Christ; the new confidence of Hindus in India as the nation moved towards independence; and the movement of the Ramakrishna Mission into the west with the subsequent advocacy of its own avatar and ideals within cultures, however secular, still underpinned by Christian perspectives.

Because the literature referring to Jesus is vast, ranging from full books to pamphlets, only a selection is given here indicating the primary foci and teachings.

*Swami Vivekananda, 1863-1902*

Swami Vivekananda was the foremost disciple of Sri Ramakrishna, pivotal in the foundation of the monastic order, and primary in bringing Vedanta and the life of Sri Ramakrishna to the west. In 1893 his message of religious unity took the first Parliament of the World's Religions in Chicago by storm.[20]

Here are some reflections on divine incarnations, Christ included, as recorded in *Inspired Talks*.[21] For Vivekananda, Christ came to reveal our own divinity

---

[19] Ram Swarup, *Ramakrishna Mission in Search of a New Identity*, Voice of India, 1986, pp 2-3. The plea was initially successful. However, in 1995, the Supreme Court formally declared the Mission Hindu. See 'Monks with a Mission,' *Hinduism Today*, Hawaii, August 1999, p 18.
[20] For full text, see Swami Vivekananda, *The Universal Religion*, Ramakrishna Vedanta Centre, UK, 1993.
[21] Swami Vivekananda, *Inspired Talks*, Ramakrishna Math, Mylapore, 1969.

and to reveal the nature of the Absolute. This requires a special manifestation. Krishna, Buddha, Christ, all of the avatars, are "drops" of *Divine Mother* or Universal Energy. "Jesus had our nature; he became the Christ. So can we and so must we. Christ and Buddha were the names of a state to be attained; Jesus and Gautama were the persons to attain it." There will be many more Christs in the future until the play is over.

"Jesus was imperfect because he did not live up fully to his own ideal and above all because he did not give woman a place equal to man's. Women did everything for him, and yet he was bound by the Jewish custom that not one was made an apostle." Whether equality for women has been fully committed to by the Ramakrishna Mission is a question of history. There are some female *sannyasins* in some of the western Ramakrishna Maths.

Christian soteriology is based on error. "Christ and Buddha are simply occasions upon which to objectify our own inner powers. We really answer our own prayers. It is blasphemy to think that if Jesus had never been born, humanity would not have been saved....Christs and Buddhas are but waves on the boundless ocean which I am."

"We are the light that illumines all the Bibles and Christs and Buddhas that ever were. Without that, they would be dead for us, not living." Clearly, the mission of an avatar cannot be completed unless it is recognized. I think confusion arises when the historical reality of an avatar appears to clash with the developed faith perceptions of him or her, a problem perhaps less pertinent to modern times when 'history' is more 'scientifically' recorded.

"The theory of the Incarnation is the first link in the chain of ideas leading to the recognition of the oneness of God and man. God first appearing in one human form, then reappearing at different times in other human forms, is at least recognized as being in every human form, in all men." Therefore, an avatar, openly revealing the nature of divine reality, awakens in others the awareness of their own innate divinity. Without the example of the avatar, this awareness might remain asleep and the divine *lila* (play) could not be consciously enjoyed. Compassion is manifested in the divine incarnation, as life without conscious awareness of our true nature is inevitably fraught with suffering. In a world of duality nothing can give permanent, unchanging happiness.

"First is existence, second is knowledge, third is bliss - very much correspond-ing to [Christian] Father, Son and Holy Ghost. Father is the existence out of which everything comes; Son is that knowledge. It is in Christ that God will be manifest. God was everywhere, in all beings, before Christ; but in Christ we become conscious of Him. This is God. The third is bliss - the Holy Spirit. As soon as you get this knowledge, you get bliss. As soon as you begin to have

Christ within you, you have bliss; and that unifies the three."[22]  Swamiji de-anthropomorphizes the Christian Trinity, turning it *Vedantic*, at the same time freeing it from any possible exclusive references to Jesus alone as Christ. Christ here is both associated with the historical Jesus and with that Jesus being one of many realized and potential manifestations of the knowledge of God. Perhaps this explanation might equate with the original faith experiences of Christians, before they became encapsulated in rigid doctrinal formulations.

Vivekananda referred disparagingly to the many attempts to match the life of Jesus to a recognizable label – rabbi, magician, messiah etc. In a lecture delivered in Los Angeles on 7 January 1900, he complained:

> One gets sick at heart at the different accounts of the life of the Christ that Western people give. I do not know what He was or what He was not! One would make Him a great politician; another, perhaps, would make of Him a great military general; another - a great patriotic Jew, and so on. Is there any warrant in the books for all such assumptions? The best commentary on the life of a great Teacher is His own life.[23]

He concludes that, whatever is the truth about Jesus, something remains which points to a truth fit for us to imitate. This is what the Hindu worships as Christ, as God. "You cannot imitate that which you have never perceived. There must have been a nucleus, a marvelous manifestation of spiritual power." In the same lecture Vivekananda conjectured that if a person had come to Jesus and said your teaching is beautiful but I cannot worship you as the only begotten Son of God, Jesus would have responded positively:

> Follow the ideal and advance in your own way, I do not care whether you give me the credit for the teaching or not. I am not a shopkeeper. I do not trade in religion. I teach truth only and truth is nobody's property. Nobody can patent truth. Truth is God Himself.

Potential tensions arise when Swamiji decides that "Jesus was gentle and loving but to fit him into Jewish beliefs, the idea of human sacrifice in the form of atonement, that is to say of a human scape-goat, had to come in…. This cruel idea made Christianity depart from the teachings of Jesus himself and develop a spirit of persecution and bloodshed."[24] The problem lies in the sure and confident removal of Jesus from his Jewish context as well as the negative interpretation of that Jewish-ness. Perhaps, more positively, Swami Vivekananda could have focused on the solid Hindu belief in the ability of

---

[22] *Collected Works of Swami Vivekananda*, Vol VIII, Mayavati Memorial Edition, Advaita Ashrama, Calcutta, 1969, p 191.
[23] Swami Vivekananda, *Christ the Messenger*, Udbodhan Office, Calcutta, 1989, pp 13-24.
[24] Swami Vivekananda, *Inspired Talks*, p 146.

spiritual preceptors to take upon themselves the karma of their devotees and work it out in their own body, an act of love ascribed to Sri Ramakrishna himself.

Vivekananda decried what he called "text-torturing." It is the spiritual impact of Jesus on our lives that is important. He claimed Jesus' key themes are spirit rather than world orientated: the Kingdom of God is within you; all are sons of God etc. The significant information is not "how much of the New Testament is true" or "how much of that life is historical." No amount of scholarly debate can dim the Jesus manifestation, revealed in his teachings not his personality.[25] This is pertinent today, for the discovery that much of the Christian Testament texts attributed to Jesus may not have emanated from him, should not diminish the value of the teachings or the effect they have had through the centuries. Nor should the possibility be neglected that the sources of the high teachings in the Christian Testament received the insights leading to them from their own inner experiences of and attunement with the Jesus incarnation.

Finally, Swami Vivekananda's 1894 statement - "I pity the Hindu who does not see the beauty in Jesus Christ's character. I pity the Christian who does not reverence the Hindu Christ" - can be seen as very in tune with the current boundary-crossing dialogical attempts at understanding amongst religious liberals and pluralists.[26] The difficulties imposed by such aspirations should not be under-assessed. It is one thing to look at such a statement and then intellectually grasp its meaning. Far more is required to delve behind the words and realize the meaning within its own spiritual and philosophical framework, one that may lead to new reflections of God, including the divine reality of our selves as Christs. Reverencing the Hindu Christ may potentially be a far greater theological journey for Christians than the one for the Hindu admiring the beauty of Jesus' character.

## Swami Akhilananda, -1962

This swami interprets incarnations as models and redeemers, "connecting links between God and man."[27] He sets the problem immediately – most orthodox Christians will not be able to accept the Hindu belief in multiple incarnations while liberal Christians will find the Hindu retention of the divine in the human too orthodox. As others of his time, he sees Jesus as truly an oriental and, non-polemically, uses this to build bridges between Hindu understandings of him and the Christian tradition.

For Swamiji, the life, practice and example of Sri Ramakrishna gives the authority for Hindus to worship Jesus as an incarnation of God. He sees the

---

[25] Swami Vivekananda, *Inspired Talks*, pp 210-213.
[26] Swami Vivekananda, *Collected Works*, Vol. VIII, p 219.
[27] Quotes from Swami Akhilananda, *Hindu View of Christ*, Philosophical Library Inc, NY, 1949, pp 11-180.

use of Jesus' "I" language in the Gospels, expressing a consciousness of "Thou," giving the same authority. Such beings are undisturbed by outer circumstances, totally integrated, supernatural magnets to others. The time of Jesus' birth was ripe for such an incarnation to renew God-consciousness. The nature of Roman society and the effect this had on Jews in the occupied Jewish territory indicates that Jesus had a mission to the gentiles as well as to the Jews.

Divine incarnations are fully human yet not limited in any way, unless they so choose. They are always aware of their divinity. They are not forced to this world, being free from all its attractions, but come to awaken right awareness in humans. They are different from saints, ordinary beings who have become illumined, as they are "veritable embodiment(s) of divine light and power from the very beginning of their lives." Their teachings are dynamic because all their words are lived out in their lives. They are a living force, transforming all those who have ears to hear. In support of this, Swami quotes Paul's Letter to the Philippians, chapter 2, where Jesus is equal with God yet voluntarily subjects himself to human limitations.

Regarding Jesus' apparent failure to bring in the Kingdom of God, Swami comments that the disappointment is human but not experienced by Jesus. Incarnations have a longer time vision and no selfish attachment to their work. Love is their only motivation. To those truly attuned this love is more power-ful than karma. For Swami, Jesus is a yogi, one totally established in right relationship with God, a Self-realized being. He compares the transfiguration and resurrection of Jesus, events when disciples were given insights not normally available, with an incident in Sri Ramakrishna's lila when, on entering samadhi, he touched the disciples present and they too were elevated to a higher plane of consciousness. Such *yogic* transmissions to disciples are not uncommon, verified by the clearly visible impact on those affected.

Jesus was a bhakta *yogi*, a yogi of devotion, an incarnation of love: his commandments were to love, his love for God was complete, he loved all without regard for social status. Also, he was a karma yogi, stressing service and offering his aid to all, setting an example to others. He was a raja yogi, experienced in self-control and the control of natural law. His unity with God reveals him as a jnana yogi, free from the maya of duality.[28] However, "Jesus as an incarnation did not need to learn yoga from anyone. As He was a born teacher, He was intimately aware of all ways of spiritual life and develop-ment."

The incarnations exist to change everyday life, to make it God-conscious, to put God at the centre of a transformed world. The teachings of Jesus were

---

[28] These yogas - bhakti, karma, jnana, raja - are all detailed in the Bhagavad Gita.

co-inherent with his life and "He did not utter a word that He did not demonstrate." Thus, the power of such Christ-like beings is in "spiritual rather than material or scientific advance, in their ability to transform human life."

Swami, as other Hindus, believed that Jesus could have saved himself from the crucifixion. His greatest miracle was his words of forgiveness from the cross. There is no doubt about the historicity of these words for they express the highest sentiment and purpose as befits a divine incarnation. By living as a true *sannyasi* (renunciant), full of *daya* (compassion) even at such a moment as the crucifixion, Jesus has positively and lastingly affected millions of lives, something never achieved by force. He acted rather than reacted and this was his strength and enduring influence.

## Swami Ramakrishananda, 1863-1911

This swami was a direct disciple of Sri Ramakrishna and he wrote of the resurrection of Jesus and its significance for Christianity.

> Christ was a universal helper of humanity. He was truly a great savior. Without the resurrection, however, Christianity would not have been a religion. Otherwise, Christ simply would have died as any man. It is because He rose again that Christianity lives. And He undoubtedly did rise, but I do not believe that He died on the cross. All things are possible with God and despite all that was done a spark of life must have remained somewhere in the body and this rekindled in the tomb.

For this monk, divine incarnations were "perfectly clear mirrors which gave us a perfect reflection."

> They did not bring us anything new. Truth is always existent. Christianity existed before Christ. Christ was only the mouthpiece.... Each one was a reflector of eternal Truth, but one man catches the light from Christ so he says, 'Christ has given me the Truth. I belong to Christ. I am a Christian.' So each great teacher has his followers who believe that the Truth came from him alone; but all teachers reflect the same Truth.[29]

## Swami Paramananda, -1940

This swami, a disciple of Vivekananda, mirrors many of the views given in the previous chapters, that the devotee of the east best understands and receives Jesus as Christ, free from exclusiveness, dogmatism, and institutionalism with all the destructive qualities inherent in them.[30] Differences between divine

---

[29] Sister Devamata, *Days in an Indian Monastery*, Vedanta Centre, Mass. 1975, pp 22-23; pp 99-100.

[30] All quotes from Swami Paramananda, *Christ and Oriental Ideas*, Vedanta Centre, Boston, 1923, pp 19-20; pp 23-81.

manifestations are highlighted through our inability to bring their ideals into our own lives.

> It would be wonderful if all people could be converted to the lofty and beautiful teachings of Jesus of Nazareth, the Christ of the Orient, the lowly, prayerful, devoted, yearning Christ who seeks divine grace above all other things, who shows man that his first and foremost duty is to find God, to live for God, and to make God a living presence in his life.

Christ comes in accord with Krishna's promise in the Gita, to incarnate whenever human need is great. What makes a good Christian is not accepting a creed but living a Christ-like life. Many Indians live by that ideal even if they have never heard of Jesus or could not accept the Christian creed. "The Supreme Ideal can never be labeled or represented by any one creed. Living the life is its only true interpretation."

The swami considers that the great difference between Christianity and Vedanta is that "the Veda declares Truth to be one without a second."

> It is eternal and all-inclusive and cannot be limited by time, place or personality; the Christ-Ideal has always existed and will always exist, because it stands for a state and not an individual. It [Veda] admits that Christ is one of the Incarnations, but not the only one; that before Him there were other divine manifestations, and that they will continue to come according to the need of humanity.

The Incarnations do not give new messages but repeat ones forgotten. The differences lie not in the principles given but only in the outer circumstances. To understand Christ it is essential to live a Christ-life. Following any great incarnation of Truth means we follow all. Anyone living the Christ-Ideal is a follower of Christ even if not a Christian. Each incarnation represents a state of being not an individual personality and all are partial representations of the Infinite that can never be fully expressed in name or form.

> When a follower of Christ shuts his heart against a child of God in any faith, he makes a mockery of his religion, because it is contrary to what Christ taught. Christ was willing to sacrifice His life even in the service of God. When God so dominates our heart that we are willing also to give up our life, then we are true to the Ideal which He preached.

Swami tells a story to illustrate this ideal of Christ. A *mendicant* beaten senseless is found by fellow monks and taken back to the ashram where they care for him. There he is asked who had beaten him. He replied that it was the same one who is now caring for him. This highlights the belief that God is present in all beings, however disguised, and hated in none.

Incarnations are "divine enough to be in touch with God and human enough to be in touch with man, so that man may realize divine things through Him." They teach nothing which other humans cannot also accomplish spiritually. Swami indicates here that the humanity as well as the divinity of incarnations matters, even as Christians have struggled for centuries to make sense of the dual nature of Jesus, understood as both human and divine. However, there is too strong a sense of *docetism* in Hindu thought for there to be a direct comparison. With such a disinterest in historicity, the humanity of an avatar must be seen as secondary, even though the avatar sustains a balanced perspective. Swamiji brings us into a Vedantic frame with his insight that "Man is always consciously finite and unconsciously infinite, while an Incarnation of God is consciously infinite and finite."[31]

## Swami Abhedananda, -1939

Swami Abhedananda, the last to pass away of the direct disciples of Sri Ramakrishna, compares Christ to Krishna, claiming both have contributed to the shaping of religions and the Kingdom of God on earth. Both were human and divine, both known as shepherds, both have said they were the Beginning and the End, and both were like "two brothers or two manifestations of the same Divinity and two different names separated only by time and space. Whether we worship one or the other we should come to the same place if our worship be sincere and through love and unselfish motives."[32]

## Swami Ranganathananda, 1908-2005

The Swami first sets the scene with his description of the nature of an avatar as a totality of knowledge, power and beneficence, divine and human, individual and universal, incarnated to accelerate humanity's spiritual evolution. The intensity of an avatar's life defies time and makes it effective through many generations. So, the essence of an avatar is not to diminish into the past but to grow into the future present, an influence exerted by Jesus now Christ. For Jesus, as for other avatars, Swami wrote:

> His earthly being and career, with its time co-ordinates of so many years, and space co-ordinates of so much height and weight, and other indefinable co-ordinates of personality like love and knowledge, is a highly deceptive mask to cover the spaceless and timeless amplitude of his being.[33]

[31] Swami Ramakrishananda, *God and Divine Incarnations*, Sri Ramakrishna Math, Madras, 1947, p 66.
[32] *Complete Works of Swami Abhedananda* Vol. VIII, Ramakrishna Vedanta Centre, Calcutta, 1969, pp 30-31.
[33] Swami Ranganathananda, *Eternal Values for a Changing Society*, Bharatiya Vidya Bhavan, Bombay, 1971, pp 96-101.

Jesus proclaimed "a religion of wide and deep horizons; he brought God near to man and bound both with the cord of love; he eliminated fear as the medium of their relationship."[34]

The Swami contrasts the emphasis of Christianity on the death of Jesus with India's concentration on the lives and teachings of Sri Rama, Krishna etc. The latter allows a fuller picture of the depth of an incarnation, its potential for human elevation and transformation. The greatest tragedy for Swami has been the transformation of Jesus into a man of sorrow and a consequent grim and cheerless Christianity. The Christian concept of redemption had the effect that "in place of calm reason and generous love, frenzy, fanaticism, intolerance, and bigotry gripped the propagation of the life-giving message of Jesus down the centuries, destroying as many lives as it undoubtedly helped to build, with groups interchanging places as persecutor and victim."

*Swami Satprakashananda, 1888-1979*

Swamiji's book, *Hinduism and Christianity: Jesus Christ and His Teachings in the Light of Vedanta*, covers a lot of ground, more than can be summarized here so I will focus on just one part, about resurrection. Satprakashanandaji describes Hindu understanding of resurrection as not that of a particular body but a movement into a subtle (or astral) body. It is this that makes contact with the disciples. The Epistles of Paul, the earliest known written documents following the death of Jesus, seem to support this view. Paul describes his experience of the risen Jesus in spiritual rather than material language. For Swamiji, resurrection and eternal life do not depend on bodies as spirit is our true nature.

The real meaning of resurrection is revealed in and by the lives of Jesus and Ramakrishna. "By following the example and teachings of the great spiritual personalities, we too can attain resurrection and everlasting life."[35] Swami describes appearances by Sri Ramakrishna after his *mahasamadhi*. Such appearances are not uncommon in Hinduism. In *Autobiography of a Yogi* by Paramahansa Yogananda, chapter three is devoted to Yoganandaji's direct experience of his risen guru, Sri Yukteswar.[36]

*Swami Dayatmananda*

Swami is leader of the UK Ramakrishna Vedanta Centre at Bourne End and kindly completed a Questionnaire I prepared for this project. His full response can be found in Appendix 1B, alongside those from the writer, Sita Ram Goel,

---

[34] Swami Ranganathananda, *The Christ We Adore*, Advaita Ashram, Mayavati, 1991, pp 35-44.
[35] Swami Satprakashananda, *Hinduism and Christianity: Jesus Christ and His Teachings in the Light of Vedanta*, Vedanta Society of St Louis, 1975, pp 188-9.
[36] See Chapter 4 of this book.

the academic, Bibhuti Yadav, and Mathoor Krishnamurti of the *Bharatiya Vidya Bhavan* (Indian Cultural Institute).

Swamiji believes, "For Hindus all over the world Jesus Christ signifies the reality of God, the reality of religion, the true meaning and goal of life and spiritual realization." He is revered as an avatar, "the proof of God's grace." What is important about Jesus is not his historicity or ethnic and religious background but the inspiring ideal he offers us in our spiritual strivings.

> Hindu understandings of Christ were far more radical and liberal than the exclusiveness preached by mainly the missionaries....Even if there were to be no historical a person as Jesus still from the idealistic point of view he would have been equally valid and venerable for me. Christ and his teachings have proved their worth during these many centuries and will continue to do so while this present creation lasts. Latest avatars like Sri Ramakrishna amply prove the truth and validity of other incarnations.

The significance of avatars like Christ and Ramakrishna was never more self-evident than now.

> At no time in history is man in more dire danger of annihilation than at present. A right understanding of each other's religion and a sincere desire to put the teachings of the prophets into day to day practice seems to be the only option left for us, not only for a saner way of living but if we have to merely survive. Jesus, Buddha, Krishna and Ramakrishna are much more relevant today than at any other time.

SUMMARY

From the direct experience of Sri Ramakrishna to the received faith of the devotees and members of the Ramakrishna Mission, it is clear that Jesus is accepted within the fold of avatars that includes Sri Ramakrishna himself. No major distinction is made between them as effective incarnations of God. Distinctions remain in the category of time, place and specific mission.

The openness of the Sri Ramakrishna Mission is not limited to Jesus. Many religious festivals are celebrated at its ashrams and monastics include regular community readings of spiritual texts from all traditions. During one visit I made to the British ashram, the monks were reading together from Brother Lawrence's *Practice of the Presence of God*, and readings from the biography of St Therese of Avila were given during services. During the same stay, puja was offered to Lord Krishna to celebrate *Janmashtami*, the commemoration of his birthday. The ashram is sprinkled with artefacts from many faiths, with paintings of many avatars and books from the majority of religious traditions. It is open-hearted rather than eclectic for the underpinning inspiration and focus of faith lies on the altar in the forms of Sri Ramakrishna Paramahansa, Swami Vivekananda, and Sri Sarada Devi, the wife of Sri Ramakrishna, known as the Holy Mother. Meditation and prayer take place here, formally, three times daily.

In one sense, the very fact that Jesus is incorporated into the faith life of the Ramakrishna Mission community validates his legitimacy in such a context. He does exist there in the hearts of devotees, whatever theological conundrums this might create for Christians. He exists as a faith experience freed from any doctrinal constraints that might limit his revelation. The question of what or who is experienced is only as relevant here as it is in any Christian setting where the presence of Christ is also felt. The very plurality of the Christ experience, within Christianity and outside of its boundaries, invalidates any constraining theological or clerical net placed over the figure of Jesus. He is not yet known as 'one' so he cannot alone represent the 'one' face of God incarnate. For the Ramakrishna Mission, he is one among many faces of God and is revered as such.

From Ramakrishna Paramahansa to the present day, the Ramakrishna Mission has exercised this policy of including-ness, placing Jesus alongside other avatars, partly because of the direct experience of Sri Ramakrishna himself and partly because of the continuing faith of members of the community. The experience of Jesus here is thus self-validating and must be taken seriously.

CHAPTER IV

# SELF-REALIZATION FELLOWSHIP

Learn to see God in all persons, of whatever race or creed. You will know what divine love is when you begin to feel your oneness with every human being, not before.
- *Paramahansa Yogananda, The Law of Success*

## INTRODUCTION

Swami Vivekananda made a great impact on western hearts and minds but in his short life he did not stay for long periods in the West. The first Hindu preceptor to remain in the West for most of his adult life was Paramahansa Yogananda. In Los Angeles, he established Self-Realization Fellowship, known in India as Yogoda Satsanga Society. It continues to disseminate his teachings and has ashrams and meditation centres throughout the world.

## PARAMAHANSA YOGANANDA, 1893-1952

Paramahansaji was born in India in the same year that Vivekananda addressed the first Parliament of the World's Religions in Chicago. His intense search for God finally led him to the ashram of his guru, Sri Yukteswar, described by the great oriental scholar, W Y Evans-Wentz, as "worthy of the veneration that his followers spontaneously accorded to him…[of] high character and holiness."[1]

In 1917 the young Swami Yogananda founded his first school, dedicated to spiritual as well as intellectual and physical education. In 1920 he was invited to speak at the International Congress of Religious Liberals in Boston.[2] Thus began his mission to the west. "Spread to all peoples the knowledge of the self-liberating yoga techniques," Sri Yukteswar had commanded him.[3] Yogananda stayed in the USA until his mahasamadhi in 1952. He returned only once to India, for fourteen months, in 1935. Of his many writings, *Autobiography of a Yogi*, published in 1946, is the best known and has been translated into more than nineteen languages. Self-Realization Fellowship recently published Yogananda's influential insights on the New Testament in *The Second Coming of Christ: The Resurrection of the Christ Within You: A*

[1] Paramahansa Yogananda, *Autobiography of a Yogi*, Self-Realization Fellowship, Los Angeles, U.S.A. Preface, p xiv.
[2] This organization became the International Association for Religious Freedom. See www.iarf.net
[3] *Paramahansa Yogananda: In Memoriam: The Master's Life, Work and Mahasamadhi*, Self-Realization Fellowship, Los Angeles, U.S.A. P 79.

*revelatory commentary on the original teachings of Jesus*, a two-volume set that profoundly explores the esoteric truths behind the written word.

There have been many testimonies to the effectiveness of the Master's life. His Holiness the Shankaracharya of Kanchipuran said of Yogananda that, "As a bright light shining in the midst of darkness, so was Yogananda's presence in this world. Such a great soul comes on earth only rarely, when there is a real need among men."[4] Swami Sivananda of the Divine Life Society described the Master in this way: "A rare gem of inestimable value, the like of whom the world is yet to witness, H H Sri Paramahansa Yogananda has been an ideal representative of the ancient sages and seers, the glory of India."[5] Evans-Wentz, himself a devotee, included in his tribute at the Master's passing his feeling that, "It is now the mighty privilege of all those yet in incarnation who venerate Paramahansa Yogananda as their Guide and Teacher to carry forward, and so transmit to the next generation, the saving teachings that he entrusted to them."[6] Following the Master's mahasamadhi, the Forest Lawn Memorial Park issued a statement:

> The absence of any visual signs of decay in the dead body of Paramahansa Yogananda offers the most extra-ordinary case in our experience….No physical disintegration was visible in Paramahansa Yogananda's body even twenty days after death…. The physical appearance of Paramahansa Yogananda on March 27th, just before the bronze cover of the casket was put into position, was the same as it had been on March 7th.[7]

*Jesus in Self-Realization Fellowship (SRF)*

Six divine incarnations are reflected on every SRF altar: Paramahansa Yogananda, his guru, Sri Yukteswar, his param-guru, Lahiri Mahasaya (guru of Sri Yukteswar), Mahavatar Babaji, Christ and Krishna. The aims of SRF include this one:

> To reveal the complete harmony and basic oneness of original Christianity as taught by Jesus Christ and original Yoga as taught by Bhagavan Krishna; and to show that these principles of truth are the common scientific foundation of all true religions.[8]

---

[4] Paramahansa Yogananda, *Autobiography of a Yogi*, Self-Realization Fellowship, Los Angeles, U.S.A. Inner front cover.
[5] *Paramahansa Yogananda: In Memoriam: The Master's Life, Work and Mahasamadhi*, Self-Realization Fellowship, Los Angeles, U.S.A. P 51. Letter 25 March 1952.
[6] *Paramahansa Yogananda: In Memoriam: The Master's Life, Work and Mahasamadhi*. P 23.
[7] *Paramahansa Yogananda: In Memoriam: The Master's Life, Work and Mahasamadhi*. P121f. Notarised letter, 16 May 1952.
[8] Paramahansa Yogananda, *Autobiography of a Yogi*, Self-Realization Fellowship, Los Angeles, USA. P 573

In *Autobiography of a Yogi*, Yogananda describes the connection between Jesus and Babaji. It was Babaji who sent Yogananda to bring the message and practice of *Kriya* Yoga to the west.[9] Yogananda claims:

> Babaji is ever in communion with Christ; together they send out vibrations of redemption and have planned the spiritual technique of salvation for this age. The work of these two fully illumined masters - one with a body, and one without a body - is to inspire the nations to forsake wars, race hatreds, religious sectarianism, and the boomerang evils of materialism.[10]

Each Christmas SRF Centers around the world hold a six-hour meditation to commemorate the birth of Jesus, and at Easter there is a sunrise ceremony to remember his resurrection. Yogananda taught:

> The real celebration of Christmas is the realization within ourselves of Christ consciousness. It is of utmost importance to every man, whatever his religion, that he experience within himself this 'birth' of the universal Christ. The universe is the body of Christ: everywhere present within it, without limitation, is the Christ Consciousness.[11]

Yoganandaji saw special greatness, "the mightiest miracle of love," in Christ's words of forgiveness from the cross.[12] He understood the crucifixion as an event in line with action by other avatars.

> Jesus signified himself as a ransom for the sins of many. With his divine powers, Christ could never have been subjected to death by crucifixion if he had not willingly cooperated with the subtle cosmic law of cause and effect. He thus took on himself the consequences of others' karma, especially that of his disciples. In this manner they were highly purified and made fit to receive the omnipresent consciousness or Holy Ghost that later descended upon them.[13]

Yogananda's reflections on the resurrection as a movement from worldly to divine consciousness, from human to divine love, inspired many injunctions and prayers.

---

[9] Mahavatar Babaji is the Supreme Guru in the line of SRF gurus. He is believed to be still incarnate in the Himalayas, seeming always to look about twenty-five years of age. See chapters 33 and 37 of Paramahansa Yogananda, *Autobiography of a Yogi*, Self-Realization Fellowship, Los Angeles, U.S.A.

[10] Paramahansa Yogananda, *Autobiography of a Yogi*. P 347.

[11] Paramahansa Yogananda and others, *Spiritual Diary*, Self-Realization Fellowship, Los Angeles, U.S.A. 'Special Thought for Christmas.'

[12] Paramahansa Yogananda, *Whispers from Eternity*, Self-Realization Fellowship, Los Angeles, USA. P129.

[13] Paramahansa Yogananda, *Autobiography of a Yogi*, Self-Realization Fellowship, Los Angeles, U.S.A. PP 236-237. Many similar accounts of Masters taking on the karma of others can be found in Hinduism eg. in the lives of Sai Baba, Sri Ramakrishna, Yogananda himself.

Whenever you do away with ignorance and think good thoughts, Christ is being resurrected within you; that is, the Christ Consciousness which was fully manifested in Jesus is awakening within you. Resurrection is not the power of Spirit in the body of Jesus only; Spirit is in everyone. Nor does man have to die in order to resurrect Spirit. The physical resurrection of Christ was only part of the lesson of his life.[14]

The resurrection of Sri Yukteswar, Yogananda's guru, is described in Chapter 13 of the *Autobiography of a Yogi*.[15] Sri Yukteswar had passed away on 9 March 1936.

Sitting on my bed in the Bombay hotel at three o'clock in the afternoon of June 19, 1936… I was roused from my meditation by a beatific light. Before my open and astonished eyes, the whole room was transformed into a strange world, the sunlight transmuted into supernal splendor. Waves of rapture engulfed me as I beheld the flesh and blood form of Sri Yukteswar![16]

The chapter concludes with the visit of the risen Sri Yukteswar to another disciple, an elderly woman known affectionately as Ma (mother). She had not heard about his passing away and recounts how she stopped to talk with him on March 16th, just as she often did during his morning walks. The date was one week after Sri Yukteswar's mahasamadhi.[17]

Like Sri Ramakrishna, Yoganandaji also had visions and direct experiences of Jesus. One such instance is described in the *Autobiography of a Yogi*:

One night while I was engaged in silent prayer, my sitting room in the Encinitas hermitage became filled with an opal-blue light. I beheld the radiant form of the blessed Lord Jesus. A young man, he seemed, of about twenty-five, with a sparse beard and moustache; his long black hair, parted in the middle, was haloed by a shimmering gold. His eyes were eternally wondrous; as I gazed, they were infinitely changing. With each divine transition in their expression, I intuitively understood the wisdom conveyed. In his glorious gaze I felt the power that upholds the myriad worlds. A Holy Grail appeared at his mouth; it came down to my lips and then returned to Jesus. After a few moments he uttered

---

[14] *Self-Realization*, Journal, Self-Realization Fellowship, Los Angeles, U.S.A. Spring 1974. P 2.
[15] The theme of resurrection is not unfamiliar in eastern religions. See also the life of Milarepa who rose from the funeral pyre itself to prevent squabbling amongst devotees over his ashes. W Y Evans-Wentz, Ed, *Tibet's Great Yogi, Milarepa: A Biography from the Tibetan*, OUP, Oxford, 1969, p 283.
[16] Paramahansa Yogananda, *Autobiography of a Yogi*, Self-Realization Fellowship, Los Angeles, U.S.A. P 475.
[17] Paramahansa Yogananda, *Autobiography of a Yogi*. P 496.

beautiful words, so personal in their nature that I keep them in my heart.[18]

*Teachings on Christ and Avatars*

"Jesus Christ is a liaison between East and West."[19] He links and balances the best distinctive qualities of both. In one sense, this can be seen as a very positive acceptance of western response to Jesus and the sharing this could entail. It is also a very strong affirmation of Jesus as intrinsically rooted in an eastern as well as a western religious thought world.

> Christ is not the property of either East or West - an East-West bond is manifested in his life. He belongs to both, and to all the world. His universality is what makes him so wonderful. Jesus took the body of an Oriental so that in being accepted as guru by the Occidental he would thereby symbolically draw East and West together....The ideals of Christ are the ideals of the scriptures of India. The precepts of Jesus are analogous to the highest Vedic teachings, which were in existence long before the advent of Jesus. This does not take away from the greatness of Christ; it shows the eternal nature of truth, and that Jesus incarnated on earth to give to the world a new expression of *Sanatan Dharma* (eternal religion, the eternal principles of righteousness).[20]

The Master further expands the relationship between this oriental Christ and other, Indian, incarnations:

> The great masters of India mold their lives by the same godly ideals that animated Jesus; these men are his proclaimed kin: 'Whoever shall do the will of my Father which is in heaven, the same is my brother, and sister, and mother'....Freemen all, lords of themselves, the Yogi-Christs of India are part of the immortal fraternity: those that attain a liberating knowledge of the One Father.[21]

When Yoganandaji was in the west he was often asked if he believed in Jesus. His response was: "Why such a question? We in India reverence Jesus and his teachings, perhaps more than you do."[22] His emphasis, as with other Hindus, was on living up to the Christ ideal.

> Worshiping Jesus is not truly meaningful until one can expand his consciousness to receive within himself the Christ Consciousness. That is the second coming of Christ. Unless you do your part, a thousand

---

[18] Paramahansa Yogananda, *Autobiography of a Yogi*, Self-Realization Fellowship, Los Angeles, U.S.A. P 558.
[19] Paramahansa Yogananda, *Man's Eternal Quest*, Self-Realization Fellowship, Los Angeles, U.S.A. P 283.
[20] Paramahansa Yogananda, *Man's Eternal Quest*, P 284-5.
[21] Paramahansa Yogananda, *Autobiography of a Yogi*, PP 195-196.
[22] Paramahansa Yogananda, *Man's Eternal Quest*, P 289.

Christs come on earth would not be able to save you. You have to work for your own salvation.[23]

Unlike some Hindus, Yogananda does not wonder about the historical reality of Jesus: "I know that Christ is real, for I have seen him many times."[24] At a Christmas meditation in 1943, Yoganandaji taught further about the living reality of Jesus and other avatars. They are all still active, according to their missions, acting for the redemption of the world. To those who are deeply attuned, Jesus reveals himself.

> Christ has not gone. He has given his philosophy, and he is watching those souls who are practicing it. You must live the ideals of Christ, and know that he is watching you all the time....He will be drawn only to the altar of your love....Christ is all the time working for you....In every good thought is a secret home of Christ....He is like a fragrance, all-pervading. But it is only through receptive souls that he works. If you call to Christ with all your heart, and if you have learned the lesson that you must never fail to live in humility and love, and to meditate deeply upon God, Christ will come to you. You can see him in flesh and blood, even as he has come to Babaji, St. Francis, and others who are in tune.[25]

## Christ and Krishna

Yogananda draws parallels between the lives of Jesus and Krishna, citing them as examples for others to emulate not merely revere. He also describes the relationship between their human and divine natures.

> Divine incarnations such as Jesus Christ and Jadava Krishna had somewhere, sometime, developed that spiritual stature which foredestined their birth as *avatars*. Such beings are free from the karmic compulsions of rebirth; they return to earth only to help liberate mankind. Even though liberated, the divine ones play, at God's behest, their human roles in the seeming reality of the earth-life drama. They have their weaknesses, their struggles and temptations, and then, through righteous battle and right behavior, they attain victory. In this way they show that all men can be and are meant to be spiritually victorious over the forces that would keep them from realizing their inherent oneness with God. A Christ and a Krishna created perfect by God, without any effort of self-evolution on their part, and merely pretending to struggle and overcome their trials on earth, could not be examples for suffering humans to follow. The fact that the great ones

---

[23] Paramahansa Yogananda, *Man's Eternal Quest*, Self-Realization Fellowship, Los Angeles, U.S.A. P 292.
[24] Paramahansa Yogananda, *Man's Eternal Quest*. P 290.
[25] Paramahansa Yogananda, *The Divine Romance*, Self-Realization Fellowship, Los Angeles, U.S.A. PP 256, 257, 265.

too were once such mortals, but overcame, makes them pillars of strength and inspiration for stumbling mankind. When we know that divine *avatars*, in order to make themselves perfect, once had to go through the same kinds of human trials and experiences that we do, it gives us hope in our own struggle.[26]

The Master here gives a clear picture of spiritual development to which all can be linked, leading from mortal to divine incarnation. Once human, now fully divine, avatars in a final, chosen (rather than compulsory) incarnation can be viewed docetically, allowing full scope for the power of their lives and their missions, yet without loss of their humanity through which they have had to move, life after life, towards their present divinity and freedom. Avatars, one with God, are therefore different but equal manifestations of divine reality. For Yogananda, however, Christ and Krishna, stand as supreme examples – Christ, the renunciant, for the greatness of his loving sacrifice, and Krishna, the king, for his life lived fully in the world but untouched by it. Of parallels between them, Paramahansaji wrote:

> Both Jesus and Krishna were born of devout, God-loving parents. Krishna's parents were persecuted by his wicked uncle, King Kansa; King Herod's threats tormented the mother and father of Jesus. Jesus has been likened to a good shepherd; Krishna, during his early years in hiding from Kansa, was a cowherd. Jesus conquered Satan; Krishna conquered the demon Kaliya. Jesus stopped a storm on the sea to save a ship carrying his disciples; Krishna, to prevent his devotees and their cattle from being drowned in a deluge of rain, lifted Mt Gowardhan over them like an umbrella. Jesus was called 'King of the Jews,' though his kingdom was not of this world; Krishna was an earthly king as well as a divine one. Jesus had women disciples, Mary, Martha, and Mary Magdalene, who helped him and played a vital role in his mission; Krishna's women disciples, Radha and the *gopis* (milkmaids), similarly played divine roles. Jesus was crucified by being nailed to a cross; Krishna was mortally wounded by a hunter's arrow. The destinies of both were prophesied in the scriptures. These two *avatars*, both Orientals, are generally recognized in the West and East respectively as the supreme incarnations of God.[27]

Jesus taught renunciation from worldly attachments in favor of our full commitment to God who would fulfill all needs (Matthew 6.25; Luke 12.30, 31; Mark 10.29, 30; Matthew 4.18). Krishna also urged that God be put first and all activities be performed with Him in mind (Gita 18.66, 4.19). Both

---

[26] Paramahansa Yogananda, *Man's Eternal Quest*, Self-Realization Fellowship, Los Angeles, USA. P 294-5.
[27] Paramahansa Yogananda, *Man's Eternal Quest*. P 296-7.

reinforced the moral commandments of the time, principles that Yogananda sees as the foundation of the practice of religion.

> As the business-man tries to alleviate the suffering of others by supplying some need; as every man is an agent of God for doing some good on earth, so Christ, Krishna, Buddha - all the great ones - came on earth to bestow on mankind the highest good: knowledge of the path to Eternal Bliss, and the example of their sublime lives to inspire us to follow it.[28]

In the teachings and examples given by both Christ and Krishna lies the link to Yoganandaji's own avataric mission.

> Jesus Christ and Bhagavan Krishna gave to the world two of the greatest books of all times. The words of Lord Krishna in the Bhagavad-Gita and of Lord Jesus in the New Testament of the Bible are sublime man-ifestations of truth, great models of spiritual scripture. These two bibles give essentially the same teaching. The deeper Christianity that was preached by Jesus has been lost sight of today. Christ taught devotion and yoga, as did Krishna; and it was my *param-paramguru*, Mahavatar Babaji, who first spoke of showing the unity of Christ's teachings and Krishna's Yoga philosophy. To fulfill this mission is the special dispensation given to me by Babaji.[29]

The Master describes a vision he had of Christ and Krishna together:

> I beheld a great blue valley encircled by mountains that shimmered jewel-like. Around opalescent peaks vagrant mists sparkled. A river of silence flowed by, diamond-bright. And there I saw, coming out of the depths of the mountains, Jesus and Krishna walking hand in hand - the Christ who prayed by the river Jordan and the Christ-na who played a flute by the river Yamuna. They baptized me in the radiant waters; my soul melted in fathomless depths. Everything began to emit astral flames. My body and the forms of Christ and Krishna, the iridescent hills, the glowing stream, and the far empyrean became dancing lights, while atoms of fire flew. Finally nothing remained but mellow luminosity, in which all creation trembled. O Spirit! in my heart I bowed again and again to Thee - Eternal Light in whom all forms commingle.[30]

---

[28] Paramahansa Yogananda, *Man's Eternal Quest*, Self-Realization Fellowship, Los Angeles, U.S.A. P 306.
[29] Paramahansa Yogananda, *Man's Eternal Quest*. P 297.
[30] Paramahansa Yogananda, *Whispers from Eternity*, Self-Realization Fellowship, Los Angeles, U.S.A. PP 170-171.

*Christ Consciousness*

Paramahansa Yogananda differentiates between Jesus and Christ or Christ Consciousness:

> I am glad that Christianity was not called 'Jesusism,' because Christianity is a much broader word. There is a difference of meaning between *Jesus* and *Christ*. Jesus is the name of a little human body in which the vast Christ Consciousness was born. Although the Christ Consciousness manifested in the body of Jesus, it cannot be limited to one human form. It would be a metaphysical error to say that the omnipresent Christ Consciousness is circumscribed by the body of any one human being.[31]

Through his attunement with the all-pervading Christ Consciousness, Jesus was both prescient and able to perform miracles. He had full realization of his oneness with the Father so was able to do many things that deluded mortals could not do. "He raised the dead. He rebuilt his mutilated body." That same power exists in every one and is the second coming of Christ. "The first coming of Christ was at the birth of creation. Christ was born not only in the body of Jesus; Christ Consciousness was already manifest in all creation. Jesus tuned in with and manifested that Christ Consciousness." Thus the second coming of Christ materialized in the body of Jesus, a process which all must undertake and complete. "[That] same Christ must be born again in your consciousness. That is the meaning of the 'second coming' of Christ."[32]

As previously mentioned, in 2004, SRF released a two-volume set of Sri Yogananda's Commentary on the Christian Testament. It contains profound and detailed analysis of the Christian Gospels verse by verse. It may prove even more exciting and challenging for some Christians than the Da Vinci Code! Its message is as radical:

> A thousand Christs sent to earth would not redeem its people unless they themselves become Christlike by purifying and expanding their individual consciousness to receive therein the second coming of the Christ Consciousness, as was manifested in Jesus....Contact with this Consciousness, experienced in the ever new joy of meditation, will be the real second coming of Christ - and it will take place right in the devotee's own consciousness.[33]

---

[31] Paramahansa Yogananda, *Man's Eternal Quest*, Self-Realization Fellowship, Los Angeles, U.S.A. P 297.
[32] *Self-Realization*, Self-Realization Fellowship, Los Angeles, U.S.A. Winter 1995, p 4. In *Self-Realization*, Winter 1974, p 9, a quote from Angelus Silesius is given: "Were Christ a thousand times reborn in Bethlehem's stall and not in thee, thou still art lost beyond recall."
[33] Paramahansa Yogananda, *The Second Coming of Christ: The Resurrection of the Christ Within You: A revelatory commentary on the original teachings of Jesus*, Self-Realization Fellowship, Los Angeles, U.S.A. Quote published at http://www.yogananda-srf.org/scoc/scoc_frameset-des.html

Dr Quincy Howe, academic and author, reviewed the book for *Yoga International* magazine. Howe wrote that an underlying Christian mysticism has been brought to the surface by Yogananda; that in this seventeen hundred page commentary, there is now a "fully developed vision of the path of meditation and the science of God-realization;" that Jesus and Krishna are shown to have preached the "same doctrine of spiritual self-discovery." Jesus was a yogi. The Gospels reveal yogic teachings and have a "universal esoteric message that has been waiting full and systematic explication since the apostolic age." Howe decrees, "In Yogananda's commentary, what has been veiled, obscure, and oblique is fully disclosed."

How could Yogananda have 'known' the secret mysteries of the Gospels, how did he come by his interpretations of biblical passages? Howe writes, "There are no resemblances to conventional biblical exegesis."

> There is no scholarly examination of the wording. There is no attempt to recreate the intellectual climate of 2,000 years ago. Here Yogananda is speaking with the voice of the spiritual visionary, the voice of Patanjali, Shankara, and the Old Testament prophets. These are the sages who stand, not on the authority of their learning and intellect, but on their *anubhava*, their unmediated knowledge of spiritual truth.[34]

SRI YUKTESWAR, GURU OF PARAMAHANSA YOGANANDA, 1855-1936

Yoganandaji wrote that Sri Yukteswar "expounded the Christian Bible with a beautiful clarity" and that "it was from my Hindu Guru, unknown to the roll call of Christian membership, that I learned to perceive the deathless essence of the Bible, and to understand the truth in Christ's assertion – surely the most thrillingly intransigent ever uttered: 'Heaven and earth shall pass away, but my words shall not pass away.'"[35] About Christ, Sri Yukteswar told Yogananda:

> Christ had won this final freedom even before he was born as Jesus. In three stages of his past, symbolized in his earth-life as the three days of his experience of death and resurrection, he had attained the power to fully arise in Spirit.[36]

Sri Yukteswar also taught Paramahansa Yogananda that:

> Theologians have misinterpreted Christ's words in such passages as 'I am the way, the truth and the life: no man cometh unto the Father, but by me' (John 14.6). Jesus meant, never that he was the sole Son of God,

---

[34] Quincy Howe, 'Mystical Christianity: A Yogic View of Christ,' in *Yoga International*, March 2005, reprinted in *Self-Realization*, Self-Realization Fellowship, Los Angeles, U.S.A. Summer 2005. PP 30-39.
[35] Paramahansa Yogananda, *Autobiography of a Yogi*, Self-Realization Fellowship, Los Angeles, U.S.A. P 195.
[36] Paramahansa Yogananda, *Autobiography of a Yogi*. P 490.

but that no man can attain the unqualified Absolute, the transcendent Father *beyond* creation, until he has first manifested the 'Son' or activating Christ Consciousness *within* creation. Jesus, who had achieved entire oneness with that Christ Consciousness, identified himself with it inasmuch as his own ego had long since been dissolved.[37]

Sri Yukteswar's seminal book, *The Holy Science*, "explores parallel passages from the Bible and the Hindu scriptures to reveal the essential unity of all religions." The destiny of each one of us is to become Christs, saviors. Sri Yukteswar describes this state of *Kaivalya* or unification of the self with God:

In this state, all the necessities having been attained and the ultimate aim effected, the heart becomes perfectly purified and, instead of merely reflecting the spiritual light, actively manifests the same. Man, being thus consecrated or anointed by the Holy Spirit, becomes Christ, the anointed Saviour. Entering the Kingdom of Spiritual Light, he becomes the Son of God. In this state man comprehends his Self as a fragment of the Universal Holy Spirit, and, abandoning the vain idea of his separate existence, unifies himself with the Eternal Spirit; that is, becomes one and the same with God the Father.[38]

Following Sri Yukteswar's mahasamadhi on 9 March 1936, Calcutta's leading newspaper, *Amrita Bazar Patrika*, wrote an obituary that included this perceptive comment on the Master's understanding of Eastern and Western spirituality: "His interpretations of the Bhagavad Gita and other scriptures testify to the depth of Sri Yukteswarji's command of the philosophy, both Eastern and Western, and remain as an eye-opener for the unity between Orient and Occident."

SELF-REALIZATION FELLOWSHIP MONASTICS

Whilst SRF monastics regularly give lectures around the world, they are based on the teachings of Paramahansa Yogananda and the talks recorded do not deal as extensively as the Ramakrishna Order with avatars in general and Jesus as an avatar in particular. Two examples are given here of leading disciples who have engaged with this topic in recorded talks or writings.

---

[37] Paramahansa Yogananda, *Autobiography of a Yogi*, Self-Realization Fellowship, Los Angeles, U.S.A. P 198-199. Footnote.
[38] Swami Sri Yukteswar, *The Holy Science*, Self-Realization Fellowship, Los Angeles, U.S.A. P 32. See John 14:11: "Believe me that I am in the Father, and the Father in me." See also Revelation 3:21: "To him that overcometh will I grant to sit with me in my throne, even as I also overcame, and am sat down with my Father in his throne."

*Sri Daya Mata, 1914-*

Sri Daya Mata is the President of Self-Realization Fellowship, a direct disciple of Paramahansa Yogananda since 1931 when she was seventeen years old and met him for the first time. She was one of the very first monastic disciples of Yogananda and in 2005 celebrated fifty years as SRF President. Many of Daya Ma's family also joined the *ashram* or became lay disciples. Reflecting on the purpose of divine incarnations, Mataji wrote:

> It is said that when the world is at its darkest and when man's guiding light has grown dim, the Compassionate Lord takes pity on His children and sends a messenger with a teaching that will help to free humanity from its self-created cave of darkness. Jesus Christ brought such a message. It is not the monopoly of one religion, but a timeless expression of eternal, universal truth, the same as taught by Lord Krishna in India, thousands of years earlier. A revival of this message has been sent to the world, in our own troubled times, in the teachings of our blessed Guru.[39]

Hearing the messages, even recognizing their truth, is not enough. Priscilla Presley tells how Elvis, when he first discovered the "higher level of spirituality" offered by SRF, something he said he had been seeking his whole life, immediately wanted to teach it to the whole world. Daya Ma, who was with him at this time, advised him that such "evolution isn't instantaneous," there are no "short cuts." "Discipline and commitment…full-time dedication" are needed. "You have to live this life."[40]

For me, this is the great message of Hinduism. This is the enormous challenge it reveals to us. A vicarious sacrifice is not enough. The whole point is that we willingly, from our own understanding, surrender, devotion and effort, return to the Source, merge with the One, become harmonious, content, peaceful and loving beings of and for all. No one can do this for us. The *lila* or play is all about realizing this for ourselves.

While, for most of us, karma dictates our return to earth, avatars are not bound by it. In response to a *satsanga* question, Mataji referred to the connection between avatars and karma:

> To appear on earth in human form…even a master has to take on a certain amount of delusion or the very atoms of his body would not hold together; but that is not *karma*. The delusion essential for a manifested form is what Jesus alluded to when he had just come out of the tomb

---

[39] Sri Daya Mata, *Finding the Joy Within You*, Self-Realization Fellowship, Los Angeles, U.S.A. P 159.
[40] Priscilla Presley, Lisa-Marie Presley and other family members, *Elvis by the Presleys*, David Ritz, Ed, Century, London, 2005, p 118.

after his crucifixion and said to Mary Magdalene, 'Touch me not; for I am not yet ascended to my Father.' When any soul, even a Christ, descends into the world of duality and takes on a human form, he thereby accepts certain limitations. But taking on the compulsions of the law of *karma* is not one of them. He still remains above and beyond all *karma*.[41]

Thus limitations are temporary and superficial and only relate to the form itself. However, pain is an inevitable companion of the physical form, even if the mind and spirit can detach themselves from it. Therefore, avatars really can suffer, even though being able to realize the delusory nature of suffering diminishes its impact.

## Sri Gyanamata, 1869-1951

Sri Gyanamata was a direct disciple, later an SRF monastic, of whom Paramahansa Yogananda said on her passing away:

> Sister's life has been like that of St. Francis, who suffered even while helping others. So she stands as a great inspiration. In all those years she suffered, she showed that her love for God was greater; and I never saw one mark of suffering in her eyes. That is why she is a great saint - a great soul - and that is why she is with God.[42]

Sister wrote of the avatars as not in competition but incarnating specifically for those who are their own. Paraphrasing John 10.14, she declares:

> The masters, the Good Shepherds of this world, come down from their high places and give their lives to searching for disciples who are lost in the darkness. They find them in desolate and dangerous places, arouse them, lift them to a divine shoulder, and bear them with rejoicing to a safe place in the fold. They feed them with celestial food and give them living water to drink, of which, if a man eat and drink, he shall live forever. They give them power to become the sons of God. They give their own lives, to the last ounce of flesh and the last drop of blood, for the redemption of the sheep who know their voice.[43]

KESHAV SHARMA, PARAMAHANSA YOGANANDA RESEARCH CENTRE, INDIA

Although not a spokesperson for SRF or YSS, I asked Dr Keshav Sharma, a life-long educator and founder of the Paramahansa Yogananda Research Centre in Shimla, whether Christ and Christianity are part of the Indian

---

[41] Sri Daya Mata, *Only Love*, Self-Realization Fellowship, Los Angeles, U.S.A. PP 203-204.
[42] Sri Gyanamata, *God Alone: The Life and Letters of a Saint*, Self-Realization Fellowship, Los Angeles, U.S.A. P 39.
[43] Sri Gyanamata, *God Alone: The Life and Letters of a Saint*. P 232.

devotee's life today.[44] He responded: "True Christianity has relevance everywhere and will hold good for all times to come. In India, if Christ is projected in his true form and his philosophy without any bias, then Indians will appreciate." Keshav has not personally experienced any problems from Christian mission but feels that "the way these missions are operating here in India is open to criticism. They are using wrong methods to convert Hindus." Even so, the disciples of Paramahansa Yogananda in India still celebrate Christmas just as they do in the west.

For Hindus who have studied the life and teachings of Jesus, he is an avatar in the same way as Krishna or Rama. This is natural, as Dr Sharma, like many Hindus, believes "Christ was a Yogi who spent his early youth and life after crucifixion in India. He was a Yogi and disciple of some great yogis of India."

For Keshav, the most significant message for our times is Yogananda's emphasis on seeking God first, before material needs, showing us how to lead a balanced life, "the gist of all great religions."

SUMMARY

For Sri Yogananda and his disciples, Jesus is an avatar who, along with Lord Krishna and other avatars of the Self-Realization Fellowship guru lineage, is highly revered for his compassionate love and commitment to God, an example to be followed by all would-be Christs. The Christs, Babaji and Jesus, are believed to be working together for the world's redemption. Jesus as Christ is not, therefore, about someone long ago, once and for all, a final definition of God Incarnate.

The Self-Realization Fellowship teachings about Jesus arise primarily from the received wisdom of Yoganandaji himself. The focus within SRF is transformational rather than theological, the direct imbibement of wisdom by devotees rather than a concentration on faith beliefs. It integrates Jesus quite directly. It also affirms the unity of avatars, each working according to God's will for the redemption of the world. The incorporation of Jesus into a proclaimed mission of spiritual unity may be too radical for the majority of Christian institutions. It has proved attractive to many individual Christians, partly through the example of the living direct disciples of Yogananda as well as through the unsullied example of the Guru himself.

Like the Ramakrishna Mission, Self-Realization Fellowship has developed as a separate and distinct tradition, open-hearted to others but serious about its own particularity. Both movements have attracted many western Christians who retain their loyalty to Christ as guru but who find the methodology,

---

[44] All Keshav Sharma quotes from e-mail to author, 6 August 2005.

philosophy and community of both spiritually satisfying, giving as each does, a Jesus free from heavy Christian doctrinal restraints.

In both traditions, the Ramakrishna Mission and Self-Realization Fellowship, the focus is on Christ rather than Jesus, and the realization that all avatars, whatever their 'historical' reality might be, are actually manifestations of one Christ Consciousness and therefore equal and mutual. Sri Ramakrishna and Sri Yogananda's direct personal experiences of Jesus as a Christ affirm both his historicity and his status as avatar and offer a challenge to Christians to be as open to all avatars in their response. For both Masters and organizations, the only valid response to any avatar is the commitment to become similar living examples of God-consciousness for the benefit of all.

CHAPTER V

# INTERNATIONAL SOCIETY
# FOR KRISHNA CONSCIOUSNESS

In every age I come back, to deliver the holy, to destroy the sin of the sinner, to establish righteousness.

*- Lord Krishna, Bhagavad-Gita*

## INTRODUCTION

The final organization explored in some detail is the International Society for Krishna Consciousness, founded in America at the height of hippy culture by a seventy-year old Indian on his first visit there. Probably most readers will have come across a Hare Krishna devotee. Of the three organizations studied here, the Hare Krishna movement - as it is popularly known - may be the most easily recognized in the West. Let us look at how that happened, how the ancient Vaishnava tradition of India came to the West. Of the tradition itself, the great Indian sage, Sri Aurobindo, wrote:

> The Vaishnava religion especially is a religion of love and beauty and of the satisfaction of the whole delight-soul of man in God and even the desires and images of the sensuous life were turned by its vision into figures of a divine soul-experience. Few religions have gone so far as this immense catholicity or carried the whole nature so high in its large, puissant and many-sided approach to the spiritual and the infinite.[1]

## SRILA PRABHUPADA, 1896-1977

Srila Prabhupada was born in Calcutta in 1896 and became the founder of the International Society for Krishna Consciousness (ISKCON), a worldwide spiritual movement dedicated to Lord Krishna and Krishna consciousness. Fulfilling an earlier injunction from his guru to preach in the west, Prabhupada set sail for America on 13 August 1965. When he arrived to begin his mission, it was a very different place to the one that greeted Yogananda. Now, in the USA of the 1960's, eastern swamis and teachers were not such rare and exotic sights. Young people had broken free of received constraints in new and bold

---

[1] Sri Aurobindo, 'Indian Spirituality and Life' in *Arya*, October 1919, published in the Sri Aurobindo Birth Centenary Library, Volume 14, Sri Aurobindo Ashram, Pondicherry, 1972, pp 156-171.

ways that included drugs and 'free love.' Spirituality was breathed in as a kind of group youth movement even as old disciplines dissolved in the out breath. Prabhupada was 69 years old when he arrived in the west, an age when most of the great religious icons have completed their missions and left their bodies. What happened next is truly remarkable.

Before leaving India he had written three books; in the next twelve years he was to write more than sixty. Before he left India he had initiated one disciple; in the next twelve years he would initiate more than four thousand. Before he left India, hardly anyone had believed that he could fulfill his vision of a worldwide society of Krishna devotees; but in the next decade he would form and maintain the International Society for Krishna Consciousness and open more than a hundred centers. Before sailing for America, he had never been outside India; but in the next twelve years he would travel many times around the world propagating the Krishna Consciousness movement.[2]

Today, the devotees of the movement Prabhupada brought to the west are a familiar sight and sound on the streets of all major cities in the western world and a testament to the incredible success of this elderly swami who arrived alone and virtually penniless in New York. He passed away on 14 November 1977 having turned ISKCON into a global phenomenon.

Harvey Cox, author and Harvard University professor, gave the founder of ISKCON this high commendation:

[The] life of Srila Prabhupada is pointed proof that one can be a transmitter of truth and still be a vital and singular person....At what almost anyone would consider a very advanced age, when most people would be resting on their laurels, he harkened to the mandate of his own spiritual teacher and set out on the difficult voyage to America. Srila Prabhupada is one in a thousand, maybe one in a million.[3]

Another US academic, J Stillson Judah, acclaimed him thus:

[A] man who played a central role in American religious-history during the counter-cultural '60's and '70's....[You]...will be struck with Srila Prabhupada's personal qualities – his strength of purpose, his genuine humility, and his deep spirituality....Srila Prabhupada's life...is the epitome of his ideal, an ideal that he set forth for others to follow. In an

---

[2] Satsvarupa Dasa Goswami, *Prabhupada: He Built a House in Which the Whole World Can Live*, Bhaktivedanta Book Trust (BBT), Los Angeles, 1983, p ix. All quotes from BBT are © 2005 Bhaktivedanta Book Trust International; used with permission.
[3] Satsvarupa dasa Goswami, *A Lifetime in Preparation*, Bhaktivedanta Book Trust, Los Angeles, 1980, back cover.

age of pervasive hypocrisy and cynicism, it is this kind of rare model that we need.[4]

*Christ and Krishna*

Krishna is one of the greatest avatars of Hinduism, accepted by most Hindus as a manifestation of God Incarnate. For Srila Prabhupada and ISKCON devotees, he is even more than that, the Supreme Godhead Itself, highest Source. In the *Srimad Bhagavatum*, there is a list of many incarnations of the Supreme Personality of Godhead, but Krishna is described as the original, primary personality from whom many, many incarnations and personalities of Godhead expand. This Krishna is revealed to Arjuna in the Bhagavad Gita (11.1). Prabhupada puts it this way:

> All the lists of the incarnations of Godhead submitted herewith are either plenary expansions or parts of the plenary expansions of the Supreme Personality of Godhead, but Krishna is the Supreme Personality of Godhead Himself. Therefore Krishna is the original Supreme Personality of Godhead, the Absolute Truth, the source of both Supersoul and the impersonal Brahman....Krishna is not an incarnation. He is the source of all incarnations.[5]

Referring to Jesus' relationship with Krishna, Prabhupada wrote, "Sometimes Sri Krishna descends Himself, and sometimes He sends His representative."

> The major religions of the world - Christian, Hindu, Buddhist and Moslem - believe in some supreme authority or personality coming down from the Kingdom of God. In the Christian religion, Jesus Christ claimed to be the Son of God and to be coming from the Kingdom of God to reclaim conditioned souls. As followers of Bhagavad-Gita, we admit this claim to be true.[6]

For the devotee this means that "Krishna is God, and Christ is the son of God."

> We don't find any difference between the son and the father....Now either you engage your mind in Krishna or Jesus does not matter. It is the same thing....So it doesn't matter you are Christian, I am Hindu. The real point is that you think of God or God's representative always.[7]

What is important is to follow Jesus' example, to practice and preach God consciousness.

---

[4] Satsvarupa dasa Goswami, *Only He Could Lead Them*, Bhaktivedanta Book Trust, Los Angeles, 1981, back cover.

[5] Srila Prabhupada, *Bhagavad-Gita As It Is*, Bhaktivedanta Book Trust, Bombay, 1968, pp 18, 177.

[6] Srila Prabhupada, *Raja-Vidya: The King of Knowledge*, Bhaktivedanta Book Trust, Culver City, 1973, p 65

[7] *Conversations with Srila Prabhupada*, Vol. 9, Bhaktivedanta Book Trust, Los Angeles, 1989, pp 314-316.

Lord Jesus Christ revealed that he was the son of God, and Krishna revealed that He is God Himself, the Supreme Father of all living entities. So if you dedicate your life to the service of Krishna, the Supreme Father, don't you think that Lord Jesus Christ will be pleased with this? [8]

Prabhupada identified Jesus as a *saktyavesa-avatara*, "an individual directly empowered by God to do his work in the world."[9] Satsvarupa dasa Goswami, a direct disciple of Praphupada, unpacks this title, one belonging to Prabhupada as well as to Jesus:

According to Vedic literature, when a person has extraordinary spiritual endowment, Krishna-sakti, he is known as a saktyavesa-avatara. Although the word avatara generally refers to incarnations of God Himself, the term saktyavesa-avatara refers to an individual empowered by God to enact the mission of God in this world. Saktyavesa-avatara and their particular functions are mentioned in the Vedic literature.... Lord Buddha, whose name and activities are described in *Srimad Bhagavatum*, is a ...saktyavesa-avatara, and even other divinely empowered personalities outside the Vedic culture, such as Jesus Christ and Muhammad, are accepted by Vaishnava acaryas as saktyavesa-avatars. Srila Praphupada's activities during the years 1968 through 1971 establish him as a saktyavesa-avatara, and he fulfils the prediction of the scriptures (to preach everywhere on Krishna consciousness).[10]

Referring to the mission of avatars, Prabhupada wrote:

Each and every avatar, or incarnation of the Lord, has a particular mission, and they are all described in the revealed scriptures....It is not a fact that the Lord appears only on Indian soil. He can advent Himself anywhere and everywhere, and whenever He desires to appear. In each and every incarnation, He speaks as much about religion as can be understood by the particular people under their particular circumstances. But the mission is the same - to lead people to God-consciousness and obedience to the principles of religion. Sometimes He descends personally, and sometimes He sends His bona fide representatives in the form of His son or servant, or Himself in some disguised form....In all incarnations of the Lord, therefore, the same principles are taught, but they appear to be higher or lower under varied circumstances....The

---

[8] Letter to Sucendra, 8 December 1969, quoted in *Srila Prabhupada Siksamrta* Vol. 2, Bhaktivedanta Book Trust, Los Angeles, 1992, p 1252.
[9] Steven J Gelberg, 'Krishna and Christ: ISKCON's Encounter with Christianity in America,' in Harold Coward, Ed, *Hindu-Christian Dialogue: Perspectives and Encounters*, Orbis, NY, 1990, p 150. See also *A Lifetime in Preparation*, p 77.
[10] Satsvarupa dasa Goswami, *Srila Prabhupada-lilamrta Vol. 4: In Every Town and Village*, Bhaktivedanta Book Trust, Los Angeles, 1982, pp 267-8.

whole purpose of the mission of incarnations is to arouse Krishna consciousness everywhere.[11]

Krishna is Absolute Truth. Krishna consciousness is God consciousness. The founders and initiators of established religions emanate from him, work for his divine purpose. Jesus is son to his father. Krishna transcends any specific incarnation; he is the Godhead Itself, into which even Brahman is subsumed.

*Jesus and Christianity*

To a devotee who pointed out a Christian argument that if God had wanted belief in Krishna he would have revealed it on Mt Sinai and then through Jesus, Swamiji suggested that the teachings of Jesus were limited by the ignorance of those listening to him.

> Jesus Christ did not explain more to you because you are rascals. You cannot follow even his one instruction, 'Thou shalt not kill.' It is not the foolishness of Jesus Christ. But because you are so rascal, you cannot understand him. Therefore, he avoided you rascals. Because whatever he said, you cannot follow. So what will you understand? Therefore, he stopped speaking.[12]

Regarding the crucifixion of Jesus, here is a sample of Srila Prabhupada's reflections:

"Jesus Christ was such a great personality - the son of God, the representative of God. He had no fault. Still, he was crucified. He wanted to deliver God-consciousness but in return they crucified him - they were so thankless. They could not appreciate his preaching. But we appreciate him and give him due honor as the representative of God....[We] adore Lord Jesus Christ and offer our obeisances to him."[13]

"Perhaps you have marked it in my preaching that I love Lord Jesus Christ as good as Krishna, because He rendered the greatest service to Krishna according to time, circumstances and society in which He appeared."[14]

"Anyone who is preaching God's glories must be accepted as a guru. Jesus Christ is one such great personality. We should not think of him as an ordinary human being....If Jesus Christ were an ordinary man, then he could not have delivered God consciousness."[15]

---

[11] Satsvarupa dasa Goswami, *In Every Town and Village*, Bhaktivedanta Book Trust, Los Angeles, 1982, p 69.
[12] Satsavarupa dasa Goswami, *In Every Town and Village*, p 313. Vaisnavas are strict vegetarians.
[13] Srila Prabupadha, *The Science of Self-Realization*, Bhaktivedanta Book Trust, Los Angeles, 1977, p 135.
[14] *Letters from Srila Prabhupada*, Vol 4, The Vaisnava Institute, Los Angeles, 1987, p 154.
[15] Srila Prabhupada, *The Science of Self-Realization*, pp 135-136.

"Lord Jesus Christ, he was a Vaishnava. He directly gave you the idea of personal God. The personal God is the origin."[16]

"A Vaishnava is unhappy to see the sufferings of others. Therefore, Lord Jesus Christ agreed to be crucified - to free others from their suffering."[17]

"Lord Jesus Christ agreed to be crucified to free others from their suffering. But his followers are so unfaithful that they have decided 'Let Christ suffer for us, and we'll go on committing sin.' They love Christ so much that they think, 'My dear Christ, we are weak. We cannot give up our sinful activities so you please suffer for us.' Christ can take the sufferings for the previous sins of his devotees. But first they have to be sane: 'Why should I put Jesus Christ into suffering for my sins? Let me stop my sinful activities.'"[18]

"[The crucifixion] has no meaning. The people were so rascal that they attempted to kill him. Because he was speaking of God....He preached 'Thou shalt not kill,' and they killed him first."[19]

Re redemption on the cross: "This is another sinful thought - Jesus has taken contract for ridding your sinful activities....Instead of stopping sinful activities, we have given contract to Jesus Christ to counteract it."[20]

"It is not possible to kill him. Such a great personality, representative of God, he is not killed. That is not possible....He made a show that 'I am killed.' That is resurrection."[21] This reveals a common Indian belief that Jesus went into samadhi on the cross from which he later emerged. It is also common with the Islamic idea that a prophet like Jesus could not have been killed in such a way.

Although Christians can gain *moksha* (spiritual liberation) through Christ, Krishna is still a safer route. "So anyone who is speaking about God with authority - take for example, Jesus Christ, he is speaking in the western world - you accept him. We Indians, we accept Caitanya or Ramanujacaraya, Madhavacarya....That is the way because these acaryas, these authorities, they are speaking about God. None of them speaking that 'You become happy here,' no, none of them....So according to the time, circumstances, position, either you follow any one of them as it suits you or, if you can make a comparative study, you follow the best one. So therefore, our conclusion is Krishna is the best. He is God. Christ is son of God. So we don't differ son of God and God. That is all right. But when the father is speaking personally, he is speaking

[16] *Conversations with Srila Prabhupada*, Bhaktivedanta Book Trust, Los Angeles, 1989, p 237.
[17] Srila Prabhupada, *The Science of Self-Realization*, Bhaktivedanta Book Trust, Los Angeles, 1977, p 135.
[18] Srila Prabhupada, *The Science of Self-Realization,* p 135.
[19] *Conversations with Srila Prabhupada*, Vol 32, Bhaktivedanta Book Trust, Los Angeles, 1991, p 88.
[20] *Conversations with Srila Prabhupada*, Vol 32, p 88.
[21] *Conversations with Srila Prabhupada*, Vol 32, p 241.

what the son has spoken plus something because he is more experienced. So take the father and follow him."[22]

## INTERNATIONAL SOCIETY FOR KRISHNA CONSCIOUSNESS (ISKCON)

Founded by Srila Prabhupada, ISKCON has gone through many phases as it came to terms with the passing of its great inspirer.[23] Like many large and diverse communities it still has to deal with mistakes from its past. Today ISKCON is linked to scholarly journals, institutions and universities. Many of its adherents are highly educated and deeply spiritual.

For different reasons from the Ramakrishna Mission but perhaps just as controversially, ISKCON has sometimes declared itself as not Hindu. "Previously we were Hindus. Now we are Hare Krishnas."[24] The journal, *Hinduism Today*, conducted an internet survey of relevant organizations to check whether they defined themselves as Hindu, quasi-Hindu or non-Hindu. ISKCON were found to be in the last designation.[25] However, all ISKCON members that I have met have identified themselves as Hindu and have been deeply informed by Hinduism so perhaps this is mainly a semantic, used by many Indian organizations active in the west, to suggest what is on offer is primarily a spiritual methodology. This can attract Christian and secular seekers without the need to change religious labels.

Reflections on Christ and Christianity from some ISKCON members and devotees, past and present, are illustrated below.

### *Kirtananda Swami Bhaktipada, 1937-*

These teachings of Bhaktipada, son of a Baptist minister, belong to the period before he was disowned by ISKCON. They are now considered to be his personal views rather than those recognized by the organization. They are only included here as he was a direct disciple of Prabhupada, enjoined by his guru in a personal letter, 4th July 1967, to write about Jesus and Krishna. He therefore represents a certain phase of development and a link to the topic of this book so may interest the reader. Prabhupadaji wrote to him:

> Because our movement is approved by Lord Jesus Christ, at least the Christian world will accept our *kirtan* procedures (chanting and praising God's names). I have seen in the Bible that Lord Jesus Christ

---

[22] *Conversations with Srila Prabhupada*, Vol 14, Bhaktivedanta Book Trust, Los Angeles, 1989, pp 120-121
[23] For example, see Rasamandala Dasa, 'An Analysis of ISKCON Membership in the UK: Moving into Phase Three' in *ISKCON Communications Journal*, Volume 3, Number 2, December 1995, pp 83-92.
[24] Quoted in 'Can it be that the Hare Krishnas are not Hindu?' *Hinduism Today*, Hawaii, October 1998, p 32.
[25] *Hinduism Today*, October 1998, p 33.

recommends this performance of kirtan. You know better than me, and I would request you to write a small book on this.[26]

In conversations with three ministers from the United Church, Bhaktipada was asked how Jesus fits into the Krishna Consciousness doctrine. He replied that Christ is accepted as the Son of God, the son of Krishna, an incarnation of Krishna. When asked elsewhere if this superiority of Krishna could become acceptable to Christians, Bhaktipada quoted John 5.19 and 8.28 as Jesus' own admission of One greater than he, of his role as son to the Father. In another conversation, with Russell Edmunds, a Catholic Deacon and Professor of History, this clear distinction between Krishna as God, and the historical incarnations known as Jesus and Prabhupada is maintained.

> Krishna is the supreme cause. From Him expand many Vishnu-*tattvas*, all part of the same energetic source, and jiva-tattvas, the infinitesimal living entities. Prabhupada and Jesus Christ are both *jiva-tattva*, but they're empowered by God for a great mission.

Vishnu-tattvas are primary and equal incarnations of God Himself. Jiva-tattvas are "atomic parts of the Lord," therefore not full incarnations of the Supreme Personality of Godhead Itself.[27]

When asked about the second coming of Christ, Bhaktipada responded by pointing also to the current incarnation of God:

> The descent of Christ two thousand years ago was God's coming into the world for the purpose of preaching Krishna consciousness. That was not the first time God has come, nor will it be the last….One who descends into the material world from the spiritual world in order to preach God consciousness is called an avatar. The Lord will certainly come again. Whether we call it the second coming, or the third, fourth, or hundredth, coming, God comes again and again. The Lord never abandons the fallen souls…. Therefore, in this age Krishna has so kindly incarnated in the form of His name. Hare Krishna is actually the incarnation of God in the form of sound. There is no difference between the Lord and His name.

This identity of name and God is granted to Jesus also as God's representative. The names given him reveal his character eg. Jesus derived from Joshua, meaning salvation or deliverance. His titles similarly show his nature, for example 'redeemer,' bringing us back to remembrance of God and so to freedom from misery. Not only is there no difference between the Lord and

---

[26] Kirtananda Swami Bhaktipada, *Christ and Krishna*, Palace Publishing, Moundsville, 1987, p i. All quotes from this book.
[27] Srila Prabhupada, *Srimad Bhagavatam*, First Canto, Part One, Bhaktivedanta Book Trust, Los Angeles, 1989, pp 408 and 411.

His name, the sound of the name is the same as the Lord Himself. As God has many names there must be scope here for thinking about God incarnating through their sounds also. In the Prologue to John's Gospel in the Christian Testament, God's *Logos* or Word is identified as one with God from the beginning. Logos Christology was an early Christian medium for an identification of Jesus with God but in its original inception it could not ensure the uniqueness and absoluteness of Jesus as that Word so it was never fully developed or accepted.

The idea of God incarnating in different ways at different times also seems to me to offer tremendous freedom in understanding divine incarnations based more on effectiveness at a given time so unlocking us from an enduring commitment to a particular form, regardless of present circumstances. The concept is very open to fresh revelations of the divine without loss to earlier ones. Within many Hindu systems of Self-realization, there is recognition of certain practices being more efficient in certain *yugas*, ages. This does not limit the potential of their effectiveness as yugas far exceed in time any generation's lifespan and whereas time is understood as linear in Christianity, in Hinduism it revolves in cycles and the destruction and renewal of each cycle of time is part of an ongoing process of creation, sustenance and dissolution.[28] When asked about parallels to Christian *eschatological* teachings, Bhaktipada referred to this and to the coming of the Kalki avatar:

> At the end of the four yugas which make up one universal cycle, the Kalki avatar comes in judgement. During the cosmic manifestation, there are ten primary incarnations of Krishna. The first nine preach Krishna consciousness, and the last, Kalki, comes to destroy….Kalki will come riding a white horse and carrying a sword. He will destroy all the miscreants and re-establish the golden age. There is a very similar description in the Book of Revelations.[29]

*Steven Gelberg*

Because of its focus on a personal, saving God, ISKCON has, at times, exhibited a missionary zeal, creating some tension in the western situation. This has inevitably involved some competitiveness with Christianity. Steven Gelberg, a (former) member of ISKCON, identified the competitive potential between Christian and Vaishnava as having four contributing components:

---

[28] For a very detailed explanation of yugas - the cyclic ages in the life of a universe - see Swami Sri Yukteswar, *The Holy Science*, Self-Realization Fellowship, Los Angeles, U.S.A, See also chapter 16 of Paramahansa Yogananda, *Autobiography of a Yogi*, Self-Realization Fellowship, Los Angeles, U.S.A. P 194, Footnote: "The life span for a whole universe, according to the ancient seers, is 314,159,000,000,000 solar years, or 'One Age of Brahma.'"
[29] See Revelation 4:11. See also Paramahansa Yogananda, *Autobiography of a Yogi*, Self-Realization Fellowship, Los Angeles, U.S.A. PP 565-566: "The universal creative-preservative-destructive aspect of God, however, is not His ultimate or even His essential nature (for cosmic creation is only His *lila*, creative sport)."

encounter in the West itself; western converts; these converts having a strong missionary agenda; and distinct theological parallels.[30]

Gelberg confirms that, despite Prabhupada's positive response to Jesus, both Jesus and Christianity are subordinate to Krishna and Vaishnavism respectively.

> Thus, transcendental religion is defined as surrender and selfless, loving service (bhakti) to Krishna. When Christians worship Jesus Christ, who is none other than the Son of Krishna, they are practicing bhakti-yoga... and their Christianity is a form of Vaishnavism. As all souls are, by spiritual constitution, eternal servants of Krishna, sincere Christians are, to turn the tables on Karl Rahner, anonymous Vaishnavas.[31]

However, although Christians can gain liberation through Jesus, "it would be very difficult to find one who strictly follows the instructions of Lord Jesus Christ."[32] This is the main protest against Christianity, that followers of Jesus do not follow his injunctions. In this sense, as they do try to obey the divine injunctions, Vaishnavas make better Christians!

*Shaunaka Rishi Das*

Shaunaka is Director of the Oxford Centre for Hindu Studies, Director of ISKCON Communications Europe, Editor of ISKCON Communications Journal, and an ISKCON priest. In a recent interview, Shaunaka spoke about Jesus this way:

> You see, in a sense, Hindus don't really see Jesus as a Christian at all.... We can see spirituality in Hindus...by behavior and practice. We can ask are we humble, are we tolerant and are we non-violent, and can we control our senses and our mind? Are we aware of others suffering and are we willing to give up our comfort to help them? Looking at these criteria Jesus measures up as a Sadhu, a holy man....Jesus was one of those people who appealed from heart to heart, and that's what makes him such a good Hindu Saint....Acharya means 'one who teaches by example.' For Hindus, Christ is an acharya. His example is a light to any of us in this world who want to take up the serious practice of spiritual life. His message is no different from the message preached in another time and place by Lord Krishna and Lord Chaitanya.[33]

---

[30] Steven J Gelberg, 'Krishna and Christ: ISKCON's Encounter with Christianity in America,' in Harold Coward, Ed, *Hindu-Christian Dialogue: Perspectives and Encounters*, Orbis, NY, 1990, p 140.

[31] Steven J Gelberg, 'Krishna and Christ,' p 155. See also Srila Prabhupada, *The Path of Perfection,* Bhaktivedanta Book Trust, Los Angeles, 1979, p 118.

[32] Satsvarupa dasa Goswami, 'Secretary to a Pure Devotee' in *Back to Godhead*, No 68, Dec. 1974, p 134.

[33] Shaunaka Rishi Das, *Jesus through Hindu Eyes*, BBC Religion and Ethics, www.bbc.co.uk/religion/religions/hinduism/features/hindu_eyes/index.shtml

I asked Shaunaka if he could describe for me his understandings of the relationship, if any, between Krishna and Jesus, and between Krishna and Christian conceptions of the Godhead.[34]

> I would always like to imagine that the relationship between Krishna and Christ is a joyous one. As a Vaishnava, I would recognize Jesus Christ as a pure devotee of God, someone consciously striving to love God with all his words and in all his deeds. Further, someone who is willing to sacrifice everything in that service so that others may also develop their love for God. Bhaktisiddhanta Saraswati Thakur, an eminent Vaishnava teacher in the 1920s, remarked that Jesus Christ can be considered a *saktyavesa-avatar* of Krishna, which refers to someone who is specifically empowered to spread the message of God through-out the world. There is no doubt that Jesus Christ was God conscious; whether he was specifically Krishna conscious can only be a matter for academic debate, but my sense and the consensus in my tradition is that he was a pure devotee of God.

Regarding Christian conceptions of God, Shaunaka has the impression that they are too limiting and it is important not to "try to limit the unlimited."

> For instance, is there any room for us to become the father or mother of God, to become God's friend, God's consort or God's lover? May it be possible through expression of pure love, unrestrained by selfish motivation, and uninterrupted by any circumstance, to develop an intimacy with God in which the concept of God itself is forgotten? In which our only thought is to please our Beloved in whatever relation-ship or position our Beloved desires of us….It would be interesting to see Christian theology broaden its concept of a personal Godhead to include manifestations that are too radical to be sensible but incapable of being ignored.

Christian mission and evangelism have presented no problems for the develop-ment of the Oxford Centre for Hindu Studies but they have "certainly affected or tried to influence the mission and even the existence of ISKCON."

> In various countries that I had been associated with, primarily my home country of Ireland, senior clerics have tried to curtail or destroy the mission of ISKCON. The all time classic was the declaration of the Priest in a village in Ireland, who, when asked to comment on the Hare Krishna community developing on town land close to his parish, remarked, 'I don't know about them but I know they are wrong.' In other countries as far east as Armenia, such agitation has led to physical violence and political repression. Having said that, dialogue with certain

---

[34] E-mail from Shaunaka Rishi Das to author on 10 August 2005. All quotes in this section from this source.

Christian organisations, including the Roman Catholic, Anglican and Methodist Churches, has been very productive and encouraging.

ISKCON concerned itself with Christianity because many western devotees originally came from Christian as well as Jewish, agnostic and atheistic backgrounds.

That Abrahamic context still exists, so a need for ISKCON members to integrate, necessitating dialogue with Christianity and Judaism, is very important. The basic Christian commandment of loving our neighbour will always find difficulty in expression if we do not know who our neighbour is, or if we do not understand and respect our neighbour. It is as important for the Christian community to try to understand the devotees of Krishna in its midst, as it is for ISKCON members to understand, appreciate, respect and live in harmony with the Christians in their neighbourhood.

Shaunaka has been instrumental in the development of ISKCON's interfaith and educational strategies. Uniquely it ("representative of Hindu culture and religion as ISKCON, as a Vedantic, monotheistic Vaisnava tradition") has introduced an Interfaith Statement and is delivering interfaith and world religions courses, accredited by universities. The Oxford Centre for Hindu Studies in the UK and Bhaktivedanta College at Radhadesh in Belgium are new institutions that will give young Vaishnavas the knowledge and insights needed to construct informed responses to religious pluralism. ISKCON now has the confidence and the interest to explore other faiths as part of a growing agenda based on dialogue rather than *proselytization*. Recently Shaunaka made history by preaching in a UK Methodist Church. His topic? Christianity! He is following a well-established Hindu tradition, as we have seen, of sharing with Christians an enhanced version of what they thought they already knew!

ISKCON is also seriously developing Vaisnava-Christian dialogue. At one such conference in Wales in January 1996, attended by many distinguished theologians, the Conference report, written by Kenneth Cracknell, makes clear there was a serious and open listening between participants.

Vaisnavas have written to me saying that they were moved by the 'openness and humility of all the members of the Christian churches present' and … expressed gratitude for the 'real willingness to understand' the Vaisnava philosophy….Interestingly, for more than a few, our being together was a moment of encountering things they thought they had left behind when they came to Krishna consciousness …. For some, the reality of Christian faith and devotion came alive as they joined with us in the Catholic morning office and a Protestant / ecumenical act of prayer and meditation. Perhaps it was this last aspect that led a senior Vaisnava to say that he had left the weekend with a 'far stronger sense of a shared path of devotion to a personal God of grace uniting both Christian and Vaisnava. We have an important journey to travel together and we are only at the beginning.' For their part the Christian participants found the experience, in the words of one of their number 'intellectually demanding, well-organized, enjoyable and instructive.'…Christians, too, appreciated the moments when we could share in reflection and prayerfulness with the devotees.[35]

What then is ISKCON's special message / insight for those of other faiths? Three things come to Shaunaka's mind. The first relates to his earlier thoughts about relationship with the Godhead: "Expanding our consciousness, our ability to relate with God and God's ability to relate with us through means other than awe and reverence, but with more intimacy than may have been previously thought possible." The second is "to examine the chanting of God's name as an efficacious devotional process."

> I often find myself having to describe chanting or *kirtanam*, one of the nine recognized devotional processes in the Vaishnava or *bhakti* traditions, in terms of meditation and prayer, so that those of the Abrahamic faiths can comprehend the method. But chanting the name of God, alongside Prayer, Service, Self Surrender etc is esteemed as an important method of communication with the Divine in itself. Of course, I chant the Hare Krishna *mantra*, but Christians can chant the name of Lord Jesus and the effect will be the same, especially when the chanting is done in congregation. This process is an open secret of the East, but is often viewed with prejudice and suspicion by members of the Christian community. This is a sad fact because the name of God is hallowed in every religious tradition and should be chanted from the rooftops and yet has the power to bring the most intimate joy to our lives.

A third insight relates to the importance of sanga or community.

> I mean this in a very specific sense, where we recognize those devotees of God, regardless of their religious tradition or affiliation, who are actually advanced in spiritual life and we humbly take their association and guidance, so that we may also begin to approach God and learn how to love God according to the lights of these teachers, or gurus. Such a broad-minded approach to spiritual life is not obviously supportive of religious denominations but is more obviously supportive of individual spirituality which is far more important in the light of eternity. In my experience the support of a healthy *sanga* encourages commitment to

---

[35] Kenneth Cracknell, 'Extracts from Conference Report,' in *ISKCON Communications Journal*, Vol 4, No 1, June 1999.

92 CHRIST ACROSS THE GANGES

*sampradaya* or denomination. To find our appropriate *sanga,* irrespective of bodily designation or religious designation etc, can be a great spiritual challenge.

SUMMARY

Like the Ramakrishna Mission and Self-Realization Fellowship, ISKCON is open to Jesus and including in its response to him. It is the community, of these three, that has generally most clearly engaged in a positioning of the divine personalities. The focus has been less on equating Srila Prabhupada with Jesus than on the true reality of Lord Krishna, the source of all, always more than, even if not different from, Christ. It was also, perhaps, initially, the most strongly polemical of the organizations with regard to Christianity. This has measured as ISKCON has developed and matured and dialogues on parallel theology have now been initiated between Vaishnava and Christian religious leaders and scholars in a systematic way possibly unmatched by any other Hindu organization.

ISKCON is a Hindu fact of life in the west and an influence that continues to attract western seekers who find God's presence in His name as they chant it. The process, as with most Hindu paths, is ultimately self-revealing rather than faith-believing. Although ISKCON sometimes had, in the past, a reputation for quite heavy dogmatism, none of the devotees I have met in recent years have exhibited any narrow doctrinal tendencies.

Srila Prabhupada opened a meeting in Paris with a devotee reading from the Gospel of John: "In the beginning was the Word, and the Word was with God, and the Word was God." He then spoke to the audience about "the power of the holy name as transcendental sound."[36] Perhaps in the acceptance of the sound of God's name as equivalent to God Itself, there is the best scope for a Christology that can comfortably include the multiple ways in which the sound of God's name has been interpreted and systematized, the emphasis being the transformational effect rather than faith precept.

As a movement, ISKCON has a lot in common with devotional responses to Christ. It posits a personal God over and above even Brahman. Its theology is close to Christian theology in many aspects and through that closeness, more likely to come into conflict over potential shared ground. However, ISKCON is innovative in its inter-religious developments and its images of Christ and Krishna as divinely revealing God's will and character need provoke no conflict in the heart of any true devotee, Christian or Vaishnava.

[36] Satsvarupa dasa Goswami, *Let There be A Temple: India / Around the World 1971-1975*, Bhaktivedanta Book Trust, Los Angeles, 1983, p 213.

CHAPTER VI

# Contemporary responses
## from india

*I am in all hearts, I give and take away knowledge and memory: I am all that the Vedas tell, I am the teacher, the knower of Vedanta.*
                                            *- Lord Krishna, Bhagavad-Gita*

## Introduction

In this chapter we look at a variety of contemporary Hindu voices emanating from India. What do living 'avatars' think of Jesus? Who are the thinkers and writers who do not think of Christ in any positive way? What do Hindu youth believe about avatars and Hindu-Christian relations today? How do eminent Hindus of our time respond to the challenges of religious pluralism?

When the early followers of Jesus were finally evicted from the synagogue and took their prophet into the Graeco-Roman world, where even emperors had to be gods, Jesus too had to become divine in order to stand out from the crowd, to be able to compete in the godly market. The Jewish Jesus became the gentile Christ.

The same process continues today as we can see in every 'new' religion that has to compete with earlier ones. It seems to be a normal pattern of religious behavior, not restricted to any one religious community. Once the process starts then slowly but surely a whole supporting theology needs to be built up to keep one particular god ahead of the rest. The faith experience of disciples becomes mythologized and, sooner or later, ends up as claims of 'best,' 'last,' or other sadly demeaning and divisive dogmas. Distortion, corruption, quagmire are usually the results.

Hinduism, at its highest, has mainly avoided these exclusivist dilemmas and Hindus can be open to the Divine in many forms and without form. There is no need for competition. For centuries this has been the way. As Hinduism increases its spiritual impact outside of India, gathering new, western devotees, it needs to stay vigilant and not be dragged into the competitive missionary market so familiar to those fleeing from its expression in Christianity.

## VOICES OF PRECEPTORS

We start with teachings about Christ and Christianity from two Indian spiritual giants of our time. Both are widely deemed avatars by their devotees. Both extend huge spiritual influence across racial, religious, cultural and national boundaries.

*Sathya Sai Baba, 1926 -*

Sai Baba is probably the best-known living avatar or Christ of India. He has millions of devotees, worldwide. His influence is vast, prevailing even when recent controversy might have reduced one less esteemed and established. In 1996 he was named Hindu of the Year and received the Hindu Renaissance Award. His Education in Human Values course is taught worldwide. One of Swami's most enticing sayings is, "There is only one religion, the religion of love, only one caste, that of humanity, only one language, that of the heart."[1]

According to this Sai Baba, he is currently the second of three intended incarnations: Shirdi Sai Baba is claimed as the first, and the third will be Prema Sai. Swami has 'materialized' an evolving image of the latter which at least one devotee thinks will end up remarkably similar to the paintings of Jesus so familiar in the west.[2] Baba claims:

> I am not Sathya Sai Baba. It is only a name by which you know me today. All names are mine. I am the one God who answers the prayers that rise in human hearts in all languages from all countries addressed to all forms of deity.[3]

*Baba and Jesus*

The stories about Baba reveal several aspects comparable with the Gospel life of Jesus, particularly the power to perform miracles, including raising the dead.[4] Baba calls his miracles and materializations his "calling cards," ways of enticing people to come closer to find the real miracle that Swami offers – himself and the opportunity for self-transformation through his blessing. The Roman Catholic priest, Don Mario Mazzoleni, writes broadly about the miracles of Jesus and the miracles of Baba. He finds no reason why Baba's 'miracles' cannot be considered as authentic as those Jesus performed. They are in accordance with classical theology's four indispensable requirements ie.

---

[1] Peggy Mason and Ron Laing, *The Embodiment of Love*, Sawbridge, London, 1982, p 151.
[2] Peggy Mason and Ron Laing, *The Embodiment of Love*, p 33.
[3] Quoted by Swami Sai Sharan Anand in 'Sai Baba and Jesus of Nazareth.' Downloaded on 15 August 2005 from http://www.indiangyan.com/books/otherbooks/sai_baba/sai_baba_and_jesus_of_nazareth.shtml
[4] See for example: Howard Murphet, *Sai Baba: Man of Miracles*, Samuel Weiser, New York, 1971, Chp 13; John S Hislop, *Seeking Divinity*, Sri Sathya Sai Books and Publications Trust, Prashanthi Nilayam, 1998, p 186f.

they must be historical events, supernatural, reveal truth, and have no diabolical influences.[5]

In a less theological way I once did a 'miracle' experiment with a class of 13/14 year olds at a large comprehensive school. Most of the children in the class were from secular backgrounds. If they had any inkling of religion (in distinction to their own spiritual inclinations) it was of Christianity but they were fairly vague about that too. I asked the well-known class agitator to be my 'special investigator' for the experiment. A short video clip of Baba was shown to the class in which he could be seen emptying *vibhuti* (sacred ash) from a small upturned vase so that the ash fell on a statue below. His sleeves were rolled up. The vibhuti poured out of the vase in ever increasing volumes, many times beyond what the vase could possibly contain. My special detective was asked if he could see any trick that could have been used to facilitate this. He had observed the arms and hands very closely. No, he could not see how it could have been done. Was it a miracle? No! The whole class agreed. What if they had seen Jesus do this, could it have been a miracle then? Yes! The whole class agreed. I passed some vibhuti around for those interested to taste. The verdict – like a rather sweet talcum powder! The verdict on the experiment – miracles need something more than rational scrutiny!

In *Sai Baba - God Incarnate*, Victor Kanu, a former High Commissioner of Sierra Leone, spent some time establishing that the visions of the coming Deliverer in the Book of Revelation relate to Satya Sai Baba. Details of the various symbols of this Deliverer are given as evident in the life and person of Baba.[6] He is both this second coming of Christ and also, much more, "the one who made" that Christ. Baba confirmed this belief in one of his Christmas discourses.

> At the moment when Jesus was emerging in the Supreme Principle of Divinity, He communicated some news to his followers, which has been interpreted in a variety of ways by commentators and those who relish the piling of writings on writings and meanings upon meanings, until it all swells up into a huge mess. The statement itself has been manipulated and tangled into a conundrum. The statement of Christ is simple. He who sent me among you will come again! and he pointed to a Lamb. The Lamb is merely a symbol, a sign. It stands for the Voice - Ba-Ba; the announcement was the Advent of Baba. 'His name will be Truth,' Christ declared. Sathya means Truth. 'He will wear a robe of red, a blood-red robe.' (Here Baba pointed to the Robe he was wearing!) He will be short, with a crown (of hair). The Lamb is the sign and symbol of Love. Christ did not declare that he will come again, he said, 'He

[5] Don Mario Mazzoleni, *A Catholic Priest Meets Sai Baba*, Leela Press, USA 1994, pp 101-102.
[6] Victor Kanu, *Sai Baba – God Incarnate*, Sawbridge Enterprises, London, 1981, pp 3-5.

who made me will come again.' That Baba is this Baba, and Sai, the short, curly-hair-crowned red-robed Baba, is come. He is not only this Form, but he is every one of you, as the Dweller in the Heart.[7]

The parts of this text unfamiliar to some are said by Baba to have been original but omitted from the Christian Testament. When Ron Laing asked him if this meant that it was Baba who sent Jesus into incarnation, Baba replied, "Yes." When Laing then asked if this meant that Baba was the Cosmic Christ, again he replied, "Yes."[8]

Like Jesus, Baba is said to have had an immaculate conception. A Hindu pundit asked Baba if he had entered the world directly or through human conception. Baba allowed his mother to answer. She said:

> I had had a dream in which an angel of God told me not to be afraid if something should happen to me which depended on the Will of God. That morning, while I was at the well to draw water, a great sphere of blue light came rolling toward me. I lost consciousness and fell to the ground, and I felt it slip inside me.

Baba then confirmed that he was born through "a descent, not from human contact."[9] Where Jesus was sent by His father, Sai Baba was not sent but came himself; and where Jesus often prayed to his Father for help, Baba does not pray but performs miracles at will.[10]

*Jesus according to Baba*

Jesus' original name was Isa. Both Isa and Sai mean Ishvara, God, the Eternal Absolute, the Sat-Chit-Ananda. "In Christianity, the term 'Esu' (Jesus) is used to describe Christ. This term also signifies the oneness of Divinity. The inner significance of the term 'Esu' is the recognition of the One Divine in all beings."[11] Unlike Baba, always aware of his true nature, Jesus developed this understanding during his austerities in the desert. He began by thinking of himself as a Messenger of God but then came to realize himself as the 'Son of God.'

> With body-consciousness predominant, He was a messenger. With the heart-consciousness in the ascendant, He felt greater nearness and dearness. So, the son-father bond seems natural at this stage. Later as the Atman-Consciousness was established, Jesus could declare: 'I and

---

[7] Sai Baba, *Sathya Sai Speaks,* Vol XI, discourse on 24.12.1972. All Christmas Discourses downloadable from: http://www.sssbpt.info/html/sss.html

[8] Peggy Mason and Ron Laing, *The Embodiment of Love*, Sawbridge, London, 1982, p 160.

[9] H K Takyi and Kishin J Khubchandani, Eds, *Words of Jesus and Sathya Sai Baba*, Prashanti Printers, Bombay, 1986, quoted in Mazzoleni, p 110.

[10] Victor Kanu, *Sai Baba – God Incarnate*, Sawbridge Enterprises, London, 1981, p 22.

[11] Sai Baba, *Sathya Sai Speaks*, Vol X, discourse on 25.12.1978.

My Father are One.' The three stages may be …compared to the *Dwaita* (dualism), *Vishishta-adwaita* (qualified non-dualism) and *Adwaita* (non-dualism) stages as described in Hindu philosophy. The final stage is the one when all duality has been shed. This is the essence of all religious disciplines and teachings.[12]

Christmas is a special time, celebrated at Baba's ashrams: "The birthday of Jesus must be celebrated by all mankind, for such *Karana-Janmas* (Masters born with a purpose) belong to the whole human race. They should not be confined to a single country or community." Christmas signifies "a holy day, the day on which Jesus was born."

> He announced Himself as the Messenger of God. In fact, all humans are born as Messengers of God. The sole purpose of this human career is to propagate the omnipresence of God, His might and glory. No one has incarnated for merely consuming quantities of food and catering to one's senses.[13]

It is appropriate to celebrate the birthday of Jesus but these celebrations "must take the form of adherence to the teachings, loyalty to the principles, practicing the discipline and experiencing the awareness of the Divine that He sought to arouse." The way to celebrate, true to the spirit of Christ, requires sacrifice:

> People talk of Christ's sacrifice as evidenced by his crucifixion. But, he was surrounded and bound, and crowned by the crowd who captured him with the crown of thorns, and later, nailed to the cross by his captors. A person bound and beaten by the police cannot say that he has sacrificed everything, for he is not a free man. Let us pay attention to the sacrifice that Jesus made while free, out of his own volition. He sacrificed his happiness, prosperity, comfort, safety and position. He braved the enmity of the powerful. He refused to yield or compromise. He renounced the ego, which is the toughest thing to get rid of. Honor Him for these. He willingly sacrificed the desires with which the body torments man. This sacrifice is greater than the sacrifice of the body under duress. The celebration of His birthday has to be marked by sacrificing your at least one desire or two, and conquering at least the more disastrous urges of ego.[14]

On Christmas Day in 1981 Baba said of Jesus this his message was compassion and that those who love him should show it through *seva* (service). Instead, Jesus is "worshipped but His teachings are neglected."

---

[12] Sai Baba, *Sathya Sai Speaks*, Vol X, discourse on 25.12.1976.
[13] Sai Baba, *Sathya Sai Speaks*, Vol X, discourse on 25.12.1976.
[14] Sai Baba, *Sathya Sai Speaks*, Vol VIII, discourse on 25.12.1972.

Everywhere, pomp, pageantry, hollow exhibitionism! Lectures, Lectures, Lectures! Mere gas! NO activity, no love, no seva. Heroes while lecturing, zeros while putting what is said into practice. Develop compassion. Live in Love. Be Good; do Good; see Good. This is the way to God.[15]

*Word of God*

Baba claims that sound is the secret of creation. Hindus generally believe in the great cosmic vibration of Aum as God active in creation. John's Gospel alludes to the Word of God, with God from the beginning and the same as God.

> The Bible, the Koran, the Vedas, the Granth – all represent the same creation. All were following the voice of God. All arose from the whisper of God which, in the pure minds of the hearers, flowered into eight sounds, eight letters, and from this, all words evolved. The eight sounds were the vowels and consonants of language.[16]

Like Srila Prabhupada and many others, Hindu and Christian, Sri Sathya Sai Baba recommends the repetition of the chosen divine name as a spiritual practice. The name is not different from the named and so can bring about oneness, mystical union, with the Divine Beloved.

For Sai devotees, he is God, Father of Jesus, Supreme Deity. There is usually no competition! And yet, I remember when an Indian friend came with me to a Mass at Douai Abbey, a Catholic monastic and school establishment. The invitation to Mass had come from Dom Peter Bowe, Chair of the Donnington Interfaith Group of which I had been a member for some years. The friend was an enthusiastic Sai devotee, often suspicious of Christian motives for involvement in interfaith. Even so, when we arrived, he sat at the front while I sat nearer the back with a Jewish member of the group. The building is beautiful, the ambience spiritual, and group members were invited to participate in the Mass by coming to the monk-priests for blessing. To my amazement my friend was immediately a recipient! I held back. Why? It was something to do with the 'language' I heard, heavy with history, disturbing. My Jewish colleague stayed back with me. I had no doubts about the integrity of the invitation so it was a discomfiting response. Later I asked my friend why he had gone for a blessing. He simply explained that he didn't think Sai and Jesus would have any problems together so why should he. I agreed with him of course but had not had heart enough to follow through. I felt saddened, ashamed, out of kilter at not being able to fully enter into the spirit of the invitation and the occasion.

---

[15] Christmas Day Message 1981; *Sanathana Sarathi,* February 1982.
[16] John S Hislop, *My Baba and I*, Birth Day Pub Co, San Diego, 1985.

Having been rightfully put in my place, maybe we could sum up the way devotees feel about Sai Baba with these words from Swami Sai Sharan Anand.

> Sai Baba, like Jesus Christ, is a Ray from the Supreme. Incarnations, like Krishna, Christ and Sai Baba, come after epochs. The event of their coming marks the end of the sad, waste time, the degeneration of moral and spiritual values and the beginning of a new age. Krishna, the full incarnation, lived five thousand years ago and directed humanity to the pathways of peace and love. Jesus Christ came two thousand years ago. He brought the kingdom of the heaven on earth both by his teachings and by his own example. Sai Baba has a more difficult and challenging task as he has come in an age of rank scepticism and eclipse of all moral and spiritual values. But he has declared, time and again, that the task for which he has come, will succeed and the golden age would dawn upon the earth. He says: 'My life is my message.'[17]

*Mata Amritanandamayi, 1953 -*

Another living Hindu saint considered an avatar and Christlike is Sri Mata Amritandamayi, known as Ammachi. She is famous for giving her *darshan* (blessing) as hugs. She is also very active in interfaith, the upliftment of women, and charitable work. On July 24, 2005, the United Nations gave Special UN consultative status to the Mata Amritanandamayi Math because of its dedicated humanitarian activities in India. Swami Krishnananda Giri of Yogoda Satsanga Society (YSS) experienced some of this during his own YSS relief work for the December 2004 Asian tsunami. He wrote how he became connected to the camps and shelters set up by Ammachi and her disciples to help the victims. Swamiji was impressed. He also warmly described how, in the space of several hours spent with Ammachi herself, he received five hugs![18]

As required for the life stories of great souls, the parents of Ammachi had spiritually significant dreams before her birth. Her mother, Damayanti, dreamt of "giving birth to the Indian god Krishna the night before Ammachi was born." Ammachi's father, Sughunanandan, also had a dream, about "Devi, the universal mother."

> Neither parent gave much credence to their visions. Today, both of them throw their hands in the air and laugh about the times they went through with Ammachi as their child. It was not possible for them then to conceive that their strong-willed daughter would some day draw crowds from all over the world, and that they would be among those who

---

[17] Swami Sai Sharan Anand, *Sai Baba and Jesus of Nazareth.*
[18] Swami Krishnananda Giri, 'My Tsunami Experience,' downloaded from http://www.yogananda-research-centre.org/html/News/NewsHome.html on 25 July 2005.

approach her to receive her blessings of infinite love.[19]

When Ammachi was sixteen years of age she visited a Catholic chapel for sewing classes. After the class she would go into the inner sanctum to pray and came to feel that there was no difference between her beloved Lord Krishna and the Jesus she saw hanging on the cross in the chapel. Both made loving sacrifices for others and inspired her to try to do the same.[20]

> Jesus Christ set an unforgettable example of how to respond. He let his body be tortured and crucified, and even when He was dying on the cross, Christ prayed for those who were against Him. He prayed for their own good - that they may be forgiven....He accepted the suffering by his own will for the good of the others.[21]

Teachings about Jesus are given in courses taught at Amrita Institutes, founded by Ammachi. Christian devotees receive mantras reflecting their religious heritage. Amma and devotees celebrate Christmas, as at other Hindu ashrams already mentioned: "On this joyous occasion of Christmas, let us honor Lord Jesus Christ by remembering his wonderful message of love and forgiveness. Let us pray for World unity and peace and let us celebrate Christmas with joined hands."[22]

At the closing plenary of the 2004 Parliament of the World's Religions in Barcelona, Amma emphasized that, "Love and compassion are the very essence of all religions."[23] She also "stressed the importance of harnessing 'spiritual power' in an effort to rise above religious differences." She said, "The problem arises when we say my religion is right; yours is wrong. This is like saying my mother is good; yours is a prostitute." On Amma's website there is this message:

> Amma has never sought to convert anyone. Her's is not a sectarian mission. But Amma has always stressed that along with a new home, a pension, an operation or a meal, the beneficiaries of her Humanitarian activities receive a compassionate smile and a kind word from those who serve them. In this way those who give, those who receive, and those who look on - all are transformed by the selfless love and sense of universal kinship, blossoming in an experience of essential unity - the oneness in the Self.[24]

I asked Rob Sidon, a tour press liaison helper for Ammachi, for his comments

[19] Savitri L Bess, *The Path of the Mother*, Ballantine Wellspring, 2000.
[20] Judith Cornell, *Amma, A Living Saint*, Judy Piatkus, London, 2001, p 34.
[21] 'Awaken Children, Teachings of Ammachi:' www.amma.org/eServices/eNews/2003-archives/Dec03/
[22] 'Awaken Children, Teachings of Ammachi.'
[23] Downloaded on 29.6.2005 from http://www.amma.org/amma/international-forum/un2004.html
[24] See http://www.ammachi.org/amma/mission.html

on the Mother's life and teachings.

> Amma makes no claims, but only considers her role to serve tirelessly, to help alleviate suffering in every way she can....Her outreach is both individual (receiving millions of people into her arms, wiping their tears etc) and through a vast network of charities....Her approach is that of a Mother's....I've heard Amma joke, 'I've no disciples, just naughty children.' Amma does not espouse a particular religion, but suggests that all the major religions are great, if understood and followed properly. Equally, she says that the essence of all religions is love and compassion. When asked about her own religion, Amma has said, 'My religion is Love.' Amma would laugh at being compared to Christ, however she says that Christ's key teaching, 'Do unto others as you would have them do unto you,' is at the heart of all spiritual truth. By birth Amma was born into the Hindu faith, however she encourages people to go deeper into their own path, ie. be better Hindus, better Christians, better Muslims, better Jews, better Buddhists etc. 'Love and Serve' would be her fundamental example to the world.[25]

Although devotees here and there may equate her with Christ, on the whole there seems little evidence to suggest that making claims to be equivalent to or more than Jesus is part of her own agenda, despite a host of western devotees with Christian backgrounds.[26] The approach to Jesus seems less engaged than with many other Hindu Christ figures. There is confidence in a unique, non-competitive kind of mission, perhaps partly due to the feminine emphasis of this incarnation: a divine Mother, embracing all, literally.

MORE VOICES FROM INDIA

India is independent. Centuries of colonialism are behind it. Hindus are free to assess and respond to their experiences. Some do this vigorously, polemically; others are more gentle and including. Both contain important ingredients for understanding Hindu responses to Christ and Christianity. We'll start at the tough end!

*Ram Swarup, 1920-1998*

Sri Ram Swarup, once an atheist and socialist, became very influenced by Gandhian philosophy and practice. From this he moved more deeply into a study of ancient Hinduism and its long-standing traditions, coming to realize that "the task before the Hindu society is immense."

---

[25] E-mail from Rob Sidon to author on 6 August 2005.
[26] See Ethan Walker, *The Mystic Christ: About Christ and Amma*, Devi Press, USA, 2004.

It consists in self-renewal and self-rejuvenation. It has to recover and re-assert its civilizational identity. It must realize that Hindus are not just a community...but a nation, a culture, a civilization. Similarly it must realize that their 'awakening' is not 'Hindu-communalism,' as the self-styled secularists describe it, but a great world-event, and the vehicle of a great good to the world. We can now see the beginnings of this awakening.[27]

To this cause, until his passing, Ram Swarup dedicated his life, primarily as one of the major and most respected writers for the publishing company, Voice of India, which he founded with Sita Ram Goel. Voice of India aims at "providing an ideological defense of Hindu religion and culture" in the light of attacks by "monolatrous creeds claiming to be the only true religion."[28] Sri Swarup wrote:

Under Muslim rule the threat to the Hindus was of a physical kind and their temples and great centers of learning were endangered. With the advent of the British, physical attacks ceased but another kind of attack – the ideological attack – continued and quite systematically too. The British took over the education of the Hindu youth and also unleashed the missionary. The purpose of both was to subvert the culture of the land and to create a loyal base.[29]

For Swarup, Hindus had lost self-confidence. They had developed a sense of inferiority and become apologetic. This outer response to colonialism was balanced by a deepening inner response to Hindu spirituality, producing giants like Sri Ramakrishna and Swami Vivekananda who, through their lives, con-firmed the richness and truth of mainstream Hinduism. Whilst Swarup thinks the revival of Hindu confidence that then emerged helped in the struggle for India's independence from the British, he goes further:

[It] is not yet equally realized that Independence can only be preserved by a revised Hinduism. Hinduism is India's name at its deepest and noblest. It is what gives India pride and hope; it is what holds its past and future together. It is what gives it culture, spirituality, coherence and stability as a nation and preserves its unity. Take away Hinduism and very little is left of the nation and the country.[30]

Swarup very wittily responds to Christian development of the term *Neo-Hinduism*, a kind of Hinduism that is shaped by its response to European pressures and is only able to defend Hinduism in the borrowed idiom of

---

[27] Quoted in *Hinduism Today*, Hawaii, April 1999, p 25.
[28] Ram Swarup, *Hindu View of Christianity and Islam*, Voice of India, New Delhi, 1992, back cover.
[29] 'Rediscovering the Real Swamiji,' *The Telegraph*, India, 13 January 1992, p 9.
[30] 'Rediscovering the Real Swamiji.'

Europe. It always seems to be used in a derogatory way and Swarup has fun
with this, first with Europeans:

> If [Hinduism] is to engage in a dialogue with the west, it must speak in
> the idiom best understood by the listener. Though the West is an acute
> linguist and it has mastered many languages it is not so nimble-witted in
> understanding the peoples who spoke them.[31]

Then more fun, with Hindus:

> Neo-Hinduism does more than justify Hinduism; it also justifies
> Christianity, Islam and many other non-Indian cults….In its insatiable
> desire for 'synthesis' and similarities, it seeks and find Vedanta in the
> Bible and the Quran and in Das Kapital too; it says that Jesus and
> Muhammad and Marx all are incarnations and Rishis, and that they all
> say the same thing. The net result is that the Semitic prophets are as
> popular among the Hindus as their own. Western rationalism had
> rejected Christianity not only for its miracles but even more so for its
> exclusive claims which offend rationality, but it is now coming back
> under Hindu auspices and promotion.[32]

You can feel Swarup's distaste for the concept of 'Neo-Hinduism.' I share that
feeling. The term is primarily in one-way use, mainly by Western scholars
influenced by Western versions of history. All religions – and cultures - are
constantly in flux, adapting to new circumstances, inter-actions, insights etc.
Nothing is untouched by this. We might as well refer, as Swarup suggests, to
Neo-Christianity or Neo-Europe. Yet no one does. Sarvapelli Radhakrishnan
put it this way: "There has been no such thing as a uniform stationary un-
alterable Hinduism whether in point of belief or practice. Hinduism is a
movement, not a position; a process, not a result; a growing tradition not a
fixed revelation." [33]

Returning to his specific encounter with Christianity, Swarup ponders that,
while Christians claim that Jesus incarnated, he is himself not sure "what he
incarnated, but it is not difficult to see that Christianity incarnated a new
religious intolerance."

> It was with the coming of Christianity and Islam that religious bigotry
> and arrogance descended on the earth on a large scale and with a new
> power. They know so little about themselves but they claim to know
> everything about God, and in imposing their definition upon others, they

---

[31] 'Indo-European Encounter: An Indian Perspective' in *Journal of Indian Council of Philosophical Research*, Vol. VIII, Number 2, January-April 1991, p 87.
[32] 'Indo-European Encounter: An Indian Perspective,' p 87.
[33] S Radhakrishnan, *The Hindu View of Life*, Allen & Unwin, London, 1964, p 129.

have killed millions of people. They have been even more fanatic than their founders.[34]

He kept up to date with contemporary Christian scholarship on the historical Jesus and believed this has led to a Jesus of legend rather than a Jesus of history about whom very little can be confirmed. This uncertainty, he reflects, has led to a focus on the Jesus of faith. However, "the question still remains whether a gratuitous faith based on the figure of a saviour imagined or historical is rationally or spiritually tenable."[35] For Sri Swarup, most of what Christianity accredits to Jesus is borrowed, not only from Judaism, but also from creeds and mystery cults then prevalent. To all this Christians added atonement through the blood of Jesus, a once and for all solution to a perennial problem: sin. Follow Jesus and sin is no longer our problem! He refers to M K Gandhi's contacts with Plymouth Brethren in South Africa, how they felt free from their sins through their belief in Jesus' atonement. Gandhi noticed that they lived true to their faith and "committed transgressions" but remained "undisturbed by them." Swarup remarks how many Christians consider it a compliment to be called sinful, how Paul rejoiced in being "the foremost of sinners." He quotes Luke 15.7 to support this – greater joy over one repentant sinner than ninety-nine righteous people who need no repentance. "To become sinful has become a cult with them." He feels that repentance, the companion to sin, has stimulated Indulgences, threats of hell-fire, and purgatory, thus creating "spiritual terrorism." This has led to neurotic and masochistic-sadistic behavior - self-flagellations and scourgings of all kinds - as well as to burnings, anti-Semitism, everything except changing the way of living itself.

Swarup has some fun at the expense of Matthew 11.v25f: "I thank thee, O Father, Lord of Heaven and earth, that thou didst hide these things from the wise and understanding, and didst reveal them unto babes." He thinks this is false piety hiding great satisfaction.

> The claim is at heart boastful but, looked at from another angle, it has a certain kind of truth of its own. Christianity has only cared for a God known by babes and sinners; it has hardly an idea of a God revealed to understanding, wisdom and purity.

---

[34] Ram Swarup, *Hindu View of Christianity and Islam*, Voice of India, New Delhi, 1992, p 41. See also 'Dead Sea Scrolls Shatter the Christian Myth' in N S Rajaram, *A Hindu View of the World*, Voice of India, Delhi, 1998, pp 109-135. For Rajaram, "Early Christianity – a Qumranian institution – was an extremist Jewish movement that arose in reaction to the secularising influence of the Graeco-Roman world in the eastern part of the Roman Empire. Its leader in the first century was James the Righteous, an ultra-orthodox Jew. What we now call Christianity grew out of Pauline Christianity, a heresy opposed to the teachings of James. It was the result of a power struggle between Paul and James that culminated in the death of James and the destruction of the early Church of Jerusalem in the First Jewish War of 66-74AD." Rajaram also questions the historicity of Jesus, pp 126-7.

[35] Ram Swarup, *Hindu View of Christianity and Islam*, p 63.

More bitingly, this Christian God is shown to be "a guardian of criminals enjoying extra-territorial treaty rights as they did during the last centuries when Europe and the missionaries ruled the roost."[36]

For Swarup, it seems that Christians require no sadhana or spiritual praxis for their prophets have already revealed all the truths to them (while hiding them from others); beliefs are certain and fixed; and their religious dharma or duty is primarily to convert others.[37] Christian mission is not about responding to the profound questions - what is real, what is the highest Good - but how to convince others about the truth of their God, his will, and how it can be ful-filled. A missionary with this message has nothing to learn, only something to correct or punish in others. He is a persecutor, a subjugator, and a destroyer. History shows this to be true, whatever the culture, wherever Christian mission has been instigated. To demonstrate the impact of this mission, Ram Swarupji turns to figures produced in *Seven Hundred Plans to Evangelise the World: The Rise of a Global Evangelisation Movement*, a "statistical marvel."[38] He comments:

> By the time Jesus came, 5.5 million years had already elapsed and 118 billion men and women had already lived and died, all ipso facto destined for hell as they did not know Christ. But new prospects opened up for mankind after AD33 when the Kingdom of Heaven was announced and inaugurated. Heaven, empty until then, began to be populated though rather unexpectedly slowly in the beginning. But by 1990 there are already 8 billion dead believers (Church Triumphant), all qualifying for habitation in the new region. They are however still only 5.70% of unbelievers destined for hell, quarters across the street. But the demographic composition continues to improve in their favour. By AD2100 they are 8.57%, and at the end of 4 billion years, they are fully 99.90%, the Christian heaven holding 9 decillion (one decillion is ten followed by 33 zeros) believers. In AD100,000, believers are still only 85% of the total living population. But by AD4 billion, the gap practically closes and almost all are believers. The Great Commission is fulfilled and Missionaries are freed from their obligations to God and His Son.[39]

---

[36] Ram Swarup, *Hindu View of Christianity and Islam*, Voice of India, New Delhi, 1992, pp 65, 71-2, 76.

[37] Ram Swarup, *Hindu View of Christianity and Islam*, pp 74-5. Certainly many Christians today, while still drawn to the life of Jesus, look to Buddhism and Hinduism to provide a methodology, a way to live life, finding little guidance in the Christian Testament. They hear truth in the Gospels but don't know how to access it directly. The direct personal appropriation of truth is at the heart of Hinduism and countless types of sadhana have been developed to make it possible.

[38] David B Barrett and James W Reapsome, 'The AD 2000 Series, 1989,' quoted by Ram Swarup in 'Evangelisation: The Great Command and a Cosmic Auditing,' *The Statesman*, India, 25 March 1990.

[39] Ram Swarup, *Hindu View of Christianity and Islam*, Appendix 1, pp 124-5.

However, in an essay, *One God of Theology*, published posthumously, Swarup begins to see a change and a new trend emerging. Recognition and respect for Hinduism is not only coming now from nominal Christians, humanists and universalists, but also from deeply religious Christians, particularly those concerned about Christian mission activities. "All this is a welcome development and it is in keeping with the spirit of the age which demands universality and breaking down of the barriers of prejudice and insularity."[40]

Ram Swarup found Hinduism satisfied humanity's every spiritual and ethical need. Using the methods it has devised leads to a more meaningful, unitive and intuitive life. It is pluralist, compassionate and non-violent. It is both what humanity has sought and the product of that seeking.[41]

For many Hindus, Ram Swarup was truly "a man of the Vedic Renaissance in a real sense."[42]

*Sita Ram Goel, 1921-2003*

Sita Ram Goel was an active defender of Hinduism, one who felt you had to study the 'enemy' in order to refute it. Together with his friend and mentor, Ram Swarup, he founded Voice of India to disseminate his research. His writings against Christianity and Islam were highly polemical but, as his son Pradip indicated, this did not mean that he did not like Christians, though Pradip also noted that most of Goel's Christian and Muslim friends deserted him when they became aware of how he wrote about their religions.[43] Goel's critique of Christ and Christianity is more spiky than satirical, perhaps less measured than his mentor's. It is as heartfelt.

In the earlier phases of his own spiritual development, from an atheist back to a Hindu, under the influence of Ram Swarup, and when he first began to study Christianity, Goel initially thought of Jesus as a mystic and Paul as the one who brought in what he understood as the typical exclusivist theology of the Semitic prophets.[44] Later he revised this judgement finding Jesus himself responsible. The title of his book about this change, *Jesus Christ, An Artifice for Aggression*, gives us some clues about his own theological conclusions![45]

Despite the missionary zeal to promote Hinduism I had when I started this research, I confess to some alarm when I first heard that he had included my Questionnaire on Hindu perspectives on Jesus and his response to it in this

---

[40] Ram Swarup, *Meditations*, Voice of India, New Delhi, reviewed in *Hinduism Today*, Hawaii, January/February 2001, p 60.

[41] Ram Swarup, *Hinduism vis-à-vis Christianity and Islam*, Voice of India, New Delhi, 1992, p 22.

[42] Navaratna S Rajaram, *Hinduism Today*, Hawaii, April 1999, p 28.

[43] Interview, *Hinduism Today*, Hawaii, July/August/September 2004, p 54.

[44] Sita Ram Goel, *How I Became a Hindu*, Voice of India, New Delhi, 1982, p 55.

[45] Sita Ram Goel, *Jesus Christ: An Artifice for Aggression*, Voice of India, 1994.

book.[46] A student then, working on a PhD, I was not sure that my future was best secured by such an alignment! Now I am only grateful for his honesty and for the challenges he gives to Hindus and Christians to reflect on the all too frequent associations of Christianity with violence, hypocrisy and ignorance. Of course, all religions are subject to these aspects, in varying degrees and according to the wisdom of their members. Sita Ramji has passed away now but I would have liked him to review this work, even though I would surely have wilted under the weight of his polemic!

A Jesuit friend told Goel that Jesus was a solid historical figure, his miracles attested by many, no "mythological mumbo-jumbo like your Rama and Krishna." [47] Following Goel's study of the Gospels and contemporary biblical criticism he came to classify this statement itself as highly mythological! He found virtually no evidence for the historical Jesus outside of the Christian Testament, no evidence of any impact of the signs and wonders associated with stories of him, beyond the small circle of disciples, but plenty of evidence on modern bookshelves that Christians were aware of this dilemma. The real identity of this enigmatic historical figure is now up for grabs.[48] Goel quotes Albert Schweitzer to support his findings:

> There is nothing more negative than the result of the critical study of the life of Jesus. The Jesus of Nazareth who came forward publicly as the Messiah, who preached the ethic of the Kingdom of God, who founded the Kingdom of Heaven upon earth, and died to give His work its final consecration, never had any existence. This image has not been destroyed from without. It has fallen to pieces, cleft and disintegrated by the concrete historical problems which came to surface one after another, and in spite of all the artifice, art, artificiality, and violence which was applied to them, refused to be planed down to fit the design on which Jesus of the theology of the last hundred and thirty years had been constructed.[49]

With the historical Jesus dispatched, how does the Christ of faith fare? Goel finds this figure has also failed. This is mainly deduced from his interpretation of the theology of Rudolf Bultmann and his colleagues, with their focus on the risen Lord, the "Christ of Kerygma." The Gospels were faith rather than historical documents. The Jesus there is not historical but pre-existent. The cross is not biography but a saving event, revealing the true nature of Jesus. This risen Lord is thus confirmed by the "proclamation of the Christian

---

[46] His responses to the Questionnaire are also included, in full, in Appendix 1B. They are only in an Appendix because of their size and format. They are a very significant contribution to the topic of this book so please read fully.

[47] Sita Ram Goel, *Jesus Christ: An Artifice for Aggression*, Voice of India, 1994, p 1.

[48] Author: He is indeed the unknown Jesus of Christianity!

[49] Albert Schweitzer, *The Quest for the Historical Jesus*, London 1906, p 396, quoted in Sita Ram Goel, *Jesus Christ: An Artifice for Aggression*, p 31.

community."[50] You might imagine by now how Goel responds to the history of Christianity built on such belief! It is with extreme anger and distaste. He includes a reference to a supporting observation about Christian theology made by Mahatma Gandhi to Christian missionaries: "Among agents of many untruths that are propounded in the world one of the foremost is theology. I do not say there is no demand for it. There is demand in the world for many a questionable thing."[51]

For Sita Ram, neither the Jesus of history nor the Christ of Faith had any merit; both were menacing bullies. The images concocted of them as 'real' are in fact false. This was the mistake Hindus initially made. They appealed to missionaries in the name of the 'real' Jesus when in fact he was no different to the theology they were preaching. The strategy of praising Jesus, used by Gandhi and others, has "boomeranged as is evident from the freedom which Christian missions have increasingly acquired not only to aggress against but also to throw Hindu society on the defensive. They are waging a war on Hinduism with no holds barred."[52]

Goel found abhorrent such books as Raimon Pannikar's *The Unknown Christ of Hinduism* and M M Thomas' *The Acknowledged Christ of the Indian Renaissance* with their hint of Hindu unfulfilment without Jesus. He refuted any suggestion that Jesus, if he ever existed, had set foot on Indian soil. He denounced Christian interest in dialogue with Hindus as insincere, a fashion accessory rather than a faith necessity.[53] Hindus had to become more abrasive to counter the constant Christian abuse of their tolerance. Whilst his tone may, at times, seem harsh, there is truth in what he writes as well as a willingness to dialogue at this honest, totally open level with those Christians really seeking that truth. He felt that, so far, there were no takers on this invitation.[54]

> The Jesus industry in India will continue to flood the market with similar spurious products till Hindus make it clear that there is nothing in common between the Sanatana Dharma and the sinister cult of the Only Saviour, that Hindus have nothing to learn from Christianity but a lot to teach, and that the sooner the Christian missionaries close their shop in this country the better for them and their masters abroad.[55]

Do current responses to Christian theology indicate some agreement with Goel's view of its lack of integrity and consequent irrelevance? Christian

---

[50] Rudolf Bultmann, *The Primitive Christian Kerygma and the Historical Jesus*, 1968, p 254, quoted in Sita Ram Goel, *Jesus Christ: An Artifice for Aggression*, Voice of India, 1994, p 71f.

[51] M K Gandhi, *The Collected Works*, Volume 71, Publications Division, Indian Government, New Delhi, 1968, p 338; Sita Ram Goel, *Jesus Christ: An Artifice for Aggression*, p 74.

[52] Sita Ram Goel, *Jesus Christ: An Artifice for Aggression*, p 83.

[53] Sita Ram Goel, *Jesus Christ: An Artifice for Aggression*, p 84.

[54] Sita Ram Goel, *Jesus Christ: An Artifice for Aggression*, Appendix, 'Hindus vis-à-vis Jesus,' p106. See also his Questionnaire response in Appendix 1B of this book.

[55] Sita Ram Goel, *Jesus Christ: An Artifice for Aggression*, p 84.

numbers are generally in decline as are priestly and monastic vocations. Many churches are near empty. However, this is countered by a strong rise in Christian fundamentalism and evangelism, especially in the United States of America and some parts of Africa. Uncertain worlds require religious certainties so the matching theology has a certain future!

Whilst understanding the need to counter centuries of Christian aggression in India, while respecting the right to promote a Hinduism un-degraded by Christian mission, whilst admitting the courage of Voice of India writers to fearlessly face down their old oppressors, while being really interested in their approach and what can be learnt from it, still I personally feel a little uncomfortable with the kind of Hinduism this then presents. Maybe, that is because my feeling for Hinduism is too 'other-worldly,' too appreciative of its transcendental gifts, not enough aware of its social and cultural justifications.

VOICES OF HINDU YOUTH

Vivekananda said his faith was in "the younger generation, out of them will come my workers, they will work out the whole problem." With this in mind two young Hindus from India responded to some questions pertinent to this book's theme: Do you believe in avatars? Is Christ one? Has Christian mission caused you any problems? Is there such a thing as Hindu mission? What is Hinduism's primary spiritual message for the world today?

*Hiten Bhagtani*, part of the Religious Freedom Young Adult Network (RFYN) co-ordinated by the International Association for Religious Freedom, was the first to get in touch from India.[56] Hiten does believe in avatars. They are divine spirit taking human form to show us how to lead a balanced human-religious life. Christ as the son of God could be understood as an avatar but may also have a distinct identity.

Hiten comes from a small town called Rajkot in Gujarat. He was educated by Christian missionaries and used to participate in some Christian festivals like Christmas but this has fallen away. The atmosphere at school was good, "full of fun," and it was not until Hiten and friends left school that they became aware of the tensions caused by Christian missionaries targeting areas like "Gujarat (Dangs), Tamil Nadu (interior parts), and the North Eastern states." Hindu fundamentalists are now resisting Christian mission in these areas where many people were deprived of basic rights and social standing. Hiten thinks these depravations were primarily caused by the Hindu caste system. While the situation is better in some big towns and states, the Government has introduced the Anti-Conversion Bill to keep a check on Christian missionary activities. Hiten's personal view on Christian mission includes the positive as a

---

[56] E-mails from Hiten Bhagtani to author on 9 and 11 August 2005. For more on the RFYN, see www.iarf.net

friend's grandfather converted to Christianity to escape the indignity of low caste Hinduism and this had brought the family an enhanced sense of dignity and well being, a better life indeed.

Hinduism's primary spiritual message for the world? It is a living philosophy incorporating aeons of spiritual experience and knowledge. "It is a big ocean making each feel its own place among it. The best message of Hinduism as per my belief is just to live a holy and pious life making all the living beings happy."

*Atreyee Day,* a writer, artist and teacher from Calcutta, is less confident about avatars.[57] They are hard to imagine but "would have a degree of godliness or 'goodliness' taken to the greatest level of perfection." In their presence we would feel that goodness tangibly. We would feel fulfilled and loved unconditionally. Because we are unused to their levels of "consistent purity of purpose and thoughts and actions" they may seem "contradictory or perplexing to others!" Atreyee feels this because two people she has met have "stood out because of the way they were as well as in their relation to others."

> I consider them to be, I felt them to be, uncritical, loving, compassionate, laughing easily, natural, actively seeing goodness in every person and situation, willing to undergo pain but unable…I repeat *unable…* to inflict it even in retaliation, non-acquisitive about anything yet appreciating with delight, almost childlike, totally involved in the moment, be it work, play or life at large, yet intrinsically detached from gain or loss, tireless in self improvement (both would feign surprise if it were to be mentioned that they were spiritually superior) - such is their modesty, simplicity and lack of guile.

An avatar, therefore, would display these qualities in a greatly magnified way, and, yes, if there are avatars, then Christ was one, Ramakrishna Paramahansa and Sarada Ma too.

Atreyee has taken part in several Christmas and Easter celebrations, at Christian churches and at Ramakrishna Maths. She tells the story of one such occasion:

> The Christmas Eve 2004 was unique! I happened to be visiting Pune Ramakrishna Math on the 24th of December and I mentioned a little wistfully to my mother that this was a rare evening before Christmas for me – no carols or candlelights! We entered the prayer hall for the *arati* and service which proceeded as usual. After the first song I thought I heard the strum of a guitar! And sure enough there was a young sanyasi

---

[57] E-mail from Atreyee Day to author on 10 August 2005. The late Swami Ranganathananda of the Ramakrishna Mission initiated Atreyee into the Ramakrishna Order.

with a guitar and as two others busily lit an arc of candles near the altar of Ramakrishna he sang three popular carols – 'Joy to the World,' 'Hark the Herald Angel Sing,' and 'Silent Night'! I found myself smiling and singing and looking slightly silly! Later I came to know of the significance of this day in the calendar of Ramakrishna Mission – after the 12 disciples of Ramakrishna took their monastic vows at midnight, Vivekananda alerted them that it happened to be the 24th of December.

Christian mission and evangelism has caused problems for her. On several occasions she was urged to convert to Christianity. She had been approached by people feigning friendship who then turned out to be evangelists.

I felt not only cheated but at a loss trying to explain to them that wouldn't following Christ's teaching in spirit be more important than signing a formal bond with the church? I told one such person even if I were a Hindu or Buddhist if you had a measuring device I'm sure you would find a high degree of Christian spirit in many of us! But the catholicity was missing in this woman evangelist who had accosted me several times on a train commute and she could not or did not want to see certain universal values above personal differences!

What is religion about then? For Atreyee it is a "personal moment-to-moment affair."

The ability to use one's discerning faculty as well as being compass-ionate in our relationships (recognizing the myriad relations in the first place!), be it with one's self or others, to me is significant. All religions threw up their share of mystics which no one traditional belief system felt comfortable to wholly claim. To me the world has come to a juncture when we can seek the wisdom of the universal religion of mystics. In our daily dealings if we ask ourselves where do we come from, how are we unique and what are we here to do, what is our relation with others, where are we going - that should keep us busy!

## SUMMARY

There seems to be considerable diversity in contemporary Indian Hindu responses to Christ and Christianity. Some of the Hindus discussed in this chapter have moved into a different category from those we met in earlier chapters. Anger against Christianity is no longer constrained. There is, generally, no more an apologetic or even including tone. There is a strong sense of Hinduism being on the higher spiritual ground, reaffirmed as not only sufficient for Hindus but of value to all. One Hindu preceptor is clearly posited as more than Christ, Father to his Son. For another, this kind of agenda seems not to be a primary concern. Young adults seem confident and non-polemical.

Hinduism no longer needs to defend itself against or compare itself with Christianity. Some of its own leaders are living Christs. Their authoritative teachings about Jesus reveal their own equality with him. This can still be useful with western devotees from Christian backgrounds but may gradually become irrelevant and disappear, even as Christian influence may be disappearing among those turning to Eastern religions for spiritual fulfilment. First generation Western Hindus will have second-generation Hindu children.

Hinduism is on the move in India and is already established across the world. Many of its words are in western dictionaries and part of common parlance. Its sublime and expansive message fits this age. Many Westerners who have turned to it for spiritual support would agree. The religious pluralism it incorporates can help a world divided by different religious 'truths.' The Sanatan Dharma offers the wisdom, experience and space for the unity of Truth to flourish without restricting diversity.

CHAPTER VII

# Contemporary Responses From North America and England

*He who is free from delusion, and knows me as the supreme Reality, knows all that can be known. Therefore, he adores me with all his heart.*
*- Lord Krishna, Bhagavad-Gita*

### INTRODUCTION

Is Jesus or Christ a topic of interest to contemporary Hindu thinkers and activists in the West or has this become passé?

We can only explore here a selection of the responses to Christ, Christianity and the Hindu-Christian encounter emerging from North America and England. There are several Hindu academics in North America actively engaged in teaching Hinduism and Hindu perspectives on inter-religious relations. Some of these are included in this chapter. There is also an introduction to the American writer and teacher David Frawley, also known as Vamadeva Shastri. From London, a profile of the Vivekananda Centre is provided as well as some responses to my Questionnaire from a leading member of the Bharatiya Vidya Bhavan. There is much more for interested readers to discover.

### K L SESHAGIRI RAO

K L Seshagiri Rao is Professor Emeritus, University of Virginia, and Chief Editor of the Encyclopedia of Hinduism project. Earlier in his career, in 1960, he undertook some fieldwork exploring Gandhiji's concept of *Sarvodharma sambhava* (reverence for all religions). This led him to visit a Christian colony in a South Indian village. There he discovered that Christians had allegiance to many different denominations, each polemical towards the other. He found these villagers did not know where Rome was but were Catholics; they did not know where England was but were Anglicans etc. What kind of Jesus Christ could they know? Rao asked a Catholic Bishop if one could be a Christian without defining oneself by any particular group but was told this was not possible. Such attitudes were reflected in the approach of many Christian missionaries when they first came to India.

[They] used to make scathing attacks on Hinduism and dismiss it as a religion of superstition and crass idolatry, not to be taken seriously. They referred to the Hindus as polytheists, pagans and heathens. They implicitly believed that the Western nations possessed a superior religion and culture. Hence they went out to give and not to receive; their objective was to spread Christianity.[1]

Rao contrasts this with the great freedom Hindus have, free from any founder, free to revere truth in many forms. He quotes Swami Nikhilananda who stated:

Nothing wonderful will happen to the world if the entire mankind be converted to Hinduism, Christianity, Buddhism, or Islam, or to any other religion. But assuredly, something marvelous will happen if a dozen men and women pierce the thick walls of the Church, the temple, the synagogue and realize the Truth.[2]

Rao admonishes Christianity for the mistakes it has made in translating Jesus' life and example into dogmas and absolutisms, something he equates with thinking still "in terms of the chosen people, favoritism of God, ritualism, and so on." Hindus respond more to the example of Jesus, his simplicity and his spirituality, without the need to turn this into exclusivist theology and apology.

It is desirable that interpretation of Jesus Christ and His activities should be big enough as to include Him in every religion wherever truth, good-ness, and love operate. A Hindu seeks the universal and living Christ. His view of Jesus Christ might take us away from some of the narrow interpretations and make us worshippers of the eternal, the true, and the living Christ.[3]

The lack of understanding of the Hindu universal mind-set means that, "For all its hopes and opportunities, 'Christian triumphalism' of the Colonial era did not succeed."

Christianity continues to be, by and large, a minority religion in Asia; it has to live with and amidst a majority community of another faith. Western Christians do not fully realize the enormous cultural and national pressures faced by the Christian minorities in Asia. Asian Christians clearly see the practical situation and recognize that human

---

[1] K L Seshagiri Rao, 'Hindu-Christian Dialogue: A Hindu Perspective' in *Journal of Hindu-Christian Studies*, Vol 14, 2001.
[2] Swami Nikhilananda, *The Mandukya Upanishad with Gaudapada's Karika*, Sri Ramakrishna Ashram, Mysore, 1974, p XXXV.
[3] K L Seshagiri Rao, 'A Hindu View of Jesus Christ,' Address at Annual Conference of the Alumni of Harvard Divinity School, 1964. Included as Appendix 1 in K L Seshagiri Rao, *Mahatma Gandhi and C F Andrews - A Study in Hindu-Christian Dialogue*, Punjab University, Patiala, 1969.

community is religiously pluralistic. They see no signs of immediate or even distant displacement of all other religions by Christianity.[4]

Some recent Christian thinkers and groups are trying hard "to eliminate the burdens of the past, to redefine their attitudes to other cultures, religions and peoples, and to dissociate themselves from certain unhappy historical associations." However, "Asian peoples are still handicapped in their appreciation of Christianity by what has been done to them in the past by Western nations." Despite these historical disadvantages, Hindus continue to revere Christ in their own way.

> Jesus Christ is ineradicably part of modern Hinduism….Hindus adore Christ. The way in which Christ has touched their lives, and their responses to him are varied: some Hindus acknowledge Jesus as an *avatar*; some others consider him as a yogi, a *satguru* and so on. Mahatma Gandhi, for instance, showed great reverence to Jesus Christ and publicly acknowledged his indebtedness to him, but refused to limit Jesus Christ to the boundaries of this or that church.

Hindus are free to appreciate Jesus without the "appendages of theology, dogma or doctrine." They can give attention to his life, its love and forgiveness.

> What strikes a Hindu above all is his complete obedience to the will of God; the more he emptied himself the more he discovered God. The Cross is not something to be believed in and subscribed to as a dogma; but something to be lived and borne in life and experience. Jesus signifies to the Hindus the transcendence of the ego as the whole purpose of morality and spirituality. The enlightened person gains release by the surrender of his little self and its vanities by the purity of self and devotion to God.

## K R SUNDARARAJAN

Professor K R Sundararajan of St Bonaventure University believes that the impact of Christianity on Hinduism has been significant. He writes that, "Indeed one may describe 'Modern Hinduism' as that phase of Hinduism which has been a response to the impact of Christianity."[5] For Sundararajan, modern Hinduism has responded to western science, technology, education, culture, and Christian mission. It has rethought itself, in differing phases, in response to these challenges and in the face of growing nationalism. He cites Vivekananda and Radhakrishnan as primary examples of Hindu "revivalism."

---

[4] K L Seshagiri Rao, 'Hindu-Christian Dialogue: A Hindu Perspective,' *Journal of Hindu-Christian Studies*, Vol 14, 2001. All remaining Rao quotes in this section are from this paper.
[5] K R Sundararajan, 'A Hindu View of Jesus' in the *Unitarian Universalist Christian Journal*, Autumn 1974, Vol 29, No 3, p 25.

This has led to a "spiritualization" and universalization of Hinduism, and to a polarization of "spiritual east and materialistic west."[6]

> The 'essential Jesus' is what the Hindu thinkers have appropriated and not the 'historical distortions and falsifications.' The 'essential' approach one finds in the writings of Rammohun Roy, Swami Vivekananda, Swami Akhilananda, Radhakrishnan and many others. Here the Hindu thinkers have taken notice of claims that Jesus was an incarnation. But they deny Christian claims that he was either unique or the 'Final revelation.'...On the whole, one could say that Hinduism, insofar as it has appropriated Christ, has usually used the category of 'incarnation.'[7]

However, Sundararajan believes this process has been incomplete, that Hindus have not really understood the incarnation of Jesus in any Christian sense, which is why they had to hinduize him.

> Christ represented a challenge with regard to questions of suffering, death, and resurrection. Can the incarnations suffer? Probably the story of Rama displays instances of suffering and, of course, all human incarnations 'die.' But theologically speaking, the divine incarnations cannot suffer and die. So a sort of 'docetist' understanding of Hindu *avataras* and Christ came to be stressed.[8]

He believes this process is not in accord with respecting the 'other,' now part of some theological and most interfaith practice.[9] It is not enough just to understand someone or something from one's own perspective; there has to be some crossing-over, some dialogical vulnerability, to know the 'other' as itself, as it really is. My own feeling is that in the case of Jesus Christ this may be rather difficult as there are innumerable understandings of him and no clear indication of how he understood himself – under scrutiny of recent scholarship, the historical Jesus and the Christ of faith seem theologically miles apart and little is known about the former. Also, there was the 'heresy' of docetism in early Christian history so Christians too reflected on Christ in this way. Christ has always been and always will be about the inner revelation of that truth in any individual attuned to it. The Christian has to appropriate Christ in the same way as the Hindu!

Even so, deep dialogue and interreligious encounter can open us up to greater awareness of other perspectives and engender fresh insights. Differences need

---

[6] Swami Vivekananda, *The Yogas and Other Works*, Ramakrishna-Vivekananda Center, New York, 1953, p 697.
[7] K R Sundararajan, 'A Hindu View of Jesus,' *Unitarian Universalist Christian Journal*, Autumn 1974, Vol 29, No 3, pp 25-29.
[8] E-mail to author, 7 September 2005.
[9] K R Sundararajan, 'A Hindu View of Jesus,' p 31.

to be respected and taken seriously. For instance, for Hindus *moksha* is freedom from ignorance (*avidya*) of the true nature of the Self (*atman*). Freedom comes from right knowledge leading to realization; this is personal responsibility. For the Christian, freedom from sin is required and one's own efforts are inadequate for this; a savior is needed, a substitute.[10] As Professor Sundararajan states, "Appreciation comes when I understand the reasons for differences, not when I simply note down that there are differences." As within some strands of Hinduism there is also scope for 'saving grace,' dialogue may also diminish the differences.[11]

However, even a limited appropriation of Christ, in a Hindu way only, also brings with it new spiritual possibilities.

> In some way Hindus cannot avoid 'Hinduizing' Jesus if they want to understand/appropriate him. Similarly, Christians cannot avoid 'Christianizing' Yoga or Zen if they find either religiously attractive. However, we should note that even in this process of understanding, which is essentially 'seeing the other through one's own eyes' or understanding the 'other' in terms of 'one's own categories', there is a potential for the expansion of and a deepening of one's own under-standing of 'being religious'. This could be considered an authentic conversion experience since one makes fresh discoveries about others and, in the same process, possibly finds out something more or new about oneself.[12]

Professor Sundararajan was kind enough to respond to some questions I posited.[13] Firstly, I wondered if there is any serious Hindu-Christian dialogue on Christ today or if it is still based on the output from India's colonial period. He replied:

> In contemporary India, missionary work is suspect. Various Christian denominations train priests and ministers so that they might serve the Christian community. Therefore, the focus of their mission is rather internal. This is also the primary intent of Hindu missions in the West, though both of them are 'open' to converts. I believe that Christ is not the primary subject of conversation in inter-religious dialogues that take place in the West. The interest seems to be 'conceptual' and thematic. In all these cases, the Hindu scholars often rely very heavily on the source

---

[10] K R Sundararajan, A Hindu View of Jesus', Unitarian Universalist Christian Journal, Autumn 1974, Vol 29, No 3, pp 31, 33.

[11] The great Hindu sage, Ramana Maharshi, spoke of 'inherited grace.' "As the Lord denotes the Self and as Grace means the Lord's presence, or revelation, there is no time when the Lord remains unknown. If the light of the sun is invisible to the owl it is only the fault of that bird and not the sun." Ramana Maharshi, *Spiritual Instruction*, Sri Ramanasramam, Tirvvannamarai, 1939, pp8-9.

[12] See K R Sundararajan, *The Hindu Models of Inter-Religious Dialogue* at www.interfaithstudies.org/interfaith/hindumodelsdialogue.html

[13] It was too late to include them all here so please see Appendix 4 for full text.

materials in their presentations. The 'revered' persons of early times such as Radhakrishnan and Swami Vivekananda are not referred to frequently.

Do Hindu responses to Christ have any meaning for Christians?

To the question of whether this 'embrace of Christ as an avatar' has any real significance for Christians, my response is to say that I am not sure. One might suggest that the Hindu tolerance of Christians historically probably reflect this kind of understanding. Finally, the Hindu tolerance could be accounted for by the very fact that the tradition stresses that there are several ways of finding God and being united with Him. Yet what was considered by the Hindus as 'conversion by force' or 'economic incentives' has resulted in opposition to Christian missionary work in India.

Does Christ really matter to Hindus?

'Does an avatar Christ really have any significance for Hindus?' is an interesting question. At the philosophical and religious level...it raised questions regarding the possibility of a 'suffering God.' The notion of God as loving, as one who steps out of his transcendent state to embrace the devotee out of love is a common theme in the theistic traditions of India. At the level of popular piety, one may find themes of suffering in the story of Rama and in the puranic episode of Siva drinking the poison when the ocean was churned by both the devas and asuras and became the blue-throated Siva (Nilakanta). Again at the level of popular piety, Hindus pray and worship in places considered to have spiritual powers of healing. Here, I may mention a Church in Velanganni in Southern India, where Hindus and Muslims pray and worship Mary, the Mother of Jesus. I believe that the Hindu tradition, with its stress on diverse ways of experiencing God, makes it possible for a Hindu to attend Church services, if necessary, without serious discomfort.[14]

For Sundararajan, "the main thrust of contemporary Hinduism is to understand itself, rather than to dialogue with other faith communities." For Hindus today there is the feeling that "the tradition has everything one needs and there is nothing to learn from 'others.'" This is not enough. "I personally feel that the sound basis for inter-religious dialogue goes beyond mere curiosity, and should be motivated by what I would describe as 'the existential need' to learn from others and be conceptually broadened and spiritually benefited."[15]

---

[14] E-mail to author, 7 September 2005.
[15] E-mail to author, 7 September 2005. For full text see Appendix 4.

ANANTANAND RAMBACHAN

Dr Anantanand Rambachan is a Hindu scholar from Trinidad and Tobago and Professor of Religion at St Olaf College in the USA. He grew up in the religiously plural ambience of Trinidad and accepted the familiar Hindu including views on other religions and spiritual perspectives whilst noticing these were not often reciprocated. Later he came to realize that Hindu religious pluralism was not so simple.

I came to understand the exclusive character of Christian claims and the denunciation of Hinduism which often accompanied these claims. This understanding did not engender disrespect for our Christian friends or hostility towards Christianity as a tradition. Frankly speaking, we felt, on the basis of our Hindu views, that Christians were wrong on this issue. I would venture to suggest that most Hindus still feel this way. I interpreted the reality of religious plurality through popular Hindu generalizations such as 'One God, many names,' 'Many paths, one goal,' etc. In the light of such interpretations, Christian claims seemed arrogant and narrow-minded. Later on, during my studies at a Hindu monastery in India, I came to realize that religious plurality in India, and within Hinduism, was a far more complex phenomenon than that which was suggested by the generalizations cited above.[16]

These complexities included variable interpretations of the Vedas; some consequential differences in understanding human nature, the nature of God, and the relationship between God and the world; and different ways of achieving liberation. "It was difficult to hold on to the view that all paths led to the same goal when the character of the goals themselves were so different." Even the different names of God were significant and led to different constructs of reality. "Hindus understood that God was the goal of human existence and was one and the same for all. There was no unanimity, however, about the nature of God and means of attaining God."

Rambachan is now engaged in inter-religious dialogue, feeling, as many do, that this will enrich his own faith as well as better inform others. The questions raised in such dialogue are important.

They are vitally connected with my own journey for the meaning of my existence and my desire to understand the relationship between the

---

[16] Anantanand Rambachan, 'What Difference does Religious Plurality Make?' Article on World Council of Churches website: www.wcc-coe.org/wcc/what/interreligious/cd34-09.html. See also Rambachan, 'Visions of Dialogue,' WCC conference, 'Critical Moment in Interreligious Dialogue,' 7-9 June 2005, Geneva: www.oikoumene.org/Prof_Anantanand_Rambacha.1053+B6Jkw9.0.html?&MP=935-1037

claims of my own tradition and those of others. I cannot ignore the challenge of claims that are different from my own. These sorts of questions, however, would not perhaps, be significant for me without the encounter with people of other faiths. I seek insights within my tradition, knowing that the questions, which are asked in other traditions, and the wisdom which they embody, could be profoundly instructive. For if God is the one God which my tradition proclaims God to be, then, surely, what my fellow human beings are saying about God is relevant and challenging to me and requires explanation and understanding on my part. My Christian and Muslim brother or sister may be speaking differently, but they are speaking about that which is dearest to me and which is also the goal of my own existence. This is a truth of tremendous significance which unifies me with the worshipper in every tradition, in whose prayer I hear the longings of my own heart.

After many years of committed interfaith activity, fully believing the same as the professor, I am not so sure now how important inter-religious dialogue is for the development of one's own faith. Surely it is vital in understanding and caring for others, realizing they are an essential part, as are we, of the whole inter-connected reality, but can we really understand the faith of another? Can we really 'cross-over' into another's tradition as some theologians suggest? We will, of course, learn from the faith life of others – qualities and lessons helpful to our own development. This is not the same though as learning from their theological or philosophical rationales. They are probably as confused as our own! In my experience it is love rather than wisdom that is most often met at interfaith meetings, and there we meet, as humans, interpreters for ourselves of a tradition perhaps, but not representatives of it. I'm reminded of an amazing moment in a documentary film about a young Israeli woman searching for the Palestinian man employed by her family for twenty years to look after her. They had lost touch when her parents felt they had to leave Israel because of their radical views. The young woman finally re-met the Palestinian and asked him a question that had long bothered her. Like all young Israelis she had been conscripted into the army for a period. How could her Palestinian carer have ironed her uniform? He looked at her and said, 'I did it for you.' He did it from love. There was no theology, no politics, no inter-religious rationale, just love.

Professor Rambachan's personal experience is more relevant here however as he teaches in the Religion Department of a College in America associated with the Christian Church. Not everyone has been happy with his appointment there! Indeed, "One graduate of St Olaf felt that my work at a college of the church would become meaningful only if I became a convert to Christianity. Today, some Hindu extremists seem to think that my work is not meaningful because I work at a college of the church. I am comfortable in the space between these extremes since it will not surprise you to hear that I reject both."[17] Filling this space, Rambachan does not shy away from the contradictions in Hinduism. Whilst feeling it has much to offer inter-religious dialogue through its understanding of religious pluralism, not everything is rosy in the Hindu garden.

The Hindu tradition has also generated its own brand of exclusivism characterized by the unsympathetic denunciation of other traditions. The Arya Samaj founder, Swami Dayananda Saraswati (1824-83), took his stand on the Vedas which he understood to be the infallible repository of all knowledge, secular and sacred. On the basis of his interpretations of the Vedas, he launched a vigorous attack on Jainism, Buddhism, Islam and Christianity. His methods were very similar to what Christian missionaries, at that time, were doing with the Bible as a basis. He was selective in his reading of the texts of other traditions and his method was apologetic and polemic. While he demythologized the Vedas, he did not treat other texts in this manner.[18] Examples like these could be multiplied. It is not uncommon, for example, to find unhistorical descriptions of Hinduism as the 'mother of all religions,' and claims that the truths of all religions have their origin in the Indian soil. My intention is to make the point that the challenges of religious pluralism are not limited to Christianity and that our responsibilities are mutual. There are wonderful resources in Hinduism for interpreting and explaining religious pluralism, but Hindus cannot be arrogant in their attitude to others on this matter.[19]

I know from my own interfaith experiences that many more Hindus are needed to join the inter-religious movement. Too often one Hindu finds herself the sole Hindu at an interfaith meeting with everyone's expectations that she will 'represent' Hinduism. The pressure is on then to give an account of it that is almost mythical in its greatness! Professor Rambachan's honesty in the intra-faith dialogue and his sensitivity in the inter-faith dialogue will set a mature model to inspire other Hindus to join the "great debate."

---

[17] Anantanand Rambachan, 'What does it mean to me to be at a college of the church?' Remarks made Feb. 6, 2002, during Community Day. www.uniyatra.com/hinduism/presskit/anantspeech.html
[18] Rambachan adds: "The following is Dayananda's comment on the Last Supper: 'Can a cultured man ever do such a thing? Only an ignorant savage would do it. No enlightened man would ever call the food of his disciples his flesh nor their drink his blood. They eat and drink imagining all the time that their bread was the flesh of Christ and their drink his blood. Is this not an awful thing? How could those, who could not keep aloof from the idea that their food and drink were the flesh and blood of their saviour, abstain from the flesh and blood of others.'" See also 'The Response of the Arya Samaj,' in H G Coward, Ed, *Modern Indian Responses to Religious Pluralism*, State University of New York Press, Albany, 1987, pp 49-50.
[19] Anantanand Rambachan, 'Towards One World Family.' Keynote address from the Hindu-Christian consultation held in Varanasi, India, 23-27 October 1997. Full text from World Council of Churches: www.wcc-coe.org/wcc/what/interreligious/cd31-04.html

RAVI RAVINDRA

Ravi Ravindra is author of *The Yoga of the Christ: in the Gospel according to St John*.[20] He is also Professor Emeritus and Chair of Comparative Religion, Professor of International Development Studies, and Adjunct Professor of Physics at Dalhousie University, Canada. He too addresses the topic of inter-religious dialogue, offering a seemingly different perspective from Professor Rambachan:

> In my judgment, there is something wrong with interfaith dialogues. When the East-West or interfaith dialogues are too much bound by the past, the dynamic nature of cultures and religions, and above all of human beings, cannot be appreciated. If one has never met someone from another culture or religion, interfaith or inter-cultural conversation is obviously a good idea. But I wish to suggest as strongly as I can that interfaith dialogues are at best a preliminary stage of human to human dialogue and can even be an impediment to a deeper understanding. A dialogue of cultures and worldviews, in which the parties involved declare their adherence to one or another faith or culture, can fix these faiths and cultures into the entities that they were. In fact these cultures and religions are alive and dynamic and are undergoing large and serious transformations right now. An inter-pilgrim dialogue, which is of necessity somewhat trans-cultural, trans-religious and trans-disciplinary, is needed to move into a future of a larger comprehension.

Ravindra writes too of his own reluctance to be labeled, to be held by past constraints, as his spiritual and life journey evolves. Today his life, like so many others, is composed of many parts, is itself religiously and socially plural.

> I myself have now lived longer in the Western world than in India. For many years now I have thought and expressed myself in a Western language. Also, for years I was trained in Physics, which surely has been the Western yoga of knowledge par excellence, and I am married into Christianity and the Western culture. I occasionally ask my friends, or organizers of the symposia to which I am sometimes invited to represent the East, 'What makes me an Easterner?' I am happy enough to be an Indian or an Easterner, but what makes me an Easterner? Place of birth? Skin color? Certain philosophical or religious inclinations? Because I am a Hindu I can happily embrace both the Christ and the Buddha, as could any one anywhere in the world appreciate and love the

---

[20] Ravi Ravindra, *The Yoga of the Christ: in the Gospel according to St John*, Element Books, Longmead, 1990.

great creative contributions of Albert Einstein or Dogen Zenzi without having to be a Swiss Jew or a Japanese.[21]

Ravi tells the story of the Pope's audience at the Vatican with the Metropolitan of the Syrian Orthodox Church in Delhi.

> Metropolitan Gregorios asked the Pope what he thought was the reason for such a small percentage of Indians having converted to Christianity although it had been in India for such a long time. The Pope said to him the reason was that the Indian mind was not developed enough to understand the subtlety of thought of St. Gregory of Nyssa or of St. Thomas Aquinas. Somewhat taken aback Metropolitan Gregorios asked the Pope if he had read *Shankara* or *Nagarjuna*. He was immediately shown out of the room where the audience was taking place.

Ravindra adds, "I found the incident merely amusing because I did not find this surprising at all, but he had been much saddened by it, for the issue was more personal for him."

> As he said, he realized for the first time and first hand that every Indian Christian is considered to be a second class Christian in the Vatican. This was even more galling for him because he belonged to a branch of Christianity as ancient as any.[22]

Regarding Christ, "From a Hindu point of view there is no difficulty with the uniqueness of Jesus Christ." However, this uniqueness is "embedded in an underlying oneness, for ultimately there is only the One. *Ekam evadvityam* (one only, without a second)*, says Chandogya *Upanishad* 6:2,1." This Oneness has been realized by Hindu sages through all the millennia. It is realized through direct perception, actual vision, and is not "a matter of universalizing or generalizing from particulars by reasoning, inference, deduction or induction." Neither is it based on "conjecture or an abstraction subject to refutation or confirmation." The problem, for Hindus, lies in exclusive claims made about Christ that deny the "sacred uniqueness of all other manifestations of Divine Energy, small or great." As the Brihadaranyaka Upanishad (V1) says, "That is Fullness, this is Fullness, from Fullness comes Fullness. When Fullness is taken from Fullness, what remains is Fullness." [23] Ravindra feels that this verse - "I am the way, the Truth and the Life. No one comes to the Father except through me" - in Chapter 14 in the Gospel of John, taken by some Christians to support the exclusive nature of the incarnation of Christ, has been misunderstood.

---

[21] Ravi Ravindra, 'What calls You Pilgrim?' published by Metanexus, The Online Forum on Religion and Science: http://www.metanexus.net
[22] Ravi Ravindra, 'What calls You Pilgrim?'
[23] 'Hindu Encounter with Christ - Some Reflections' sent to author on 9 August 2005. Following quotes also from this. For full text see Appendix 3.

To know the real name of someone or to do something in that person's name means, both in the Old Testament and the New Testament, as it does in many ancient traditions, to be able to participate in the being and to share in the power of that person....When the disciples believed in the name of Christ, it meant that they understood the real nature of Christ and were able to participate in his being and power, and could act on his authority....Since Jesus Christ was one with the Father, he could speak with the authority and the power of the secret name of God....It is in this mode that Christ uses I AM, to indicate his identity with God and his participation in His power and being, and not as an identification of his own particularity or specialness....In spite of the mutual indwelling of the Father and the Son and the essential oneness of their fundamental energy, there is a discernible and proper internal order, so that it is right to say both 'The Father and I are one' (John 10:30) and 'The Father is greater than I' (John 14:28). Similarly, if there is a mutual indwelling of the Christ and a disciple, they are essentially one, but not without hierarchical order....But, the disciples do not always understand the subtle teachings of Christ. They are continually looking outward, as if the goal and the way were outside. And Christ has to remind them repeatedly that the Way and the Truth and Eternal Life are within themselves; if they do not find these there at the threshold of I AM, connecting the higher and the lower worlds within themselves, they will not find them anywhere.

As for the crucifixion of Christ, Ravindra believes that "the Christian notion that Jesus Christ sacrificed himself in order to take away the sins of humanity is of fundamental importance."

This needs to be understood in its cosmological sense in which sacrifice is continually needed in order to maintain the cosmos. The preservation and maintenance of *rita* (cosmological order) depends on the proper relation between earth and Heaven. This proper relation is based entirely on *yajña* (sacrifice)....To sacrifice...is to make sacred. It is by yajña that one participates in the right order. As far as (Christ) is concerned, the right preparation for sacred action (*yajña karma*) consists in dying to one's self-will, and in denying oneself, so that one could obey the will of God. His *yoga* consists of this; and of this the cross is the supreme symbol....As he repeatedly told his disciples, no person is worthy and capable of being his disciple unless he takes up his own cross - not only as an idea but as a daily practice - and follows him.

BIBHUTI YADAV

Sri Yadav, a Vaishnava and Associate Professor at Temple University, was one of those who kindly participated in my Questionnaire and his detailed replies can be found in Appendix 1B with the other responses.[24] He has now passed away.

Bibhuti questioned what Jesus, whose Jesus, was usually described. He thought the egalitarian Jesus that seemed committed to social justice was of great significance to India's underprivileged, inspiring Hindu reform movements. The "gentleman" Jesus, moving in academic and elitist circles, is not so appreciated. This Jesus was "appreciated by *bhadraloka* ie. the urban upper caste and westernized Hindus who joined the administrative services." They belong to the "neo-vedantic culture of Rammohan Roy, Vivekanand, Tagore, Mahatma Gandhi and Radhakrishnan."

Neo-Vedanta "alienated the Christ from historical Jesus." The Vedantic Christ has "no memory of historical Jesus, no concern for social justice." This Christ "performs yoga in the spiritual space of Vedanta and features very much in Hindu-Christian dialogue today." This yogi-Christ "has tactical significance for elite Hindus both in India and abroad, including Hindu religious movements in Europe and America." Hindu reflections on Jesus are still primarily associated with this strand of Hinduism today.

> The association has to do with the Indianisation of the raj and the conscious and organised steps the traditional elite took towards westernization in defence of their social and political interests. This association is linked to the 19th and 20th century ruling circles in India. Hinduism in the West is a product of the encounter between Vedantic and Western elites in the 19th century.

Yadav was critical of Hinduism as expressed and experienced in the West. It "emanates from pseudo-Westernized Indians. Most of its devotees in the West are pseudo-Easternized Americans and Europeans." As for the dialogue between Hindus and Christians, it is "too unhistorical, too untextual, too spiritualistic, and too superfluous. It is thick in interreligious smile, too thin in substance."

In India, the social reality is changing with potentially explosive implications.

> Never before in India did the marginalised Hindus have the right or ability to formulate their social concerns. Now they do. Given the social-ethical relevance of Jesus, and given the increasing prominence of the so far marginalized Hindus in the historical debate, new formulations of national identity and this-worldly visions of salvation may emerge. The social critique of poets and philosophers like *Ravidas*

---

[24] Especially interesting are his remarks on Indian thinking about avatars and the potential there for a very early form of inclusivism that could lead to a revised understanding of Jesus as an 'anonymous' Hindu. See also Bibhuti Yadav, 'Vaishnavism on Hans Kung: A Hindu Theology of Religious Pluralism' in Paul J Griffiths, *Christianity Through Non-Christian Eyes*, Orbis, NY, 1990, pp 234-246.

and *Tathagata* are being revived. In the emerging discourse, a post neo-Vedantic Indian Christology could very well be formulated.

If there had been no encounter with British imperialism and the raj, would there have been a natural Hindu interest in Jesus? Yadav speculated that most probably "Jesus would not have been alienated from Christ; neither would he have been incorporated into a Gentleman and a yogi....Quite possibly, Jesus would have wandered in the company of poets like Ravidas, those who composed and sang songs of God, demanding social equality on religious grounds."

## DAVID FRAWLEY (VAMADEVA SHASTRI), 1950-

David Frawley is Director of the American Institute of Vedic Studies and one of the "few Westerners ever recognized in India as a Vedacharya or teacher of the ancient Vedic wisdom."[25] Like Swarup and Goel he writes for Voice of India. In 1991 he was named Vamadeva Shastri and in 1995 he was given the title of Pandit. He has been a visiting professor for the Vivekananda Yoga Kendra in Bangalore, India, and also a teacher with the Sringeri Shankara-charya Math, a traditional Vedantic centre in India.

Born a Catholic, Frawley has described his absorption into Hinduism in his autobiography, *How I Became A Hindu.*[26] By his mid teens he had already begun to develop the attraction for eastern mysticism that was to transform his life.

> [The]...Christian fixation on Jesus seemed almost neurotic. It was clear to me that there have been many great sages throughout history and Jesus, however great, was only one of many and that his teachings were not the best preserved either. I failed to see what was so unique about him or what his teachings had that could not be found with more clarity elsewhere.

Frawley's primary complaints against Christianity are linked to aggressive mission, especially in South Asia. Even where liberal Christians disagree with such mission they do little to prevent or criticize it. Where Hindus have honored Christ, missionaries have abused this to aim at conversions. Christians do not offer reciprocal honor to the great Hindu preceptors. They have not apologized for their denigration of other faiths. The dominant missionary impulse has come from an authoritarian, jealous God who metes out rewards and punishments. There is a focus on sin and exile and a strong exclusivist tendency. This God is at war with other gods. The Bible is too humanly

---

[25] David Frawley, *How I Became a Hindu,* Voice of India, 2000, Inside cover. For more information on the American Institute of Vedic Studies, see www.vedanet.com
[26] All quotes from David Frawley, *How I Became a Hindu,* pp 35-168.

constructed, historical, outdated. Christianity has proved a religion of oppression, evident in many countries and situations in the world.

Christian mission in India is a real bane of contention with its target of poor, uneducated Hindus and its lack of serious, open dialogue with Hindu leaders. Hindu "fundamentalism" rather than the underlying impact of the mission field on tribal peoples is wrongly blamed for tensions in India. In 1999, Frawley and the Catholic Archbishop of Hyderabad were invited to dialogue together. Frawley referred to the Pope's message about the evangelization of Hindus and Buddhists that stated, "While expressing esteem for the elements of truth in these religions, the Church must make it clear that Christ is the one mediator between God and man and the sole Redeemer of humanity." There is no equality or tolerance in such a statement. Other religions are rejected.

When the Pope visited India in 1999, Frawley was one of many Hindus interviewed and quoted in newspapers, opposed not to the Pope or his visit but to his intolerant and unacceptable stand on Hinduism. He was one of many Hindus who wanted the Pope to apologize for the forced conversions in India. Where racial superiority has been dropped, religious superiority continues. Christians dress up in Hindu clothes and create ashrams, not out of respect for Hinduism but to attract local people. Inside the conversion goes on as before. Frawley compares this with McDonalds selling veggie burgers in India to attract custom! Let Christians come to India to learn not to preach.

For Frawley, mission is big business. It is triumphalist, not concerned with religious freedom. India, with its huge population, is vulnerable and targeted because of its tolerance, an invitation not extended by many non-Christian countries. Mission has a bloody history of genocide on many continents. As long as Christians keep the same idea about Jesus as they always had this system will continue whereas, if we really love people, it is not their conversion we seek.

> If we love God, if we love our fellow human beings, we will love them regardless of what their religious belief is. We will love their religion as well. We will honour and respect their religion….We will not see any need to convert them….True love of God does not seek converts. It is not based upon names, forms or identity. It is based upon recognising the Divine presence in all.

Frawley quotes Swami Rama Tirtha who, on coming to America, was asked about religion. His response: "You do not belong to any religion. All religions belong to you."

## MATHOOR KRISHNAMURTI

When I first met Mathoorji he was head of the *Bharatiya Vidya Bhavan* or Indian Cultural Institute in London.[27] Our initial encounter was at the 1992 annual conference of the Modern Churchpeoples Union, an organization of progressive, inclusive Anglican priests that meets annually.[28] On this occasion it was to engage with Eastern religions and Mathoor was one of their Hindu speakers.

In fact, it was an event that also included one of my most positive encounters with Christians. The special conference chaplain, Derek Barnes, arranged the worship sessions. Derek is married to a Hindu and their two children enjoy immersion in both parents' traditions. The conference worship gradually built up over the three days to the final all out Hindu rendition! Ranchor Prime, a Vaishnava and leading exponent of the Vrindavan re-forestation project, led the way and asked me to help with *arti* (act of worship celebrating light).[29] I took the arti lamp around the room while all present chanted Hare Krishna. I was so moved by everyone's participation. All but one person took the light. John Hick was there and Keith Ward plus around fifty priests and participants. It was so impressive. I shall never forget those wonderful people and the example they set - faith without fear, love without limitation!

Mathoor is now working for the Bhavan in Bangalore. However, he kindly responded to my Questionnaire when he was in London and his full response can be found in Appendix 1B. For Mathoor, Jesus is an avatar on a par with other avatars. He came for the same reasons as those given in the Gita: "To protect the good and punish the wicked...to establish Dharma." Western influence has not changed Hindu perception of Jesus. Hinduism can absorb and welcome all.

> Before Christianity came to India, Buddha came – and opposed the Vedas. Even so, Buddhism was welcomed in India and not perceived as a threat by the Hindus. Similarly other religions came and developed, like Jainism and Islam. Christianity was relatively a newcomer to impinge on the Hindu consciousness. Even so it was absorbed within the Hindu framework. It is the unique nature of Hinduism to accept and absorb new ideas and appreciate them. Hinduism has an open mind, respects all other faiths and sentiments and embraces them.

Mathoor, as so many Hindus, is not satisfied by the way missionaries have materially enticed the poor and illiterate in India in order to gain converts. "This is considered, even today, as a disservice for which many Hindus cannot

---

[27] For more information on the Bharatiya Vidya Bhavan, UK, see www.bhavan.net
[28] For more information on the Modern Churchpeoples Union, see www.openchurch.info
[29] For more information on Friends of Vrindavan, see www.fov.org.uk

excuse the missionaries." Better would be discussion of the similarities between the faiths. "Christians need to broaden their vision and develop respect for freedom of faith rather than misuse/abuse the economic backwardness of a society to propagate the Christian faith." There is much common ground that could enrich such a dialogue and development.

VIVEKANANDA CENTRE, LONDON

Jay Lakhani of the London Vivekananda Centre, and his daughter, Seetha, an anthropology student at University College London, kindly responded to some questions I asked about the current situation for those who continue the work of Swami Vivekananda in the world.[30]

*Jay and Seetha Lakhani*

Is there currently any meaningful engagement of Hindus with Christ and Christianity or are Hindu responses (positive and negative) primarily based on original responses to colonialism and now out-dated or irrelevant? Seetha responded, "I think it is only safe to say that Hindus have an engagement with Christ to the extent that they accept his validity and recognize that he was a highly spiritual individual who has influenced Christians for thousands of years."

> It would not be correct to say that Hindus worship Christ. That would be a contradiction in terms. Hinduism states that if you are a Hindu, become a better Hindu. If you are a Christian, become a better Christian. Because Hinduism teaches religious pluralism, it does not mean that Hindus must worship Christ, but that they should become more steadfast in their own religion while accepting the validity of others. Some Hindus who were forcefully converted to Christianity (or Islam) have become fanatic in their new faith, and become the greatest enemies of Hinduism as an (unconscious) way of justifying their conversion.

Both Jay and Seetha feel comfortable with the way the Ramakrishna Mission has included Christ as an avatar but uncomfortable with the way some Christians treat Hindus and Hinduism. Jay wrote, "The Vivekananda Centre or the Ramakrishna Order have no difficulty with Christ the avatar but have great difficulty with the organized church that continues to promote conversions and exclusivist agendas." Seetha continued, "At present the Vivekananda Centre faces resistance from stodgy Christian ideologies that do not accept the validity and relevance of Hinduism."

---

[30] All Jay and Seetha Lakhani quotes from e-mails to author, 28 July 2005. For more about the Vivekananda Centre London, see www.vivekananda.co.uk

Christian missionaries have not died out but are still manifesting themselves through the Western media which puts a lot of effort into presenting Hinduism in as distorted and twisted a way as possible. They make documentaries on weird peripheral cults and tell the world that this is Hinduism. They dig out verses from ancient literature that no longer have any relevance and make Hinduism sound primitive and backward. Swami Vivekananda said that the amount of mud slung at India is more than the mud found at the bottom of the Indian Ocean.

With regards to Christian mission and evangelism, the Vivekananda Centre London works hard to promote good relations through an informed understanding of Hinduism.[31] This is not always easy, as Jay mentioned.

We have mixed experience in this field. Some have been reasonably friendly and have allowed us to make presentations at mainstream churches. Some have actively promoted us but after discovering a very positive reaction such presentations produce from their congregation have discontinued further interaction.

Now that Hinduism has a significant spiritual presence in the west, how does Hindu 'mission' differ from that of Christian and other religious groups? Jay indicated that, as the aim of the Ramakrishna Order that Swami Vivekananda established is "to revive and refresh the message of spirituality worldwide, it is far wider in its scope and application." Seetha added:

The world has shrunk to a global village, and it is no longer possible to claim absolute and exclusivist authority of any one religion. Spirituality has been central to the Hindu tradition for thousands of years. It carries a unique message that is proving to become increasingly relevant for the world we live in today, ie. religious pluralism. It states that *all* religions, and all sects within religions are equally valid routes to the same one ultimate reality. Taking on board spiritual democracy is the only way that all world religions can live side by side with each other peacefully.

The model of religious pluralism embodied in Hinduism could be a strategic key for addressing global concerns. Education is important for this. Jay wrote, "We are actively involved in modifying some aspects of Religious Education in the country by incorporating ideas of religious pluralism. Such ideas are now becoming acceptable and will enter the education system."

For Seetha, "The importance of religious pluralism today is evidenced by the late terror bombings in London. The issue cannot, like so many secular lobbies say, be resolved through economics or politics because it is a problem of

---

[31] See Seetha Lakhani, *Hinduism for Schools*, Vivekananda Centre London Ltd, 2005. Edited by Jay Lakhani.

religious fundamentalism that can only be resolved through religious pluralism." Jay agrees.

> Pluralism no doubt can be found in all religions; in Hinduism it is very explicit and far more comprehensive than one can image. For example it is prepared to take on the challenge of reconciling truth claims between different religions including non-theistic religions and between religious and non-religious (science oriented) worldviews. You can appreciate how wide can be the scope of this kind of pluralism. Of course, this form of pluralism will be very critical on all exclusivist claims. *Caution and steadiness* are the necessary and crucial attributes needed to allow such ideas to be explored sensibly and on a rational footing. Not only is this nation geared to take on and develop such ideas, it also possesses the educational infrastructure to allow these ideas to reach its young. I have already tried out these ideas on a vast number of youngsters in this country and I can confirm that they generate tremendous acceptance and enthusiasm. The panacea of how many world religions can co-exist peacefully and how religions can become the unifying force rather than the dividing force in our society lies firmly with this form of pluralism. The reason I sometimes use robust language is because I feel very concerned. I also feel quite sure that all political, economic, diplomatic or military efforts are not going to work or offer a lasting resolution. The resolution to the serious issue that has arisen in the name of religion lies firmly in religion.

A unique opportunity arose from the London bombings and attempted bombings in July 2005 as faith communities sought enhanced ways to build bridges of cooperation and understanding. Jay wrote:

> Last night we (together with many other faith representatives) were invited to the Al Khoi Shia Mosque in London for a prayer meeting for the victims of the London bombings. We recited and translated *Shanti-paths* (peace invocations) from the Vedas. We have in the past presented Hindu teachings from quite a few mainstream church pulpits but this must be a first where Hindu prayers are recited and explained in a mainstream mosque![32]

## Vikram Seth

Vikram is a student at the Vivekananda Centre London who kindly responded to some questions sent to him. Vikram believes avatars are "God's presence in our world or universe in the form of something that we can relate to." This has to be a tangible presence but not necessarily human. The purpose of an avatar is "specific to the context of the time, but generally may be to direct towards

---

[32] Regular London Vivekananda Centre news update e-mail, sent on 5 August 2005.

God, like a reminder or setting the people back on the path towards God. In that sense Christ was an avatar."[33]

Many of Vikram's friends and peers are Christians so there is some celebration of Christmas and Easter but "the religious aspects of these festivals are not as prominent as they may be in most Christian homes." He has not experienced any difficulties with Christian mission and believes that "the purpose of the Christian missionaries today is to promote spiritual and religious ideals, which fortunately no longer involve forced conversions, at least in this country." Hindu mission has the same motives.

> I believe the underlying purpose of each religion is to lead the people to the ultimate truth. Be this the 'Self' or 'God' or 'Mother Nature.' This remains the purpose of Hinduism and all the other religions, the means by which the people are made aware of this purpose may differ and even within each religion there may be many different ways. I feel that it makes no difference whether there is an ultimate body known as the 'Hindu Mission;' the mission in itself is led by the people.

Hinduism has an important message for our times: "Pluralism, Non-violence and Celibacy (at least until marriage)." Living a life of Truth is "the most basic requirement before one can begin any sort of spiritual journey; forget being truthful to others, many of us are not even truthful to ourselves!"

SUMMARY

Hindu voices from the West, like those from India, also show some diversity of approach. Amongst some of the Hindu academics in North America an inter-religious or trans-religious approach can be discerned. Other Hindu voices, from America and England, are more vigorous in their promotion of Hinduism as the faith that can provide apposite and potent messages and methodologies for our troubled times. Most Hindus would agree that the Sanatana Dharma has such breadth and diversity that it can encourage and support all sincere efforts to realize Truth, whatever form or formlessness we are drawn towards in our search for Wisdom and Love, whatever troubles we encounter on that way.

Contemporary Hindu thought on Christ and Christianity has been sampled. There seem to be two major trends. Do either have any universal significance? Is anyone really bothered by or about either today? The final chapter will look at these two trends against the background of continuing Christian mission in India and Hindu mission outside India.

---

[33] Vikram Seth quotes from e-mail to author on 11 August 2005.

CHAPTER VIII

# JESUS THROUGH HINDU EYES

Oh God! Reveal Thy most valuable truths to all
so that Your own may not be numbered with the fanatics and the crazed
and that the whole of humankind may be admitted as Your own.
*- Srila Bhaktivinode Thakura, Pure Love of God*

## INTRODUCTION

Two distinct trends in Hindu responses to Jesus can be discerned: the spiritual/ transcendental and the cultural/historical or communal. The former embraces Jesus in its own way. The latter reacts against the impact of conversion by colonial force. Some readers may find some Hindu descriptions of Christian missionary behavior hard to believe. Some readers may find some Hindu tendencies to include Christ as something akin to Christian inclusivism. Some readers may wonder if what Hindus think about Christ and Christianity is, in any way, relevant to Christians and if Christ and Christianity are in any way relevant to Hindus.

### CULTURAL / HISTORICAL / COMMUNAL TRENDS

Hindu responses to Jesus began on the mission fields of India as a response to the encounter with Christianity. Conversion to Christianity meant ostracism from caste and culture so Hindus drawn to Jesus found it easier to detach him from Christianity and claim him as their own, one misunderstood and mis-represented by the Church. As P C Mozoomdar put it: "Christ has reached us; the missionaries have missed us."[1] Those Hindus who did convert usually did so, as Himalayan Academy's Satguru Sivaya Subramuniyaswami put it, "to have food on the table, to gain access to schools for their children or to a hospital for health care, to qualify for employment or a promotion, to protect their lands from confiscation or their families from harm."[2]

There are many examples of such 'persuasions' but they are beyond this study. As stated above, conversions caused terrible ostracism from families and communities and converts were not usually welcomed back to the Hindu fold when they sought to return. This situation is changing but is still fraught with

---

[1] P C Mozoomdar, 'Lectures in America,' p 87, quoted in Hans Staffner, *The Significance of Jesus Christ in Asia*, Gujarat Sahikya Prakash Anand, India, 1984, p XIV.
[2] Conversion by Conviction' in *Hinduism Today*, April/May/June 2002, p 50.

difficulties. The journal, *Hinduism Today*, reported a mass re-conversion to Hinduism, in 2000 CE, of 33 men, 28 women and 11 children in the tribal village of Manoharpur in the state of Orissa.[3] The *Shankaracharya* of Puri, one of Hinduism's highest spiritual authorities, presided over the ceremony of re-admission. Even so, these 'new' Hindus were not accepted by some other Hindus and were denied access to Hindu temples, even though significant figures like Vivekananda and Radhakrishnan have argued that 'reborn' Hindus should have the same rights as all Hindus. Hindus still have to agree a mechanism by which all strands can embrace new and returning Hindus.

Professor Arvind Sharma spoke about some of the related issues when he addressed the United States Commission on International Religious Freedom in 2000 CE. He detailed some of the different understandings of religious freedom that could influence the way laws to protect it are implemented in particular countries. His primary focus on this occasion was India. Only part of his thinking, where religious freedom relates to the conversion agenda, is described here:

> Mahatma Gandhi was once asked: What if a Hindu comes to feel that he can only be saved by Jesus Christ? Gandhi's reply may be paraphrased thus: 'So be it, but why should he cease to be a Hindu?' (Harijan, 28-11-1936.) Thus in the Eastern cultural context, freedom of religion means that the person is left free to explore his or her religious life without being challenged to change his or her religion. Such exploration need not be confined to any one religion, and may freely embrace the entire religious and philosophical heritage of humanity.

Sharma identifies two principal Hindu responses to the threat of conversion in the period since 1800 CE:

> 1. Most modern Hindus are opposed to the idea of conversion from one religion to another per se. This opposition is rooted in the neo-Hindu doctrine of the validity of all paths to the divine. If all paths are valid, then conversion from one religion to another does not make much sense.

> 2. Some modern Hindus also believe that while conversion from Hinduism, like conversion from any religion, is undesirable, yet conversion to Hinduism in India should be tolerated and even encouraged. According to them, the conversion of Hindus to Islam and Christianity, specially during Islamic and British Rule, took place during Hinduism in times of trouble, and therefore such reconversion is now valid, as it represents the righting of a historical wrong.

---

[3] *Hinduism Today*, November/December 2000, p 59.

Sharma concludes: "If the first position may be described as the neo-Hindu position then this second position could be called the Hindu nationalist position. It should be noted though that both are equally opposed to conversion from Hinduism."[4]

Manoharpur, the village where the mass re-conversion to Hinduism took place, is the same village in which the Australian Missionary, Graham Staines, and his two sons were burnt alive whilst sleeping in their car during an evangelical 'Jungle Camp.' Whilst the media naturally concentrated on the horror of the deaths, few focused on why such a camp was functioning and its legality. There was no mention of the provocative actions of missionaries in these tribal areas, the desecration of Hindu shrines, the violence sometimes used to induce conversions, the loss of culture and community caused by such conversions. Dr R S Thangkhiew stated, "The British policy of sending us missionaries didn't do anything for us except weaken our culture."[5] In a report about Hindu-Christian conflict in this region, made on 7 January 1999 to India's National Human Rights Commission, Ghelubhai Nayak reminded that Gandhi had denounced conversion activity by Christian missionaries as "a blot on humanity in the name of social service."[6] Swami Dayananda Saraswati is as robust:

> Missionaries slaughter religions, slaughter traditions, slaughter cultures …slaughterhouse love it is. If you really love people, just give charitably and forget about it. Don't talk about your religion. Keep your sacred religion in your heart. I find it is not a happy thing to talk about, the vulgarity of it. Even to talk about it is rather staining my tongue and leaves a distaste.[7]

In August 2000, I attended the Millennium World Peace Summit of Religious and Spiritual Leaders held at the United Nations and the Waldorf-Astoria Hotel in New York.[8] It was an important symbolic and historical occasion with its own collection of challenging moments provided by the unique gathering of holy (wholly) pre-eminents! During one of the workshops, enlivened for us all by what happened, the opportunity was taken by some Hindu Swamis and their disciples to forcefully bring to the agenda their views on the activities of Christian missionaries in India. As I later wrote for the International Interfaith Centre Newsletter about the Summit, "The real work and development was done behind the platforms and preaching."

---

[4] Arvind Sharma, Birks Professor of Comparative Religion, McGill University, 'Religious Freedom: A Hindu Perspective,' Testimony provided to the *United States Commission on International Religious Freedom*, September 18, 2000.
[5] 'Tribal Tribulations' by Dr Mihir Meghani, *Hinduism Today*, April 1998, p 37.
[6] 'What happened in Dangs' in *Hinduism Today*, June 1999, p 18.
[7] 'Countering Conversion' in *Hinduism Today*, January/February/March 2004, p 68.
[8] Find out more about this prestigious event at www.millenniumpeacesummit.org

One important instant result of this was a statement signed by some of the Hindus and Christians present that altruism should never be connected to conversion. Many of the Hindus at the Summit did not accept the corruption of aid with mission: 'we prefer to stay poor and keep our dignity!' These tensions forced behind-the-scenes meetings over six hours that were partly mediated by a Dutch rabbi.

From these meetings came a statement, 'Informal Working Understanding: Freedom from Coercion in Religion,' that was endorsed by three Hindus, five Christians, and Rabbi Avraham Soetendorp from the Summit's International Advisory Board. It contained the following points:

1. We agree that the free and generous preaching of the Christian Gospel is welcome in India.
2. We condemn the use of coercion and religious proselytism; we particularly reject the exploitation of the issue of poverty in religious outreach and missionary work.
3. We agree that the giving of aid to those in need is a primary commandment of all our religious and spiritual traditions; we are resolved that this act of justice should never be tied to compulsory conversion.
4. We commit ourselves to a continuing dialogue in the spirit of interreligious harmony, mutual respect, and the cooperative common effort to build a better world.[9]

K L Seshagiri Rao reminds us why narrow evangelical Christian mission in India causes such a stir. It is totally unnatural to Hindus.

Hindus have expressed an ecumenical spirit in religious matters throughout history. Never have they claimed to be exclusive possessors of truth. It is not necessary to be or become a Hindu to obtain salvation. They recognize revealing and saving powers in all great religions. Hindus respect all prophets and sages who come to guide humanity. In the context of the diversity of human needs, they hold that the great religions of the world are not only relevant but also necessary. Hindus have shown willingness to learn from other traditions. They are at liberty to draw inspiration from any source in their spiritual quest. Actually, the Hindu tradition encourages its followers to celebrate each other's way of God-realization. Reverence for other religions is an essential element of the Hindu spiritual vision.[10]

---

[9] International Interfaith Centre Newsletter No 14, December 2000.
[10] K L Seshagiri Rao, 'Hindus in America and the Emerging World Culture,' paper presented at the Symposium of *Hinduism: Past, Present, and Future* organized by the Sri Venkatesvara Temple, Pittsburgh and sent to author, August 2005.

Why is this lesson so difficult to learn for Christian missionaries? Why do they continue in the same old, unproductive ways with the same limited goals? What kind of Christ are they bringing to India? In India, in July 2005, Dena Merriam, disciple of Paramahansa Yogananda and Convenor of The Global Peace Initiative of Women, attended the Women Thinkers of India conference, where issues of mission and conversion raised the usual passions. Dena was a Vice Chair and primary instigator of the Millennium Peace Summit of Religious and Spiritual Leaders, conceiving and developing the women's peace initiative after that event. Writing about the conference in India, she told me:

> There seems to be a growing, and rather deep, wound around the issue of conversion, which has become quite intense in the villages and especially in the tribal regions….The evangelical churches are everywhere ….There was a delegation at the conference from Assam and they told us that the missionaries, after converting the village people, tell them the Hindus are witches and must be banned from their villages. There have been a number of murders of villagers who wouldn't convert - because they were regarded as witches. I heard one story of a missionary who had a school of children. He told them to pray to Shiva and see what he will give them. Then he told them to pray to Krishna and see how he responds. Then he said now pray to Jesus and see how much he loves you - at that moment he put on the overhead fan, behind which he had put candies, and candies fell all over the children. We heard many such stories. I heard another story of a young Hindu girl in a Christian school who when the teacher said that Jesus walked on water, she said Krishna also walked on water. She was punished by the teacher for saying this….The women at the conference were concerned about preserving Hindu values and culture for their children, in light of the intense missionary activity, globalization and the allures of the west.[11]

However, it is not only in India where problems exist for Hindus. The Editorial of the August 2005 edition of *Sevashram News*, published from London, bemoans the European "continuous conspiracy and effort to denigrate the Hindu's religious and cultural values and hurt their sentiment." This tendency often reveals itself through the marketing of material goods using sacred Hindu symbols and images of deities in inappropriate and insensitive ways. Whenever Hindus respond to such attacks they are usually branded as "fundamentalists, fanatics, fascists." In the same journal, T R Jawarhar writes of the "conversion curse." He urges Hindus to wake up to it: "Careless vegetarian sheep end up in wolves' stomachs!"[12] Indeed the sheep have needed

---

[11] E-mail from Dena Merriam to author, 28 July 2005. For information on The Global Peace Initiative of Women, see www.gpiw.org
[12] T R Jawarhar, 'Crusade Against Crusaders – Their Genesis, Our Nemesis,' in *Sevashram News*, Issue 32, pp 20-22.

to stay alert as one of the 2005 Christmas stamps issued in the UK by the Royal Mail revealed. It depicted two Hindus worshipping the baby Christ and awakened a furore in the Hindu community with the result that the Royal Mail apologized for its introduction, halted distribution, and offered those stamps already in UK Post Offices only to those who specifically asked for them.

So, in India today, as elsewhere, Christian aspirations and strategies for conversions are still considered highly controversial and undesirable, as are the Christian monastics blending Hinduism into their Christianity. "Present day missionaries...have created a cultural hybrid of Hindu and Christian symbols and practices, deliberately fostering confusion as to their true intentions."[13] On the brighter side, those Christians who lead Hindu life styles in India but still remain Christian may, as a result of their practices, end up being absorbed into "the all embracing arms of Hinduism."[14] However, many Christians highly revere these hybrids. I remember, when working in the International Interfaith Centre's office that a visitor, on learning I was Hindu, was thrilled to recommend Bede Griffiths to me and suggest that I read Bede's commentary on the Bhagavad Gita! There was absolutely no awareness that a Hindu commentary on this most sacred Hindu text might be more appropriate.

Adding insult to injury in the arena of Christian mission in India, a recent Baptist pamphlet, *Divali, Festival of Light, Circle of Darkness*, issued this appeal and called for special prayers over a twelve-day period:

> More than 900 million people are lost in the hopeless darkness of Hinduism....Walking the streets of India during *Divali* is a sobering reminder of the power of darkness that lies over this land....If you and your Church would like to 'adopt' one of these un-reached Hindu groups for extended prayer and ministry that they might receive the Gospel, please call us.[15]

The previous Pope's visit to India also reinforced old anxieties about modern mission. Catholic expansionist theologies did not go down well – for example, "Asia is thirsting for the living water that Jesus alone can give" - and there were many Hindu demands for retractions and apologies, including those from David Frawley. *Hinduism Today* writers saw the bright side however, feeling that the Pope actually did Hindus a favor with his visit, uniting Hindus and Buddhists, awakening those who had not previously believed Hindu warnings about Catholic mission plans, creating world sympathy for Hindus, and putting Indian Catholics on the defensive.[16]

---

[13] Book review, 'Conversion to Christianity, Aggression In India' by Dr M S Srinivasan, *Hinduism Today*, January/February 2001, p 60.

[14] 'When Not in Rome..,' *Hinduism Today*, March 1997, p 49.

[15] 'How They Prey on Hindus' in *Hinduism Today*, January 2000, p 37: www.imb.org/resources/HPG.pdf

[16] 'Pope: Convert all Hindus' in *Hinduism Today*, February 2000, p 24.

The Hindu response to Christian mission and colonialism has led to a heated debate on the kind of religious education children receive in Indian schools. This is beyond the scope of this study but is a major concern in India where colonialism left behind an educated elite with English as a first language and a sense of Europe as the initiator and innovator of all important intellectual, scientific and cultural developments. Whilst groups like the BJP (Bharatiya Janata Party) and RSS (Rashtriya Swayamsevak Sangh) want to Indianize/ Hinduize education, others feel that such reforms would lower standards. The perception of many is that a British style education is the best in the world. Modern Britons may wonder at such a myth!

Despite such struggles, taking place at governmental levels, there is a revival, a re-assertion of Hinduism at informal levels of education. Much more is being done to promote Hinduism, to re-entrench its ancient traditions and wisdoms, to make it a living force in people's lives. This extends far beyond India's borders. It could be described as mission, a non-aggressive, spiritual kind that does not require conversion to a particular religion (though that does happen) but offers a new or renewed spiritual perspective and praxis. Indeed, times have certainly changed from earlier eras. Anti Christian mission 'education' is now highly organized and extensively available online. The old agitations continue but are now dealt with firmly, without any apologetics or defensive responses from the Hindu side.

In a paper given by John Zavos at a Bristol University Graduate Seminar I attended many years ago, he referred to Ashish Nandy who identified "two consistent incarnations of religion across post-colonial South Asia." These are: "Religion-as-faith, a way of life and a tradition which is non-monolithic and operationally plural; and religion-as-ideology, an identifier of communities contesting for or protecting non-religious – usually political or socio-economic – interests."[17] This second incarnation has led to inter-communal tension in India and to a newly strengthened sense of Hindu identity, even to a call for India to be a Hindu *Rashtra* – State or Nation. The term 'Hindu' not only defines a broad range of religious practices and philosophies but is much more - it is nationality.[18] Sri Aurobindo, many years ago, made this link so it is not

---

[17] Ashish Nandy, 'Politics of Secularism and the Recovery of Religious Tolerance' in Suranjan Das, *Communal Violence in 20ᵗʰ Century Colonial Bengal: an analytical framework*, p70; quoted in John Davos, *Situating Hindu Communalism*, paper, undated, p 5. John Zavos is now Lecturer in South Asian Studies at the University of Manchester.

[18] See, for example, Abhas Chatterjee, *The Concept of Hindu Nation*, Voice of India, 1995; David Frawley and Navaratna S Rajaram, *Hindutva and the Nation*, Naimisha Research Foundation, Bangalore, 2001. Chatterji writes (pp 2-5): "We Hindus are a nation....The term 'Hindu' is the name of our nationality....We are the oldest surviving nation on earth....There are many points of difference within the Hindu fold, caused by caste, language and religious tradition. But the fundamental sense of Hindu identity, unity, and harmony cuts through all differences and prevails over the community on account of the common spiritual current of the Sanatan Dharma which is the distinguishing feature of the Hindu nation."

so much a new idea as better established and more robustly promoted.[19] It is perhaps strange that all this has been classified as Hindu 'fundamentalism' rather than understood as the natural development of a people with anciently rooted traditions, refreshed with freedom after centuries of colonialism, a massive majority in their own country, who naturally want to express themselves holistically again and manifest Sanatan Dharma.

SPIRITUAL/TRANSCENDENTAL TRENDS

This second strand of Hindu response to the threat or promise of Christianity may also be conditioned by culture and history but it engages at another, less material, level. Examples of how Hindus have included Jesus in their pantheon of divine incarnates dominate this study. Some Hindus, whose primary focus has been the cultural/historical impact of Christianity in India, have denounced this approach as fervently as they have decried the imperialist and arrogant agenda of Christian mission. Others feel that this 'including-ness' is naturally as Hindu as any of its aspects and has contributed to Hinduism's indefatigable survival.

The development, by some Hindus, of spiritual inculturation of Jesus, from reactionary to embryonic, is paralleled by Hinduism's original incorporation and conception of the Buddha as an avatar (in the Vishnu Purana and the Bhagavata Purana). His incarnation was initially understood as one that was specifically intended to mislead the unwary and only later, as the threat of Buddhism subsided, did he gradually become the beloved avatar known today. Although Jesus was never viewed negatively this way, all associated with him were and only as the threat of Christianity subsided could the polemic cease and Jesus be handed back to Christians in the light of Hindu understanding, an enhanced model!

Many leading religious and political Hindus, including Radhakrishnan and Gandhi, began interpreting the life and teachings of Jesus within a Hindu context, feeling they could legitimately dislocate him from the Christian packaging so clearly confirmed as erroneous by the praxis of the British in India. There was little Hindu concern with Jesus as a figure of history.

For Hindus, the teachings and example of the life painted in the Gospels exist to stimulate right praxis regardless of how they may have originated or who initiated them. Whatever special needs at a special time may have been addressed by Jesus' incarnation, he is accepted as a highly evolved spiritual

---

[19] "When therefore it is said that India shall rise, it is the Sanatan Dharma that shall rise. When it is said that India shall be great, it is the Sanatan Dharma that shall be great. When it is said that India shall expand and extend itself, it is the Sanatan Dharma that shall expand and extend itself over the world. It is for the Dharma and by the Dharma that India exists....I say that it is the Sanatan Dharma which for us is nationalism." Sri Aurobindo, Uttarpara Speech, 1909, quoted in Chatterjee, *The Concept of a Hindu Nation,* footnote, p 9.

being transcending any particularity of time, place or context, providing a message and example of universal relevance. Such beings deliberately 'descend' and are not conditioned by their earthly circumstances or situations. They are free from such limitations, either having worked through that in previous lives or, as God Itself incarnate, are beyond the maya or dualities that affect other life forms. Indeed, in 1979, Dr Gokak, a devotee of Sai Baba, criticized John Hick, the Christian pluralist philosopher and theologian, for denuding Christology of its divine aspect. Gokak argued that the Council of Chalcedon, where Jesus' humanity and divinity were inextricably blended, was closer to the truth than modern quests for the historical Jesus. This belief is illustrated by Hindu understandings of Jesus as an avatar.[20]

As avatars became rather more frequent in modern times, their link with historical reality becomes more natural. For example, Ramakrishna was evidently both an historical being whilst also claimed by many, during his own lifetime and since, an avatar. His experience of Truth, corroborated by the example of his life, confirms for the devotee her own spiritual aspirations and experiences. As Judith Brown relates:

> A prominent leader in the Ramakrishna Mission told me in 1978 that Hinduism was a scientific religion because it rested on the empirical method, in that the believer based his belief on his own experience and on that of such experts as Ramakrishna and Vivekananda, much as one would trust the authority of an atomic scientist on his subject.[21]

This is an important point to remember in any evaluation of Hindu perspectives on Jesus: the line of authority begins and ends with verified personal experience of religious truths. These can then be slotted into appropriate, more formalized structures of belief if needed. Even then, for Hindus there are no rigid boundaries and much legitimate cross-referencing. What we are is more important than what we believe. To be what we truly are permits free access to all resources. The life-transforming, beatific participation in God shown in the lives of many Hindus irrevocably disproves Christian claims of absolute authority for Jesus. Religious truth has to be uncovered in each life and not merely read or believed. Infallibility lies not in the static written word but in directly revealed experience and renewal.

Even the Vedas, of primary scriptural significance for many Hindus, are secondary to experience. As *Sruti*, directly heard truth, they have to be directly heard, internally, by everyone and not just intellectually appropriated.

---

[20] V K Gokak, *In Defence of Jesus Christ and Other Avatars*, M Gulab Singh & Sons, Lahore,1979.
[21] Judith M Brown, *Men and Gods in a Changing World*, SCM, London, 1980, p 97.

Seshagiri Rao described them as not the goal but the means to the goal of God-Realization.[22] Radhakrishnan affirmed this.

The Hindu attitude to the Vedas is one of trust tempered by criticism, trust because the beliefs and forms which helped our fathers are likely to be of use to us also; criticism because, however valuable the testimony of past ages may be, it cannot deprive the present age of its right to inquire and sift the evidence. Precious as are the echoes of God's voice in the souls of men of long ago, our regard for them must be tempered by the recognition of the truth that God has never finished the revelation of His wisdom and love.[23]

Some Hindus have found harmony between Christian and Hindu texts. Sri Yukteswar explored links between *Samkhya* (dualistic) philosophy and the Book of Revelation.[24] John's Gospel has been understood by some Hindus as Vedantic in nature. In *The Yoga of the Christ: in the Gospel according to St John*, Ravi Ravindra wrote: "I am happy to find light wherever I can, without thereby having to deny other sources of illumination or other colors of the spectrum, which together can more fully express the glory and abundance of The Vastness than any one can alone."[25]

Some Christians have tried to fit Jesus as Christ into the *Purusha Shukta* or Cosmic Person model of the Rig-Veda and Upanishads.[26] Some see Jesus as their guru.[27] The term 'guru' has been adopted somewhat loosely into western parlance but traditionally indicates far more than just an ordinary teacher of which one may have many during a lifetime. A guru, in the full sense, is one who unconditionally promises to guide the true disciple to Self-realization, through life after life and life after death, however long it takes. No ordinary being can do this.[28] It takes a true spiritual Master. In *Autobiography of a Yogi*, Yogananda described such a being.

---

[22] K L Seshagiri Rao, 'A Hindu View of Jesus Christ.' Address delivered at the Annual Conference (1964) of the Alumni of the Harvard Divinity School, Harvard University. Published as Appendix 1 in K L Seshagiri Rao, *Mahatma Gandhi and C F Andrews – A Study in Hindu-Christian Dialogue*, Punjab University, Patiala, 1969, p 79.
[23] S Radhakrishnan, *The Hindu View of Life*, Unwin, London, 1988, pp 15-16.
[24] Sri Yukteswar, *The Holy Science*, Self-Realization Fellowship, Los Angeles, U.S.A. See also Chapter 4.
[25] Ravi Ravindra, *The Yoga of the Christ: In the Gospel According to St John*, Element Books, Longmead, 1990.
[26] See, for example, Bede Griffiths, *A New Vision of Reality*, Collins, Glasgow, 1989; Raimon Panikkar, *The Unknown Christ of Hinduism,* Orbis, NY, 1989; Ian Davie, *Jesus Purusha*, Lindisfarne, NY, 1985.
[27] Guru comes from the Sanskrit, 'gu', darkness and 'ru,' that which dispels.
[28] Ramana Maharshi describes the effect of the guru's grace as "like that of an elephant which wakes up on seeing a lion in its dream. Even as the elephant wakes up at the mere sight of the lion, so too is it certain that the disciple wakes up from the sleep of ignorance into the wakefulness of true knowledge through the Guru's benevolent look of grace." Ramana Maharshi, *Spiritual Instruction*, Sri Ramanasramam, Tirvvannamarai, 1939, p 2.

Proof that one is a Master…is supplied only by the ability to enter at will the breathless state (*sabikalpa samadhi*) and by the attainment of immutable bliss (*nirbikalpa samadhi*). The rishis have pointed out that solely by these achievements may a human being demonstrate that he has mastered *maya*, the dualistic cosmic delusion. He alone may say from the depths of realization: '*Ekam sat*' ('Only One exists').[29]

Ramakrishna links the true guru to God and warns of the false teacher: "Anyone and everyone cannot be a guru. A huge timber floats on the water and can carry animals as well. But a piece of worthless wood sinks if a man sits on it and drowns him. Therefore in every age God incarnates Himself as the guru to teach humanity. Satchidananda alone is the guru."[30] Karan Singh confirms that the guru is a gateway to God but the devotee must walk through the gate herself.

[The guru] can point out the way, inspire and guide the disciple lovingly on the path, help to save him from myriad temptations and dangers that lie on the journey. But the actual traveling has to be done by the disciple himself. A guru cannot be a substitute for the *sadhana*, the sustained work and effort on so many levels, which alone can actually move us along the inner path.[31]

Some Hindus and Hindu organizations include Christian Testament teachings amongst their own and celebrate Christian festivals as well as their own, particularly Christmas and sometimes Easter, as described in earlier chapters. Pictures of Jesus may be found on some Hindu altars. At the Sanatan Deevya Mandal in Bristol, UK, a large picture of Jesus, with a 'bleeding heart' in the Catholic fashion, is displayed among images of avatars, gurus and deities, Hindu, Sikh, Jain and Buddhist. At a village school near Bangalore in India, I saw a similar selection of pictures displayed.

Some Hindus like Gandhi were drawn to Jesus as an Ideal, one who's life exemplified service to others. R Gopal Krishna wrote, "One of the greatest blessings that India received from Christianity is the idea of serving man as fervently as serving God."[32] However, the idea of Hinduism being without a code of *seva* or service, and needing someone like Jesus to wake it up to its social commitments has been generally overplayed by most Christian commentators. As Anantanand Rambachan remarked:

[29] Paramahansa Yogananda, *Autobiography of a Yogi*, Self-Realization Fellowship, Los Angeles, U.S.A. P 238.

[30] M, *The Gospel of Sri Ramakrishna*, Ramakrishna-Vivekananda Center, New York, 1973, p 98. Translation by Swami Nikhilananda.

[31] Karan Singh, 'The Bridge to Immortality' in Karan Singh, *Mundaka Upanishad*, Bharatiya Vidya Bhavan, Bombay, 1987. Extract printed in *Self-Realization*, Journal, Self-Realization Fellowship, Los Angeles, U.S.A. Spring 1990, p 31.

[32] R Gopal Krishna, 'India and Christianity' in *The Illustrated Weekly of India*, Christmas 1976. Quoted in Hans Staffner, *Significance of Jesus Christ in Asia*, Gujrat Sahikya Prakash Anand, India, 1984, p 7.

> What initially attracted me in the personality of Jesus is the embodiment in him of what I considered to be, from my Hindu viewpoint, the ideals and values of the authentic spiritual life….Perhaps in its concern to stress the uniqueness and originality of Jesus, Christianity has ignored some of the identities in the definition of the spiritual life which Jesus shares with the tradition of Hinduism.[33]

A condition for seva is always present, if underlying, in the Hindu concept of every being having an Atman, an individualized aspect of Brahman, so all are inter-connected. Even the Hindu greeting – namaste - makes obeisance to that indwelling Reality in all. Many Hindu organizations exist to do service. In 2005 the seeds have been sown for a Forum for Compassionate Hinduism. The Ramakrishna Mission, Ammachi's ashrams, and Yogoda Satsanga Society each conduct educational and medical programmes for the poor, the sick and the disadvantaged. Other Hindu organizations that have active social service programs include Seva Dal set up by Sai Baba and the London Sevashram Sangha, headed by Swami Nirliptananda. The latter asserts:

> In the light of modern conditions, a continuing exposition and inter- pretation of the philosophy of the Hindu scriptures…as a guide to a sublime way of life would provide peace and spiritual tranquillity and a consciousness of Self. It would spread the ancient message of love towards all beings and create a harmonious atmosphere in our present disturbed world society.

Hindus generally place more emphasis on long-term, sustainable change than on short-term fixes. The former can only be realized by living a spiritually aware life. Charity is important but secondary, yet India is famous for its hospitality and lack of attachment. Many visitors have legendary stories of how they have been received by the poorest who, when the visitor shows the slightest interest in, say, a devotional calendar on display, one of the few items in the home, offer that item unconditionally to the guest. In India the guest is God.

This devotional concept has been developed by Pandurang Shastri Athavale to energize a global grassroots movement known as Swadhyaya Pariwar, "a role model for the entire world based on indigenous Indic concepts. Swadhyaya Pariwar is a global family of volunteers who follow Swadhyaya, a holistic Vedic philosophy based on Gnaan (knowledge), Karma (Action) and Bhakti (devotion)."[34] Swadhyaya was recognized as the best sociological model at a United Nations seminar in Rome in 1986. It has won many awards including the Templeton Prize for Progress in Religion in 1997, delivered in London's

---

[33] *My Neighbour's Faith – and Mine*, World Council of Churches, Geneva, 1986, p 19.
[34] www.goodnewsindia.com/Pages/content/newsclip/swadhyayaPankajJain.html and www.swadhyay.org

Westminster Abbey. On the Templeton Foundation web site, this description is given:

> In 1954 in the villages around Bombay, nineteen of Athavale's most dedicated co-workers, primarily professionals, began *bhaktiferi* - devotional visits to the villages to spread the message of love for God and others. Through *bhaktiferi*, Athavale and his co-workers developed the practice of *swadhyaya*, a form of self-study that inspires each individual to recognize an inner God, cultivate an increased self-respect, and abandon immoral behavior. By believing that God also dwells within others, those who pursue self-study can develop a loving relationship with all persons, resulting in a reduction of crime, the removal of social barriers, and an alleviation of poverty, hunger and homelessness.[35]

RELEVANCE OF HINDU THOUGHT ON JESUS, FOR CHRISTIANS AND HINDUS

Has Hindu thought on Jesus, Christ and Christianity any serious relevance for Christians? The Christian academic, Clifford Hospital, argued, "An adequate Christology must be sensitive both to what Christians have had to say about the significance of Jesus and to the views of participants in the religious communities, particularly in relation to figures who are analogous to Jesus."[36]

There are many implications in this for Christians now that Hindus, Buddhists, Muslims, Jews, Sikhs and Baha'is have offered reflections on the life and meaning of Jesus and Christ. The very fact of such reflections suggests a global theological perspective emerging in which Jesus can no longer be fully claimed or understood within any single faith community. Just a cursory glance at bookshelves indicates a certain uncertainty about who he is, his true nature and identity.

As we have seen, Hospital's point is particularly pertinent to the dialogue with Hindu participants where many figures analogous to Jesus are claimed and where Jesus has, on occasion, been absorbed into the Hindu scheme of things. It is not transparently clear, however, that many Hindus have fulfilled the first part of Clifford's maxim, to be also sensitive to what Christians have had to say about Jesus. A confident Swami Vivekananda, returning to India from the West, said:

> Spirituality must conquer the West....They are waiting for it....Where is the supply to come from? Where are the men ready to go out to every country in the world with the message of the great sages of India?...

---

[35] Downloaded on 22 August 2005 from http://www.templetonprize.org/bios_recent.html
[36] Clifford G Hospital, 'Towards a Christology for Global Consciousness' in *Journal of Ecumenical Studies,* 26.1 Winter 1989, p 46.

Such heroic souls are wanted to go abroad and help to disseminate the great truth of Vedanta. The world wants it; without it the world will be destroyed.[37]

The Hindu Jesus is just one of a series of supremely moral, archetypal and exemplary, divinely imbued humans who have fulfilled the destiny for which all are intended. He is primarily described as an avatar. All avatars come to restore dharma. The title of avatar avoids competitive and all-inclusive claims for particular historical beings as all such incarnations are for specific God-given, salvific missions: each comes for his or her own flock. Hindus point to John's Gospel as evidence of Jesus' self-understanding in this light.

Whilst there has been much philosophical debate on avatars, there is not so much focus on the *ousia*, *fousia* and *hypostases* so loved by early Christians debating the mysteries of the Christ Incarnation![38] For Hindus, Christ is important for what he demonstrates to the world and not for his ontological status. Recent intra-Christian debates on the nature of Jesus and Christ have themselves undermined traditional claims and opened some Christian doors to other perceptions and faith events. Bishop Cragg's affectionate moan about Hinduism that it can be "sharply exclusivist about its non-exclusivity" and has "anathemas but reserves them for anathemas" and wants to be "rejectionist only of rejectionism" can, perhaps, be enjoyed by Hindus, aware that such attitudes have, on the whole, produced a tolerance unmatched elsewhere and have not, generally, led to condemnation, alienation or acrimonious division.[39] SwamiVivekananda wrote, "Unity in variety is the plan of nature and the Hindu has recognized it."

To the Hindu, the whole world of religions is only a travelling, a coming up of different men and women through various conditions and circumstances to the same goal. Every religion is only evolving a God out of the material man and the same God is the inspirer of them all.[40]

For Seshagiri Rao, this unity of being, as understood and taught by Hinduism, could be a major factor in establishing global consciousness and harmony. It encourages a way of life in tune with the Infinite; transcends individual ego barriers; promotes love and non-violence; establishes moral order; and enables reconciliation, human fellowship and peace.[41]

[37] Swami Vivekananda, *The Complete Works of Swami Vivekananda*, Advaita Ashrama, Calcutta, 1970, Volume III, pp 276-277.
[38] "Hypostatic Union... the union of the two natures... in the person of Jesus....He is 100% God and 100% man. ...He continued to exist as God when He became a man and added human nature to Himself. Therefore, there is a 'union in one person of a full human nature and a full divine nature.' Right now in heaven there is a man, Jesus, who is our Mediator between us and God the Father (1Tim. 2:5)." From Dictionary of Theology at http://www.carm.org/dictionary.htm
[39] K Cragg, *The Christ and the Faiths*, SPCK, London 1986, p 237.
[40] Quoted in Marcus Braybrooke, *Together to the Truth*, CLS-SPCK, Madras, 1971, p 107.
[41] Workshop, Parliament of the World's Religions 1993, Bangalore.

"The spiritual gift of India to the world has already begun. India's spirituality is entering Europe and America in an ever-increasing measure. That movement will grow; amid the disasters of the time more and more eyes are turning towards her with hope."[42] Those religions that cling to divisive doctrines, singular and particular revelations, are perhaps increasingly out of touch with aspiring global togetherness, holism, even the new physics. Hinduism can help in breaking down unnecessary and unsustainable tendencies, can encourage an emphasis on orthopraxy based on personal and universal spiritual experience. Gandhi thought the praxis of people was the key to their spirituality. Perhaps this is the only acceptable universal validation. Applying such a key would surely reveal a selection of achievers within each religious - and secular - community. Paramahansa Yogananda wrote, "Distinctions by race or nation are meaningless in the realm of truth, where the only qualification is spiritual fitness to receive."[43] Radhakrishnan tells us something about that truth: "The universality of the great facts of religious experience, their close resemblance under diverse conditions of race and time, attest to the persistent unity of the main spirit."[44]

How to achieve right praxis? Devotees may use various and diverse beliefs and practices to access Divine Reality but it is always realized as One. Unity is its dynamic. Kabir, the great Hindu-Muslim poet, mystic and saint, warned: "Behold but One in all things; it is the second that leads you astray." The great Hindu *rishis* stated: *Tat tvam asi*, Thou art That. That One may be mediated to the world through avatars of equal status, incarnated in unique conditions and situations, but all with the same mission, expressed in religiously pluriform ways: to restore all to Oneness.

So, has the Christian Christ really any special relevance for Hinduism; does he have something to teach us that is not already in our multiple traditions? Do Hindu interpretations of Christ really have any special transformative significance for Christianity? Probably the honest answer to both is no, not really. Individuals of both faiths may gain some insight on their spiritual journeys but generally speaking, Hinduism has Christs enough of its own and Christians are far removed from the pluriform christologies so appreciated by Hindus – although it could be said there are as many Christs as there are Christians believing in him. Much Christian theological study of Hindu responses to Christ leaves those of us outside such immediate circles with an uncomfortable feeling that the incentive is to offer him back to Hindus in an acceptable form as THE savior. Such ploys, however sincerely intended, will never bear much fruit. Hindus have a totally different mind-set and world-view. Continuing

---

[42] 'A Message from Sri Aurobindo,' 15 August 1947, in Adwaita P Ganguly, *Vedanta Philosophy for the Unity of Mankind*, Vikas Publishing House, Delhi, 1995, p 102.
[43] Paramahansa Yogananda, *Autobiography of a Yogi*, Self-Realization Fellowship, Los Angeles, U.S.A. PP 568-569.
[44] S Radhakrishnan, *Eastern Religions and Western Thought*, Oxford University Press, Delhi, 1991, p 296.

Christian mission in India is causing great disturbance, even violence, and brings few, if any, benefits to the vulnerable converts that are generated. Under prevailing conditions it can be of little benefit to Christianity either.

However, even the most militant Hindu can find satisfaction today in some Christian writings. Klaus Klostermaier, closely associated with Vaishnava-Christian study and dialogue, is the subject of a pamphlet by Ashok Chowgule, a supporter of the Rashtriya Swayamsevak Sangh (described by Klostermaier as an organization that has "intimidated and often provoked non-Hindus.")[45] The pamphlet quotes from Klostermaier's book, *A Survey of Hinduism*, to help people "appreciate the ethos of Hinduism and its relevance in today's world." Professor Klostermaier wrote:

> It would not be surprising to find Hinduism the dominant religion of the twenty-first century. It would be a religion that doctrinally is less clear-cut than mainstream Christianity, politically less determined than Islam, ethically less heroic than Buddhism: but it would offer something to everybody, it would be a delight by its richness and depth, it would address people at a level that has not been plumbed for a long time by other religions or prevailing ideologies....[It] will spread mainly through the work of intellectuals and writers, who have found certain Hindu ideas convincing and who identify them with their personal beliefs. A fair number of leading physicists and biologists have found parallels between modern science and Hindu ideas. An increasing number of creative scientists will come from a Hindu background and will consciously and unconsciously blend their scientific and their religious ideas. All of us may be already much more Hindu than we think.[46]

The religious pluralism embedded in the Sanatana Dharma may indeed prove the remedy for an era deeply disturbed by religious difference.

CONCLUSION

What is really needed today for deeper understanding between Hindus and Christians, deeper exchange on the significance of Christ and other avatars, is some mutuality. The focus is still almost exclusively Christocentric. Where are the Christian appreciations of Krishna or Rama or other Hindu Christs? Where can we find Christian study on the great avatars of Hinduism as a means for greater spiritual understanding of the Christian tradition? Ravi Ravindra feels sadness that Christians, in the main, are still not ready for this mutuality.

---

[45] Ashok Chowgule, *Shri Klaus Klostermaier on the Ethos and the Future of Hinduism*, Hindu Vivek Kendra, Mumbai, 1995, pp 2-3.
[46] Klaus Klostermaier, *A Survey of Hinduism*, Munshiram Manoharlal Publishers Pvt Ltd, Delhi, 1990, pp 413-414.

[In] my experience of more than forty years living in a nominally Christian country, I rarely meet Christians who find delight in discovering any great insight or wisdom in another religion. On the contrary, it seems to deflate them to find that another tradition may have some wonderful things to teach, as if it somehow shows Christianity in a poorer light. There is a conviction among most if not all Christians that there can be only one true religion and one true savior and that naturally theirs is it. Christianity has the Truth, and for someone else to have a nugget of truth seems for them to take away from the fullness of Christianity.[47]

Maybe, at individual experience level, there is some evidence of a break-through, in the cross-over of many from Christianity to Hinduism, perhaps in far greater numbers than may ever be expected from Hinduism to Christianity. Many westerners have been attracted by the naturally religious pluralism of Hinduism, by the freedom and openness it allows to move across and between different Hindu (and other) paths without risk or condemnation or loss, and by the ancient and well-tested methodologies it provides for enlightenment and *Self-realization*. Maybe not all of those crossing that Rubicon (or Ganges!) initially realized that it would take intense discipline and efforts for moksha or true and lasting freedom from *avidya* (ignorance). No real religion offers easy routes, even those that seem to suggest a vicarious option. Finally, a true religion will allow us to transcend its narrow boundaries and dwell in the unbound Infinite. This never includes future promises or threats or has labels of any kind.

However, the sound advice not to compare the best of our own tradition with the worst of another is also pertinent. When it comes to Hindu encounters with Christ and Christianity, it could indeed be argued that, on the whole, the best of Hindus have dealt with the worst of Christians! Yet, if we took the same encounter to other arenas, there may seem more of a balance or even a reverse polarity. David Frawley sets out to guide Hindus towards a more mature dialogical encounter in his book, *Awaken Bharata*. There is much of interest here, much that will be familiar to Western thinkers in the chapter entitled 'The Dangers of Hindus Speaking in the Name of Other Religions.' There is the plea for serious listening to the 'other' acknowledging that they are not the same and we cannot just say so; that we must learn about others in order to understand them as they are and not just as we see them; that there is a need for Hindus to learn their own religion thoroughly before articulating it to others or attempting to identify other religions as the same as Hinduism; that

---

[47] Reflections on 'Christ and the Hindus' sent by Ravi Ravindra to author on 9 August 2005. See full text, Appendix III.

there must be a genuine mutuality from all sides for the encounter to have integrity, for any hope of realizing true unity.[48]

It seems to me that all people of faith have to work much harder to be truly mutual. Perhaps for many of us it will not be possible; others of us may think we have arrived there; and just a few may genuinely stand on that threshold, fully aware of their vulnerability as they take their first steps across it. This is real faith. This is the Sanatan Dharma, true religion. It does not belong just to Hinduism but to all who love God enough to find or be found by that Divine Beloved. In some ways it has nothing to do with religion or inter-religious relations. It is much more than both and much simpler than both. It is all about relationship, the fundamental building block of life in any sphere; the relationship with each and every being, with Truth Itself.

Let Swami Vivekananda have the last words. Swamiji spoke over one hundred years ago of the broad religion needed to embrace all spiritual needs and approaches. Here is the essence of the Hindu response to Christianity and all religions. Here is the key to making the most of spiritual wisdom wherever it is revealed. Here is the heart of the including response of Hinduism as it best expresses the Sanatan Dharma.

> Our watchword, then, will be acceptance, and not exclusion....I accept all religions that were in the past, and worship with them all; I worship God with every one of them, in whatever form they worship Him.... I shall keep my heart open for what may come in the future. Is God's book finished? [An] infinite number of pages remain yet to be unfolded....Salutation to all the prophets of the past, to all the great ones of the present, and to all those that are to come in the future![49]

---

[48] David Frawley, *Awaken Bharata*, Voice of India, Delhi, 1998, pp 117-119.
[49] Swami Vivekananda, 'Universal Religion: Its Realization,' Sermon at Universalist Church, Pasadena, USA, 28 January, 1900, printed in Swami Vivekananda, *The Universal Religion*, Ramakrishna Vedanta Centre, UK, 1993, pp 45-6.

# EPILOGUE – A PERSONAL JOURNEY

When I first began this research, many years ago, I had a strong feeling that Hindu understandings of Jesus and Christ were far superior to those of most Christians. From my theology studies I had come to think that Christianity had perhaps gone further from its source than any other religion I knew. Hinduism, the faith that had nurtured and sustained me in my adult life, seemed to glow with insight and wisdom by comparison, though I was sometimes disappointed by Hindus I met who did not seem to live up to these high expectations and behaved in old, familiar ways: my guru is best, supersedes yours etc.

Today many sensitive and spiritual Christians are both setting a new praxis and establishing new interpretations of old Christian truths. They are beacons of light in these fresh directions. Indeed, with so many global challenges to religious identity and their impact on Hindu communities, there is a kind of reversed situation with many Hindu voices sounding strident and closed and some Christian voices sounding soft and open.

Maybe it's time to leave behind all dependencies. When we pass from this world to the next, we leave religions behind along with everything else.[1] Only Love remains and it cannot be limited or stifled by this name or that, this belief or that. It is already whole and holy and we are all called to be Christs, avatars, embodiments of wisdom and love, true Selves, divine beings.

Some are far ahead in this, those we look to for inspiration and guidance at times in our lives – the Christs, the Bhagavans, the Masters, the advanced rishis, yogis, yoginis, Mothers. We must all catch up. That is our destiny, our truth, our reality. In Jesus and others we catch glimpses of that. This is what attracts us, compels us to 'follow.'

In following we should be careful not to let our religious maps lead us to false destinations – Christianity, Hinduism etc. We have become so used to needing these maps - even though our spot on the map rarely matches the place where our religions say we should be! It seems to me now that life is more about unknowing, unlearning, throwing off all the conditioning we have acquired through this and other lifetimes, leaving maps behind so as to be here, now.

---

[1] See Jael and Sandy Bharat, *Mapping the Cosmos: An Introduction to God*, Sessions, 2006.

Even so, I don't hesitate to say that the Sanatan Dharma is not a narrow map, is not a map at all. Whilst shaping Hinduism (a mix, like all religions, of spirituality, cultures, history, nationality), it is much more than it, transcending any religious label. It is 'the eternal truth' that exists in and for each one of us. Everyone is part of it. If none of us affirmed a religion – I am Hindu, I am Christian – religions would not exist. But Eternal Truth always exists, with or without acknowledgement. We just have to discover, uncover, and recover it in ourselves.

There are many examples of Christians realizing this. In the beautiful book, *In Sweet Company*, the Rev Lauren Antress tells how she learnt from Marcus Borg, the Christian theologian, about 'first-hand religion' or the personal experience of God. "Borg said first-hand religion is what people are looking for, but the Christian tradition teaches 'second-hand religion:' religion imposed from the outside-in – if you only just believe, then, lo and behold, you'll have the faith you need. It's a white-knuckle approach to God that doesn't work. We all need our own personal knowing, our own first hand religion, to make sense of things and to handle the stress of modern life in a more fluid and graceful way."[2]

In *Hinduism Today*, Swami Bua told how, hundreds of years ago, one of India's great Tamil saints, Thayumanivar, said:

> It is easy to tame the rogue elephant. It is easy to tie the mouth of a bear. It is easy to mount the back of a lion. It is easy to charm poisonous snakes. It is easy to conquer the celestial and the non-celestial realms. It is easy to trek the worlds invisible. It is easy to command the angelic heavens. It is easy to retain youth eternally. It is easy to enter the body of others. It is easy to walk on water and sit in burning fire. It is easy to attain all the *siddhis* (yoga powers). But to remain still is very, very difficult indeed.[3]

Remaining still opens us up to higher, un-labeled revelation. It is indeed very difficult – to fully understand as well as to realize – but the Sanatan Dharma reveals many ways we can try to make this deep peace our own and so be a blessing to our troubled world.

May I wish all readers ever-increasing stillness, the joy of the moment, the peace of contentment, the wisdom of realized being.

Om shanti. Om Satcitanand.

---

[2] Margaret Wolff, *In Sweet Company: Conversations with Extraordinary Women about Living a Spiritual Life*, Jossey-Bass, San Francisco, 2004, p 73.
[3] Swami Bua, *Hinduism Today*, April / May /June 2003, p 41. For more about Thayumanivar see http://www.tamilnation.org/sathyam/east/saivaism/thayumanavar.htm

# APPENDIX 1A

In 1994 I sent a few Hindu scholars and religious a copy of a Questionnaire I had devised to accompany my research. More people would have been approached had I continued the research at that time. I have re-contacted the respondents and invited them to add a postscript to their original comments. Sita Ram Goel and Bibhuti Yadav have recently passed away.

The questions asked and the responses (unabridged) are presented here and, as you will read, present quite a diversity of position and inclination.

## QUESTIONNAIRE

1. What significance, if any, do you think Jesus has for Hindus around the world today?
2. If there is a significance, how is Jesus primarily understood – as Jesus or as a Christ, and if the latter, is this the equivalent of avatar? If not, how is avatar best understood today?
3. With what strand of Hinduism is Jesus most closely associated today? Is such association primarily linked to Hinduism in the West or does it also apply to the Indian situation?
4. Have Hindu understandings of Jesus changed since Hinduism's expansion into the West and the movement towards it of many western devotees?
5. Many liberal Christian theologians criticise Hindu interpretations of Jesus as being out of touch with recent Christian 'discoveries' of the Jewish-ness of Jesus and his historical context. What would be your response to this critique, arising as it does from a very different world-view?
6. Study so far suggests to me that Hindu interest in Jesus arose initially as a reaction against western Christian imperialism in India; this later changed to an incorporation of Jesus within a Hindu framework divorced from received western Christianity. Since the threat of Christianity subsided, there appears to have been no real development of Hindu responses to Jesus. How would you assess this critique?
7. Would there have been a natural interest in Jesus without the encounter in India during British rule there? If so, how might this have differed from current interpretations? If it had arisen within a friendly interfaith exchange, would the Hindu response have been different?
8. Could you please summaries your personal perspective as a Hindu to the Hindu-Christian dialogue and the relevance of Jesus to that?

# APPENDIX 1B

## SWAMI DAYATMANANDA, RAMAKRISHNA MISSION

1. For Hindus all over the world Jesus Christ signifies the reality of God, the reality of religion, the true meaning and goal of life and spiritual realization.

2. Jesus is revered by all Hindus as an incarnation or Avatar (unlike some Christian thinkers Hindus do not make any distinction between these words). He is revered and worshipped like other Avatars such as Rama, Krishna, Buddha and Chaitanya. He is one of the doorways leading man to the One, Infinite, Ultimate Reality. An Avatar is the highest manifestation of divinity. As such he is the actuality of what each one of us is in a potential form. Hence Christ's name, form and teachings gradually help his followers to be like him. An Avatar is also the proof of God's grace. An avatar has immense power, capable of removing the ignorance of man and granting him Salvation or Eternal Life. This is the significance of an Avatar.

3. Christ is primarily associated in popular Hinduism with the path of devotion. But the followers of even *Advaitism* (the path of non-dualistic philosophy) consider him as the best example of a true Advaitin. The saying of Christ "I and my father are One" is taken as proof of their contention. Both these interpretations are right. The view one takes depends on individual feeling and attitude. Christ helps an aspirant according to one's attitude. This is true of East or West.

4. I do not think this understanding of Christ changed much. Perhaps now he is better understood than before since the narrow interpretations of the dogmatic missionaries no longer hamper the Hindus.

5. As has been said earlier Hindus revere Christ as a most perfected of spiritual beings. Hence the criticisms of Christian theologians do not disturb Hindus. Christ is an ideal and is as significant and valuable today as he was in the past. He will be so in the future. The criterion of any interpretation is the help it can give one in progressing toward the ideal. Hinduism has always given full freedom to understand saints in our own way. Any attempt to force particular interpretations is dangerous leading to unwarranted quarrels and narrowness. It is immaterial whether a person called Jesus was a historical being or a Jew or not. It is enough if he can be of a sufficiently inspiring ideal helping man toward the goal of perfection or the attainment of the Kingdom of Heaven. Hindus have ever entertained this view in regard to all Avatars and saints. They will do so in future. The criterion is not the certificate of a

particular theologian but one's heart. "A tree is known by its fruits." Incidentally this also would indicate the two world-views of Hinduism and Christianity.

6. It is true that interest in Christianity had increased with the arrival of the British and the Dutch. But Christianity was being practiced by a small minority since a long time, though it was confined mainly among the so called lower caste people. It is only with the advent of the British that educated people started to take a deeper interest. Even then Hindu understanding of Christ was far more radical and liberal than the exclusiveness preached by mainly the missionaries. Raja Ram Mohan Roy, Keshub Chandra Sen, Mahatma Gandhi, Aurobindo are instances. Hinduism is likened to an octopus. I think it is true. It is not that Christianity has lost its interest for Hindus. Merely it has been accepted as a valid path for the realization of God. As such it is for the aspirant to quietly assimilate Christ and manifest the innate divinity. Since it is in the very life-blood of Hindus to regard all religions and all paths as equally valid they do not make much fuss of Christianity. For the same reason Hinduism does not show such an avid interest in inter faith dialogues etc.

7. If the British were not there perhaps Hindus would have taken more time to have a deeper interest in Christ and Christianity. But this is merely speculation. History cannot be reversed. Now that the whole world has come together every faith and every religion is bound to spread everywhere. The response, of course, depends on the culture and ethic of each particular nation. India ever welcomes every true religion. The more religions the better. Only it begs to let it accept religions according to its own understanding and need. Interpretation is bound to change, to become progressively better depending on the development of the interpreter. This is as it should be. No religion can be a fixed entity for ever. Every religion, like a living organism, grows. Hinduism has changed much over time. So too Christianity. Hence even the present interpretations of theologians are also bound to change. If this is accepted there would be a much better harmony between people of different faiths.

8. I am a Hindu and a follower of Sri Ramakrishna and Swami Vivekananda. I regard Christ the same as Sri Ramakrishna, as another incarnation of God who descended into a human body to show the way to God to ignorant humanity. Even if there were to be no historical a person as Jesus still from the idealistic point of view he would have been equally valid and venerable for me. Christ and his teachings have proved their worth during these many centuries and will continue to do so while this present creation lasts. Latest avatars like Sri Ramakrishna amply prove the truth and validity of other incarnations. I am sure you are aware of the fact that Sri Ramakrishna had practiced Christianity and had the blessed vision of Christ. This should be the greatest assurance to

the followers of Christ. Now that men have come closer the need and value of a true dialogue with sincerity of heart on the part of all religions needs no emphasis. At no time in history is man in more dire danger of annihilation than at present. A right understanding of each other's religion and a sincere desire to put the teachings of the prophets into day to day practice seems to be the only option left for us, not only for a saner way of living but if we have to merely survive. Jesus, Buddha, Krishna and Ramakrishna are much more relevant today than at any other time.

# Mathoor Krishnamurti, Bharatiya Vidya Bhavan

1. Jesus is held in high esteem by the Hindus, on a par with some of our Avatars.

2. Jesus is an Avatar, like Krishna or Rama of the Hindus.

3. Just as Rama and Krishna did, Jesus also came to protect the good and punish the wicked.

4. No, the Hindu perception of Jesus has not changed with western influence.

5. Hindus believe that God appears in human form or any other form to protect the Good and establish *Dharma* (Righteousness). Jesus is thus seen in a similar light by the Hindus.

6. Before Christianity came to India, Buddha came – and opposed the Vedas. Even so, Buddhism was welcomed in India and not perceived as a threat by the Hindus. Similarly other religions came and developed, like Jainism and Islam. Christianity was relatively a newcomer to impinge on the Hindu consciousness. Even so it was absorbed within the Hindu framework. It is the unique nature of Hinduism to accept and absorb new ideas and appreciate them. Hinduism has an 'open mind,' respects all other faiths and sentiments and embraces them.

7. 52 years after Jesus, a church was built in India. Christianity made inroads. Hindus became aware of this new religion and some of them accepted and converted to Christianity. I do not think that British rule had a deep impact, except in the sense that churches got bigger support. Missionaries adopted the method of approaching the poor and downtrodden, offering food and clothing and thus converted many to Christianity. This is considered, even today, as a disservice for which many Hindus cannot excuse the missionaries. On the whole, however, Hindus respect all religions and Christianity is no exception.

8. I personally feel that Hindus and Christians should meet and discuss similarities between the sayings of the Bible and Hindu scriptures. Christians need to broaden their vision and develop respect for freedom of faith rather than misuse / abuse the economic backwardness of a society to propagate the Christian faith. The teachings of Jesus are parallel to those which we find in the Hindu scriptures. As mentioned before, he is considered as an Avatara, a personification of God, representing Righteousness. Hence I feel that there is much common ground for Hindu-Christian dialogue.

# BIBHUTI S YADAV, ASSOCIATE PROFESSOR, TEMPLE UNIVERSITY

1A. What Jesus? Whose Jesus? What kind of Hindus? And particularly, where in the world? If it is an historical Jesus, with his commitment to social justice, then yes. This Jesus is of great significance for the underprivileged of Hindu society. This Jesus was introduced in India by some very thoughtful Christians in the 19th century, building hospitals and schools for those who had nowhere else to go. Intellectuals and reformers of lower caste background in Maharastra and elsewhere were inspired by the social egalitarianism of Jesus. Mahatma Phule and Dr Babasheb Ambedkar are notable examples. Ambedkar introduced fundamental issues in his encounter with Mahatma Gandhi. What kind of India? Is it an India where all human beings regardless of caste, gender and religion are equal before God? Or, is it an India where Santana Dharma equals the nation? Ambedkar's legacy is very much alive for the issues he introduced in the discourse on freedom are at the centre of the political debate today. A number of political forces, organised by and for the marginalised majority, are inspired by the works of Mahatma Phule, Ambedkar, and the social and secular commitments of historical Jesus.

1B. Then there is the 'gentleman' Jesus who moves in the circles of doctors, professors, journalists, lawyers and politicians of the Congress culture. This Jesus was introduced by the ruling elite in the West, among them liberal orientalists and utilitarians, of sacred and secular sorts. They wanted to immortalise the raj by indianising the administration. The 'gentleman' Jesus was appreciated by bhadraloka ie. the urban upper caste and westernised Hindus who joined the administrative services. The bhadraloka belong to the neo-vedantic culture of Rammohan Roy, Vivekanand, Tagore, Mahatma Gandhi and Radhakrishnan. Classical Vedanta of Shankaracharya believed in the doctrine of two planes, *parmartha* and *vyavahara*. The former is a metaphysical plane where there is no consciousness of difference, no I and other, and no society or history. There is only stillness of spiritual universality. The latter is a social historical plane, the sphere of Sanatana Dharma, where inequality in the name of karmic will prevails. The Vedanta of Shankaracharya alienated the spiritual from the social in defence of the historical identity of Sanatana Dharma. Neo-Vedanta inherited the legacy of Shankaracharya. It also alienated the Christ from historical Jesus. The Vedantic Christ has no memory of historical Jesus, no concern for social justice. The Christ performs yoga in the spiritual space of Vedanta and features very much in Hindu-Christian dialogue today. The yogi-Christ has tactical significance for elite Hindus both in India and abroad, including Hindu religious movements in Europe and America.

2A. Yes, Jesus is primarily understood as Christ in Hindu discourse, which virtually means neo-Vedantic discourse. See Question 2B. I address 2 issues here: (1) Is Christ equivalent of avatar? (2) If not, how is avatar best understood today?

2B. I respond to the second question first. There is no serious theology or philosophy of avatar today. Theology of avatar has, traditionally, been best done by Shaiva and Vaisnava thinkers. The last serious theologian to do serious reflection was Vallabha. He affirmed a God (Krishna) who speaks scriptural words, who speaks differently, and who lives through the contra-dictions of his own words. Vallabha tested his theology of avatar on Buddha, demonstrating hermeneutically that it was Krishna who spoke through the body of Tathagata. God is a magician, transferring his logos to his bodies that are the historical agents of speaking fundamentally different and mutually incompatible scriptural or revelatory words. Would Vallabha have the same stance towards Jesus? Has Krishna spoken through the body of Jesus? Interesting thought!

3A. Modern Hindu discourse on avatar is dominated by neo-Vedantins, the westernised Hindu apologetics who have no access to the serious texts and technical categories of Sanskrit thought, not even of Vedanta. The neo-Vedantins are for 'transcendental unity,' not immanent complexities of history. There is very little substance (or relevance) in the neo-Vedantic recognition of Christ as avatar.

3B. With what strand of Hinduism is Jesus primarily associated today? Obviously, neo-Vedantic Hinduism. The association has to do with the Indianisation of the raj and the conscious and organised steps the traditional elite took towards westernisation in defence of their social and political interests. This association is linked to the 19th and 20th century ruling circles in India. Hinduism in the West is a product of the encounter between Vedantic and Western elites in the 19th century.

4. Have Hindu understandings of Jesus changed since Hinduism's expansion into the West? No. Hinduism in the West emanates from pseudo-Westernised Indians. Most of its devotees in the West are pseudo-Easternised Americans and Europeans.

5A. Apparently, yes. But forgive my rhetoric. The line between the liberals and conservatives, in my view, is not clear. Did not the 19th century liberals, both Christian and secular, espouse imperialism on ethical grounds? Did they not contribute to the rise of neo-Vedantic spiritualism for utilitarian reasons? Why should they complain now?

5B. Neo-Vedantins would care less about the critique. Why should they? Precisely how many liberal Christians have understood Krishna in his

Vedicness? Is not the neo-Vedantic devaluation of Vedic Hinduism (read textual and historical Hinduism) enclosed in the 19th century liberal Christian rejection of the pre-Christian as useless and irrelevant? This rejection of real Hindu past is very much evident in the life and works of Rammohan Roy, Keshub Chandra Sen, the Tagores etc. Keshub Chandra called Veda (Vedic Hinduism) an "old hag." He implied the same thing about the Hebrew Bible.

5C. I agree with the liberal Christian theologians that Hindu interpretations of Jesus are out of touch with recent 'discoveries' of the Jewishness of Jesus. But why should Hindu intellectuals make themselves up-to-date by following the Western Jewishness of Jesus? Is it not more interesting and creative if serious Hindu scholars keep the Jesus discourse in the context of Sanskrit thought, possibly tracing the Vedicness or Puranicness of Jesus? Also the alleged liberality in the Jewishness of Jesus may not be universally liberal. That may be liberalism in the context of Western Christianity, and for Western historical reasons. From non-Western perspectives, in this case an Indian perspective, the return to Jewishness of Jesus may well be a sign of cultural conservatism. Neo-Vedanta too claims to be liberal, although its cultural and social con- servatism is only too evident. For historical and political reasons, it may 'discover' Krishna (or Rama) in a Jewish context. There are signs saying that this may already be happening.

6. You make valid observations. However, the social reality is changing in India. Never before in India did the marginalised Hindus have the right or ability to formulate their social concerns. Now they do. Given the social- ethical relevance of Jesus, and given the increasing prominence of the so far marginalised Hindus in the historical debate, new formulation of national identity and this-worldly visions of salvation may emerge. The social critique of poets and philosophers like Ravidas and Tathagata are being revived. In the emerging discourse, a post neo-Vedantic Indian Christology could very well be formulated.

7. Would there have been a natural interest in Jesus without the encounter in India during the raj? Too hypothetical a question. I can only speculate in the absence of historical experience. Most probably, Jesus would not have been alienated from Christ; neither would he have been incorporated into a 'Gentleman' and a yogi. Quite possibly, Jesus would have wandered in the company of poets like Ravidas, those who composed and sang songs of God, demanding social equality on religious grounds.

8. Could I surmise my personal perspective to the Hindu-Christian dialogue? In my view (and it is just a view), Hindu-Christian dialogue is too unhistorical, too untextual, too spiritualistic, and too superfluous. It is thick in interreligious smile, too thin in substance.

# SITA RAM GOEL, AUTHOR

My letter and questionnaire and a responding letter from Sri Goel, as well as his responses below, were all published as Appendix 4 in his book, *Jesus Christ: An Artifice for Aggression*, Voice of India Press 1994. Both his letter and Questionnaire responses are included here.

"Before I take up your questions one by one, I prefer to give a little background about the intellectual atmosphere in post-independence India. This may help you in sizing up your subject.

The scene in post-independence India has been dominated more or less completely by Communists and socialists and Leftists of all sorts. They have shown no interest in religious subjects, least of all in Jesus Christ. It is only recently that the Ayodha Movement has drawn the attention of our educated elite towards what they call religion. But in this context too they have proved that they are either equally ignorant about all religions or equally indifferent to them.

Of course, there have been Hindu parties and platforms present on the scene all along. But they have hardly mattered until recently. The Arya Samaj seems to have lost its fire and has become more or less moribund. The Hindu Mahasabha, the Rashtriya Swayamsevak Sangh (RSS), and the Vishva Hindu Parishad (VHP) have never been interested in doctrinal Christianity or Jesus Christ as such. Their headache has been the conversions by Christian missions. If you ask them about Jesus, they are most likely to say that he was a good man. Some of them may even call him a mahatma or rishi or even an avatar. But that means nothing. They will say the same about Muhammad or about any other prominent figure for that matter.

Thus there is no truth whatsoever in the Christian missionary propaganda abroad that a Hindu-Christian dialogue is on in India at present. I am totally unaware of any such dialogue being in the forefront. Of course, there are some Christian groups across the country who are holding 'dialogues' with 'Hindus' and reporting them in the Christian press, here and abroad. But the whole thing is a farce, in any case a far cry from the Hindu-Christian dialogues during the long period from Raja Rammohun Roy to Mahatma Gandhi. First of all, there are now very few Hindu thinkers who are interested in Jesus Christ, one way or the other. Secondly, Hindu thinkers who have studied Jesus Christ in depth, and who thus qualify for the dialogue, are fewer still. Thirdly, knowledgeable Hindus are hardly the Hindus whom Christian groups are likely to invite for their dialogue. They pick up Hindus who suit their purpose, with the result that Hindu participants are no more than mere presence reported in the Christian press. For all practical purposes, the current Hindu-Christian dialogue is a

Christian monologue. It seems that Christian theologians in India have lost completely their self-confidence of earlier days.

Nor is there any truth in the missionary propaganda abroad, namely, that Hindus are hungering for Jesus or that, in the words of Mother Theresa, Hindus need Christ. This may help the missionaries raise funds and gain other types of support from their western patrons. But the fact remains that this is as big a lie in the present as it was in the past. Hindus have never been hungry for Jesus nor have they ever been in need of Christ, notwithstanding the 'harvest' which missionaries have reaped from time to time. The force and fraud and material allurements involved in the missionary methods tell the true story.

Now I will take up your questions.

1. Jesus as such has never had any significance for Hindus at large. At best he means to them one religious teacher among many others. The educated Hindus have been fed for a long time and by some of the best Hindu leaders on the Jesus of the Sermon on the Mount, the Jesus who saved an adulteress from being stoned, and the Jesus who cried from the cross that those who have wronged him may be forgiven. But for Hindus like me who have studied him first-hand and in the context of the history he has created all through these two thousand years, he means death to Hinduism and all that it stands for, the same in the case of many Pagan religions and cultures around the world.

2. To the best of my knowledge, no Hindu thinker has ever accepted Jesus as the Christ. Some Hindu thinkers may have called him an avatar, but no Hindu thinker has ever equated him with Rama or Krishna, or the Buddha. Hindus who know the shastric meaning of *avatara* as also the theological meaning of Christ, will never equate the two terms. In any case, I have not come across any Hindu literature on the subject. Christian theologians have tried to put their own words in Hindu mouths, or their own meanings in Hindu terms. But that is another story. Hindu scholars are not at all eager to get credit for such exercises.

3. Christian theologians have tried for many years to relate Jesus to practically every strand of Hinduism – from Advaita to Bhakti. But I wonder why they have not been able to make up their mind and say for sure that this is the strand of Hinduism which needs Jesus as its crown. So far it has been a free for all, which shows what they are about. They are out to try different Hindu versions of Jesus on different sections of Hindu society. There have also been a few Hindus who have tried to see this or that strand of Hinduism in Jesus. But they have done so in order to prove that Jesus was some sort of Hindu, or that Christianity has borrowed from Hinduism. I have yet to know of a Hindu who has asked Hindus to rally round Jesus because he is close to some strand of Hinduism. For Hindus like me who have studied Hinduism as well as Jesus,

he can be related to no strand in Hinduism. We see in him a dark force arising from the lower levels of human nature. Hinduism in its essence can have nothing to do with the likes of him except as villains a la Vitra or Ravana of Kamsa.

4. I am not competent to answer this question because I really do not know anything about Hinduism's expansion into the West. All I know is that some Hindu swamis are getting audiences, even followers, in the West. I know the Hare Krishna movement also to a certain extent. I was told by friends in the USA that some Hindu swamis start with fulsome hymns to Jesus before they come to their subject proper or tell their audience that they are not saying anything which was not said by Jesus long ago but which the Christian West has missed. I can understand the strategy witting or unwitting. But I cannot approve of it. I want Hindu swamis to be more self-confident, and not lean on Jesus. I met some converts to Hinduism in the USA. They came under the influence of another convert turned guru. They did not tell me that they were dissatisfied with Jesus, only that the new guru was more satisfying. The other type of western converts to Hinduism I have met in India. In their case the rejection of Jesus and the whole Judeo-Christian tradition is total. But all this is not sufficient for me to draw any firm conclusions. In any case, I am not aware of any new understanding of Jesus dawning in this country simply because some people in the West feel drawn towards Hinduism.

5. I am afraid I have not understood your question. Which are the Hindu interpretations of Jesus that liberal Christian theologians are criticising? So far I have only known one Hindu interpretation of Jesus, namely, that he was a good man, preaching humility, compassion and forgiveness. Thus Hindus have remained out of touch not only with recent Christian 'discoveries' but with all Christian 'discoveries' at all times. Jesus has never meant so much to them as to make them go into Christological researches. I have not come across a single book on Christology written by a Hindu. Even educated and modern Hindus are not aware of the subject. But I am sure that once they get informed they will feel more at home with Jesus the Jewish preacher in a historical context than they have done with Jesus the Christ. For instance, I am conversant with the latest researches. I find Jesus the Jew more acceptable than the Jesus of Christian theology.

6. You are quite correct that Hindus were forced to take interest in Jesus only because he came with western imperialism and threatened Hinduism in all sorts of ways. But you are not correct when you say that they incorporated Jesus in a Hindu framework. Before western imperialism came to this country Hindus had lived with Islamic imperialism for several centuries, and learnt the art of flattering the bully out of his crude hectoring and cruel deeds. They appealed to the mullah and the sufi in the name of 'true' Islam and the 'real' Muhammad. The art also became a belief in some sections of Hindu society

with the passing of time. But it will be untrue to say that Muhammad was ever incorporated into the Hindu framework. The same applies to the Jesus of Western imperialism. Hindus have only tried to beat the missionaries with their own stick, that is, by inventing a 'true' Jesus and praising him to the skies while denouncing proselytisation in his name. That is all. And that also has come to an end with the coming of independence. Christian missionaries can no more afford to be bullies. Hindus are no more in need of the 'true' Jesus. Now they are bothered only about the Christian missions as a political problem. No new response to Jesus is called for. Christian theologians are deluding themselves if they think that Jesus has ever meant anything much to the Hindus.

7. Hindus had heard of Jesus even before the British advent. Jesus was very much present in Islamic theology. But I am not aware of any Hindu taking notice of him in the mediaeval times. They would have shown the same indifference to him had he come with preachers without any backing of bayonets. Hindus have never denied to anyone the freedom to preach what one likes. They have their own way of smiling at only sons and sole saviours. They remained indifferent to Muhammad so long as it was only some sufis settling down among them and presenting him as the last prophet. But they had to take notice of Muhammad when the sufis invited the swordsmen of Islam. So also in the case of Jesus. Even today, take away the financial and political backing which the powerful West provides to Jesus and see the result. Hindus will have no objection to Christian preachers trying to make converts. But I am very doubtful about the Hindu response to Jesus being more positive or substantial than it has been so far. Hindus have thousands of saints, and Jesus comes nowhere near even the most minor of their spiritual teachers. If all the military might, financial largesses, and media power of the West has failed to impress Jesus on the Hindu mind all these years, there is no reason to believe that he will fare better without this equipment.

8. The most worthwhile Hindu-Christian dialogue took place when Raja Rammohun Roy, Swami Dayananda, Swami Vivekananda and Mahatma Gandhi spoke from the Hindu side. John Mott and the Tambaram conference of the International Missionary Council (1938) found the Christian missionaries at the end of their wits in the face of Mahatma Gandhi. They would have been nowhere if Nehruvian secularism, a continuation of Western imperialism, had not rescued them out of the tight corner into which they had been driven. They resurged forward, and devised new mission strategies of Indigenization and Liberation, etc. They also achieved some notable success, particularly in the North-East. But they never felt the need of a Hindu-Christian dialogue anymore. Why are they in need of it now? The Second Vatican is invoked as the new inspiration. But the Second Vatican itself has to be explained. We have not been taken in by the airs of condescension in the papal declaration of 1965 about Hinduism. We know that Christianity has

never made concessions out of an inner seeking. In fact, the word 'inner' is not applicable in the case of Christianity. It has always used or bowed down to outer circumstances. The Second Vatican saw that Christianity was in a bad shape in the West, and had to find a new home in the East. Dialogue with Hinduism and Buddhism became the new mission strategy. But unfortunately for the new Christian mission, Hindus have shown no interest in the dialogue. Nor are they likely to show any interest so long as the missionary apparatus is maintained intact and the right to convert is insisted upon. It amounts to picking my pocket after making me look the other way. I have told my friends such as Raimundo Panikkar that, if they are sincere about a dialogue with Hindus, they should denounce the missionary apparatus. They smile and dismiss me as a Hindu chauvinist. Even so, we are prepared for a dialogue provided the Christian side does not lay down the ground rules. That is not acceptable to them. What they want us to accept in the first instance is that Christianity is a great and unique religion, that Jesus is a spiritual power, and that Hindus should have no objection to Christian missions. We will not walk into the trap. In any case, we are in a dialogue with them through Voice of India publications. They have refused to respond so far. We do not know whether the silence is prompted by the fear of losing the argument, or by the self-satisfied smugness of those who wield big money, big organisation, and big influence. Jesus has a relevance to the dialogue if the Christian side allows us to present him as we and not they see him. Why should we not have our say?"

# Appendix 2

## Jesus Darshan: sandy bharat
Published in *World Faiths Encounter* No. 6, November 1993.[1]

There is a paradox about the interreligious dialogue between Hindus and Christians. Mostly such meetings involve liberal Christians and Vedantic Hindus. Liberal Christians tend to emphasise the humanity of Jesus. Vedantic Hindus, placing this humanity within a cosmic Christness, assert the divinity of Jesus. Both get along well because Jesus, in both views, is part only of a wider salvific scene. Some Christians appreciate hearing Jesus acclaimed and affirmed by Hindus and some Hindus are joyful that the way now seems open for the Christian assimilation of Krishna and other spiritual giants of the Hindu tradition into a welcoming Christian community. However, such two-way traffic does not, as yet, seem a consequence of interfaith mutuality.

Hindus in India began developing christologies in earnest at the turn of the 20th century, mostly in reaction to the imposed partnership of western imperialism and Christian missionising. Whilst Christians sought ways of inculturating Christ, Hindus were busy detaching him from his western travelling companions, claiming Jesus, an Asiatic, as their own, one misunderstood and misrepresented by the West. Affirmations such as Hans Staffner's that Jesus "was the fulfilment of the desires expressed in the Asian religions" could not be earthed in deeply rooted Hindu religious experience.[2] The empirical claim of Ramakrishna Paramahansa, 'passing over' into Islam, Christianity and various forms of Hinduism, that an essential unity underlay all religions, was a far more powerful force in the hinduization of Jesus than missionaries who did not appear to demonstrate a praxis that matched their proclamations.

Gandhi argues that the rigid structure of Christian allegiance was against the spirit of Christ who "wished to give everything, asking nothing in return, and not caring what creed might happen to be professed by the recipient."[3] Many Hindus accepted Jesus as their preceptor, without any allegiance to Christianity. Those who did enter the Church became ostracised from caste and culture and, many, like Gandhi, found such a move unnecessary. Jesus fitted naturally into Hinduism whereas Hindus were very uncomfortable

---

[1] This journal is now Interreligious Insight. www.interreligiousinsight.org
[2] Hans Staffner, *The Significance of Jesus Christ in Asia*, Gujarat Sahitya Prakash Anand, 1984, p 173.
[3] R Ellsberg, Ed, *Gandhi on Christianity*, Orbis Press, New York, 1991, p 27.

within fixed Christian boundaries. Paramahansa Yogananda's view sums this up: "The precepts of Jesus are analogous to the highest Vedic teachings, which were in existence long before the advent of Jesus. This does not take away from the greatness of Christ, it shows the eternal nature of truth, and that Jesus incarnated on earth to give to the world a new expression of that Sanatan Dharma."[4]

This understanding of Jesus, placed within a multiform, ongoing salvific context but affirming a unique God-given mission, is now established as a Hindu response. It offers a relational inter-play between the Jesus of history and the Christ of faith which retains the Father/Son link, removes the 'scandal of particularity,' and stresses the right relationship of each human with the Real. It binds together what we know of the historical Jesus and the influence of that figure across the years through his perceived indwelling in the hearts and minds of those attracted by him, whatever their religious grouping. Christians have found in the life of the Hindu Gandhi an inspiring expression of discipleship, suggesting that any holistic christology must arise from the faith interface and not be constrained by fixed dogmas. A holistic, dialogical Christology needs both east and west even as it needs both history and faith.

Hinduism offers a balance between the Jesus of history and the Christ of faith which is perhaps overlooked by liberal Christians now stressing the humanity of Jesus. The Hindu starting point is the life of Jesus, which so unfolds and develops that Christness is realised, part of every human destiny, thus generating the metaphysical focus authenticated by its reception and response in other individuals. The gap between the Real is thus exposed as temporary, erasable and unreal and such revealers become more than perfect examples but verifiable forces in the spiritual world. Gandhiji believed that Jesus, Nanak, Muhammad, the Buddha and others "exercised an immense influence over and moulded the character of thousands of men. The world is richer for their having lived in it." Again, it is the praxis of preceptors and followers that act as the guide to their spiritual effectiveness and integrity. Such a measurement surely reveals a selection of achievers within each religious community.

Kenneth Cragg's comment that it was "a Hindu instinct both to welcome Jesus and to detach him from the Christian context of his historical meaning and indeed from the Jewish context of his story" is paralleled by the Christian extraction of Jesus from his historical meaning within his Jewish story.[5] Only recently has action been taken to redress this neglect and to begin reconciliation. The full repercussions of the rediscovery by Christians and Jews together of the Jewishness of Jesus have yet to be felt in the wider dialogical arena. They will surely be impressive and, as all Christological perspectives

---

4 Paramahansa Yogananda, *Man's Eternal Quest*, Self-Realization Fellowship, Los Angeles, U.S.A. PP 284-285.
5 Kenneth Cragg, *The Christ and the Faiths*, SPCK, 1986, p 177.

emerging from the world religions are born out of a response to an encounter with Christianity, a redefined mainstream Christian understanding of Jesus may well prove a genesis factor. Hindu-Jewish dialogue, notable for its absence, could make a valuable contribution to the advent of any new paradigm. Both religions emanate from the far horizons of history though both relate to that very differently. Both contain a history partly shaped by confrontation with the power of Christendom. Both contain beneficial balances to extravagant Christian claims. Like the dervish, both point hands to earth and heaven, turning on this axis, an intertwining spiral which has not yet truly touched the other in the cosmic dance.

Jesus *darshan* may not be a present possibility for Jewish people of faith but, like the woman confidently touching Jesus' robe, Hindus have reached out to experience the saving grace of one who transcends man-made confines. This inclusive gathering-in of spirituality wherever it is discerned has no affinity with Christian inclusivism which attempts to suck in those outside Christianity against their will. The Hindu embrace of another's spirituality is based on the belief that Brahman is everywhere and in all things, breaking through in all those who have put God first in their lives. Such evidence for the Real cannot be exclusively or finally exhausted by any one historical being so appreciation should not be limited to only one exemplar, even though loyalty must be so restricted if spiritual indigestion is not to follow! If liberal Christians do now think of Jesus as one saviour among many, perhaps it is time not only to borrow the methodology of eastern religions but also to enter into the heart of their devotional focus. Perhaps this would create a challenge for us as Hindus if we find our own great preceptors being detached from their Hindu context and Christianised! A truly global inter-connectedness and awareness would transform our religious boundaries and highlight our common, sacred ground. Differences that remain could be enjoyed as not divisive but, like the rainbow's spectrum, various interpretations of the light which arch together harmoniously towards the treasure now hidden from our view.

The Hindu Jesus emerges as one of a series of supremely moral, archetypal and exemplary, divinely imbued humans who have 'fulfilled the destiny for which all are intended.' The *avatara* model usually enshrining this under-standing has an affinity with logos Christology, except where the latter, illogically, maintains one absolute Incarnation. The historical Jesus is placed inside a greater cosmic Christness and, as Yoganandaji discerned, it would be a "metaphysical error to say that the omnipresent Christ Consciousness is circumscribed by any one human being." Each particular incarnation of the logos or Christ Consciousness is in harmony with the universal 'creator' and so acts in the world as a 'saviour' recalling all things to Itself. The anticipated incorporation into the logos of those not yet Christs is the Second Coming, or the second birth of John's Gospel. This Christ Consciousness, active in creation, enables all to be 'sons of God,' a divine invitation none can finally circumvent for it is the call of the unbound Self to the enclosed Self to be whole again and free. The relationship between the Christ and Jesus is thus spiritual, not ontological, and open to all. Testimony to such a fulfilled relationship is demonstrated in the lives of avatars so providing a conceptual base which avoids competitive and all-inclusive claims for particular historical beings as all such incarnations are for specific, God-given, salvific missions: each comes for his or her own flock.

Where traditional christology focuses on the divine reaching out to the human, an avatar understanding of Jesus highlights the human realising the divine so initiating compassionate return. Both encompass two-way travel in an oscillating spiritual universe. An avatar, free from karmic compulsion, exhibiting truly free will, is the finished product of what all must become and shows the way back to Reality-centredness, declaring through his or her own integrated example, the possibility of such travel. Such figures are worthy of worship, are salvific, for they have been self-emptied and Self-filled so becoming perfectly transparent reflections of the Divine Reality. The avatar helps to stimulate and direct the movement of others back to that Source, action which cannot be restricted to Jesus without denying the faith experience of countless devotees of God. Unlike Christian interpretation, even where historicity is part of the package, the purpose is not to give history ultimate meaning but to free human consciousness from such limitations. The descent into history of the Cosmic Christ is to shatter its momentum, to reveal it as *maya*, a present with no future. The divine energy pulls out of history and back to Itself. Jesus can be placed in such a transcending, timeless exposition for his influence has clearly overcome all transient boundaries.

Clifford Hospital wrote that "an adequate Christology must be sensitive both to what Christians have to say about the significance of Jesus, and to the views of participants in the religious communities, particularly in relation to figures who are analogous to Jesus."[6] This is particularly pertinent to Hindu-Christian dialogue where the former claim many such figures. Hindu christologies maintain the significance of Jesus without demoting the truth-claims of others. Where absolute, universal significance is not upheld, it may be evident, in the overall failure of mission, that nothing can be gained by its retention. The recent insights into historical, cultural and sociological factors affecting the development of early Christianity, and the closeness of the world religions in neighbours and friends, make such claims increasingly difficult to defend. They present difficulties with the Christian concept of God and the commandment to love one another without judgement. They have proven countereffective in the meeting place between religions, turning people away from Christ as well as Christianity. They do not fit with the newly awakened, if

---

[6] Clifford G Hospital, 'Towards a Christology for Global Consciousness' in *Journal of Ecumenical Studies*, 26.1, Winter 1989, p 46.

struggling, social and political global awareness. Those seeking a one world ethic may find aggressively conflicting religious claims of any kind better left outside the new world order.

Keith Ward has recently explored the dynamics of breaking free from traditional constrictions into a new sharing of spiritual vision. This could engender a belonging to "more than one religious tradition, thereby widening one's sources of inspiration, one's range of symbols for the divine, and one's understanding of human life as it is experienced." He wonders if this may mean "the end of religion, in the sense of monolithic blocks of belief or authoritative institutions which oppose one another as competing vehicles of absolute truth."[7] With this freedom, with the enhanced immediate, unmediated, self-affirming, self-directing human-Divine relationship it promotes within each community response, Hindus and Christians can witness together to the meaningfulness of the life, teaching and influence of Jesus. We can share his *darshan*. Christians are now invited to join Hindus at the feet of our great spiritual preceptors to know the love and grace they, like Jesus, also bestow. Om shanti.

---

[7] Keith Ward, *A Vision to Pursue*, SCM Press, 1991, p 7.

# APPENDIX 3

## HINDU ENCOUNTERS WITH CHRIST: SOME REFLECTIONS
## BY RAVI RAVINDRA

Professor Ravi Ravindra kindly sent me these reflections on the theme of this book. Extracts are included in Chapter 7 but the full text is given below.

A. Idolatry of the Christians: It has been a matter of sadness for me that in my experience of more than forty years living in a nominally Christian country, I rarely meet Christians who find delight in discovering any great insight or wisdom in another religion. On the contrary, it seems to deflate them to find that another tradition may have some wonderful things to teach, as if it somehow shows Christianity in a poorer light. There is a conviction among most if not all Christians that there can be only one true religion and one true saviour and that naturally theirs is it. Christianity has the Truth, and for someone else to have a nugget of truth seems for them to take away from the fullness of Christianity.

There are some well-known exceptions to such attitudes. Wilfred Cantwell Smith, my esteemed colleague at Dalhousie University where I had the privilege of co-teaching a course with him many years ago, was one such exception. He was the Founding Director of the Center for the Study of World Religions at Harvard University, and before that the Founding Director of the Institute for Islamic Studies at McGill University in Montreal. Many of his ideas had been shaped by his long stay in India. He used to think of himself as a missionary to the West and he was often being singled out by well-meaning Christians for remedial help in discovering the true faith. On one occasion, after he had been much hassled by a strident Christian for the softness of his commitment to Christ, he said to me, "I hope that my Hindu friends are right in thinking that one of these days these Christians will grow up and realize that God is much more than their theology can capture." He continued to be a thorn in their side with his writings. Since Christians have been fond of speaking of the Hindus as idol worshippers who bow down to wood and stone, he undertook to examine the notion of idols. In one of his papers he observed that, "For Christians to think that Christianity is true, or final, or salvific, is a form of idolatry." He concluded:

> With a comparative perspective, one sees that 'idolatry' is not a notion that clarifies other religious practices or other outlooks than one's own;

yet it can indeed clarify with some exactitude one's own religious stance, if one has previously been victim of the misapprehension that the divine is to be fully identified with or within one's own forms. Christians have been wrong in thinking that Hindus are formally idolaters. We would do well, on the other hand, to recognize that we Christians have substantially been idolaters, insofar as we have mistaken for God, or as universally final, the particular forms of Christian life or thought.

Christianity--for some, Christian theology--has been an idol. It has had both the spiritual efficacy of 'idols' in the good sense, and serious limitations of idolatry in the bad sense.[1]

B. I AM the Way: Jesus said, "I AM the Way and the Truth and the Life. No one comes to the Father except through me....Do you not believe that I am in the Father and the Father is in me? I am not myself the source of the words I speak: it is the Father who dwells in me doing His own work. Anything you ask me in my name, I will do" (John 14: 6, 11, 14).

These remarks of Jesus Christ have been the scriptural authority for the Christians to regard him as the exclusive and unique saviour. It is therefore useful to make a few comments about this.

We have an indication here of the power and the majesty of I AM, the sacred name of God. To know the real name of someone or to do something in that person's name means, both in the Old Testament and the New Testament, as it does in many ancient traditions, to be able to participate in the being and to share in the power of that person. This is true even in the present day English usage: if someone speaks in the name of someone else, for example, if the Secretary of State speaks in the name of the President of the United States of America, it is done with the President's authorization and authority, with the backing of the power of the office. When the disciples believed in the name of Christ, it meant that they understood the real nature of Christ and were able to participate in his being and power, and could act on his authority. In the Greek original, the word for 'name' is *onome,* which also has the connotations of power and being. It may also be remarked here, somewhat parenthetically, that for the Jewish philosopher Philo, name was equivalent to *Logos.*

*Moses said to God, "Who am I that I should go to Pharaoh and lead the Israelites out of Egypt?" He answered, "I will be with you; and this shall be your proof that it is I who have sent you: when you bring my people out of Egypt, you will worship God on this very mountain." "But," said Moses to God, "when I go to the Israelites and say to them, 'The God of your fathers*

---

[1] Smith, Wilfred Cantwell, 'Idolatry in Comparative Perspective,' in *The Myth of Christian Uniqueness*, Ed. John Hick and Paul F. Knitter, 553 -68. Maryknoll, NY, Orbis Books. 1987.

*has sent me to you,' if they ask me, 'What is His name?' what am I to tell
them?" God replied, "I AM WHO I AM." Then he added, "This is what you
shall tell the Israelites: I AM sent me to you"* (Exodus 3:11-14).

I AM itself has been declared by God to be his most mysterious and sacred
name; and the real power of this name seems to have been shown and given to
only two great persons in the entire Biblical literature; namely, Moses and
Jesus Christ, to the former only temporarily whereas to the latter permanently
after the descending of the Holy Spirit on him. Since Jesus Christ was one
with the Father, he could speak with the authority and the power of the secret
name of God. Only because of that and certainly not in isolation from God
could he manifest I AM which functions as a proper name of God, with His
power and being in it.[2] It is in this mode that Christ uses I AM, to indicate his
identity with God and his participation in His power and being, and not as an
identification of his own particularity or specialness.

Whenever exalted statements are made by Christ, he reminds the disciples that
he has become so transparent to the Divine Ground that those who have seen
him have seen the Father, for he has nothing of his own, neither the words nor
the works. All he says is what the Father tells him to say, and all he does is
done by the Father living inside him. Furthermore, any of the disciples can do
what Jesus does if they understand him truly and dwell in him.

The important point to be emphasized again and again is that a person can do
nothing of any value in their own name, which is to say based on their own
energy and for their own sake. Jesus Christ himself does nothing in his own
name; he speaks and works only in the name of the Father. In spite of the
mutual indwelling of the Father and the Son and the essential oneness of their
fundamental energy, there is a discernible and proper internal order, so that it
is right to say both "The Father and I are one" (John 10:30) and "The Father is
greater than I" (John 14:28). Similarly, if there is a mutual indwelling of the
Christ and a disciple, they are essentially one, but not without hierarchical
order. More than anything else, it is a matter of the right flow of energies--
from above downwards, or from the inside outward, or, to use a metaphor used
by Christ himself, from the vine to the branches.

*Abide in me, as I abide in you. No more than a branch can bear fruit of itself
apart from the vine, can you bear fruit apart from me. I am the vine, you are
the branches. He who lives in me and I in him will bear abundant fruit, for
apart from me you can do nothing. He who does not live in me is like a
withered, rejected branch picked up to be thrown in the fire and burnt* (John
15:4-6).

---

[2] See Raymond Brown's *The Gospel According to John I-XII*, in the Anchor Bible, vol.29, appendix iv.

But, the disciples do not always understand the subtle teachings of Christ. They are continually looking outward, as if the goal and the way were outside. And Christ has to remind them repeatedly that the Way and the Truth and Eternal Life are within themselves; if they do not find these there at the threshold of I AM, connecting the higher and the lower worlds within themselves, they will not find them anywhere.[3] There is no other way to the Father except I AM, where the Son of Man meets the Son of God, at the very core of the soul in each person, for "the Kingdom of God is within you" (Luke 17:21).

C.  Uniqueness and Oneness: From a Hindu point of view there is no difficulty with the uniqueness of Jesus Christ. However, this uniqueness is embedded in an underlying oneness, for ultimately there is only the One. *Ekam evadvityam* (one only, without a second), says Chandogya Upanishad 6:2,1. Over a period of at least four thousand years – as reckoned by Western scientific chronology – the sages in India have repeatedly said that there is an underlying unity of all that exists, including everything we call animate or inanimate, and that the cultivation of wisdom consists in the realization of this truth. The expressions of this fundamental insight vary in time, but the insight itself is said by the sages to be a part of Eternal Order (*Sanatana Dharma*). It is not only coexistent with the cosmos but it provides its stable foundation.

The unitary insight of the sages is not a matter of universalizing or generalizing from particulars by reasoning, inference, deduction or induction. It is primarily a matter of perception – an actual vision. It is an insight based on direct perception, not a conjecture or an abstraction subject to refutation or confirmation. This perception is possible only when the doors of perception are cleansed of all fear and fantasy. The cleansing of perceptions is not the same as a quantitative extension of the perceptions by scientific instruments. As William Blake simply remarked, the world that a sage sees is not the world which an ordinary person sees. It requires the sacrifice of the individualistic clinging to a separation from the All. The sacrifice of the separate ego is the *sine qua non* of this perception.

Apart from the selflessness (and the accompanying absence of pride) and the natural feelings of compassion and love, which are characteristic of all the sages, there is one feature which needs to be underscored, and which is rarely remarked upon. A sage simultaneously sees the *oneness* of all there is and the *uniqueness* of everything. One cannot be unmindful of the seeming paradox implied here. However, we are speaking about the experience of the sages and

---

[3] For some discussion of I AM please see chapter 6 and 11 of R. Ravindra: *The Yoga of the Christ*, Element Books, Shaftesbury, England, 1990. (This book has been reprinted under the title *Christ the Yogi* by Inner Traditions International, Rochester, Vermont, in 1998 and as *The Gospel of John in the Light of Indian Mysticism* in 2004. The revised edition has been published under the original title *The Yoga of the Christ* by Theosophical Publishing House, Adyar, Chennai, India in 2005.)

not about the limitations of our ordinary minds. It is a fact of their existence and behaviour that, in relationship with others, the sages are aware that each human being is a manifestation of One Divine Energy, but that at the same time each person presents a unique potential (and corresponding particular difficulties) and is a wondrously unique expression of the Vastness. Each person is related with the oneness, but no person is replaceable by another. The One is unique in each manifestation. Everyone is seen by the sage as both one with the Source as well as uniquely oneself.

The perception of a sage is holistic in the sense that what is seen is seen both in its oneness with all there is and in its uniqueness. Quite often the thorough-going Vedantists are so dedicated to the idea of oneness that they ignore the uniqueness of the individual which to them seems like a mark of ignorance. Uniqueness is there – even Krishna could not replace a single child – but it is seen as embedded in the whole. It is a quality of this mysterious oneness that it expresses itself in endless unique forms. The same Divine Energy is manifested in myriad forms and at different levels of consciousness and being, much as the same light from the Sun is reflected uniquely by each leaf and each drop of water, forming quite wondrous and varied patterns.

The Hindus do not object to the uniqueness of Jesus Christ but only to an exclusive claim that denies the sacred uniqueness of all other manifestations of Divine Energy, small or great. As the Brihadaranyaka Upanishad (V,1) says,

> That is Fullness, this is Fullness, from Fullness comes Fullness.
> When Fullness is taken from Fullness, what remains is Fullness.

D. The Lamb Slain from the Foundation of the World: The Christian notion that Jesus Christ sacrificed himself in order to take away the sins of humanity is of fundamental importance. This needs to be understood in its cosmological sense in which sacrifice is continually needed in order to maintain the cosmos. The preservation and maintenance of *rita* (cosmological order) depends on the proper relation between earth and Heaven. This proper relation is based entirely on *yajña* (sacrifice) by which alone an act or the whole life can be made sacred. To sacrifice (derived from the Latin *sacer* + *facere*) is to make sacred. It is by *yajña* that one participates in the right order. *Yajña* is the 'abode of *rita*,' 'the home of *rita*,' 'the dwelling of *rita*,' or 'the path of *rita*' (Rig Veda I, 43,9; I, 84,4; III, 55,14). *Yajña* becomes the cause, the origin and the beginning of all righteous acts and it prescribes obligations of the world (Rig Veda I, 164,50; X, 90,16).

*Yajña* is the very navel of the universe (Rig Veda I, 164,35). *Yajña* is the central thread binding together human souls with the souls of the gods for everywhere and in everything "the all pervading Brahman is ever established in *yajña*" (Bhagavad Gita 3:15). The creation is sustained through *yajña*.

The *Yoga Sutra* continues the Vedic sacrifice (*yajña*) by the sacrifice of the limited and limiting mind (*citta*) for the sake of *Purusha* who is the only true seer. This *Purusha* is not personally yours or mine; it is the pure power of seeing. One sacrifices the limitation for the unlimited power to see, a sacrifice of one's separated self – with all of one's fears and hopes, likes and dislikes, sorrows and pleasures, failures and ambitions – for the sake of the Only One who truly sees. Then follows the sacrifice of the seen for the sake of the Only One who truly is. Then there is no separate object but the *Purusha,* there is no separated subject but *Purusha,* there is no knowing except *Purusha.* The seer, the seen and seeing are all One; there is no other. This is the state of *kaivalya* – of aloneness, not because there is an opposition or a separation but simply because there is no 'other.' As Ramana Maharishi said simply, "There are no others."

Thus sacrifice permits Order. *Yajña,* born of *Rita,* is the ground for the re-establishment of *rita.* As Shatapatha Brahmana (I.3.4.16) says, '*Yajña* is the womb of *rita.*' In the *utsava* (festival) of life, all of *sadhana* (practice, effort) is *yajña.* In the movement from *asmita* ('I am this' or 'I am that') to *Soham* (I AM), from a limited self to the Self, from the identification with *citta* to that with *Purusha*, from the self-will of Arjuna to his willingness to carry out Krishna's will, one places oneself in the right internal order. The resulting insight (see *Yoga Sutra* 1:48-49; 2:15; 3:54) is naturally full of truth and order.[4]

Christ said, "When I speak, I speak just as the Father told me" (John 12:50). As far as he is concerned, the right preparation for sacred action (*yajña karma*) consists in dying to one's self-will, and in denying oneself, so that one could obey the will of God. His *yoga* consists of this; and of this the cross is the supreme symbol. Whether or not it corresponds to the actual method of killing Jesus, the enormous psychological and spiritual significance of the cross cannot be exaggerated. Every moment, whenever one is present to it, one is at a crossing; at this point of crossing one chooses whether to remain in the horizontal plane of the world or to be yoked to the way of the Christ and follow the vertical axis of being.

The way of the cross consists in surrendering oneself completely to the will of God, and emptying oneself of one's self-importance. Jesus Christ himself set an example of this. He became so transparent to the Ground of Being that anyone who truly saw him saw God. He had nothing of his own; he did not speak in his own name, or on his own authority. To use an analogy given in the *Yoga Sutras,* the mind and being of those who are truly liberated are like a

---

[4] In this connection please see '*Rita* Is Founded on *Yajña*' in R. Ravindra: *Yoga and the Teaching of Krishna*, Theosophical Publishing House, Adyar, Chennai, India, 1998.

perfectly polished clear diamond, without any blemish at all, so that the glory of God can be reflected as it is. The words and actions of the Father are transmitted then without any distortions introduced by the personal ego. Since his words are not his own, to hear him is to hear God.

It is important to remember that Jesus was a crucifer before his arrest and trial, which eventually led to his death by crucifixion. The way of Christ is that of the cross. As he repeatedly told his disciples (see Matthew 10:38, 16:24; Mark 8:34; Luke 9:23, 14:27), no person is worthy and capable of being his disciple unless he takes up his own cross--not only as an idea but as a daily practice-- and follows him. In the language of symbols, the only one appropriate to these realities, a fact not lost to the early Christians, crucifixion is the only just manner of death of the Crucifer. Naturally, he who is "the Light of the world" (John 8:12) must be born on the darkest day of the year, just as "the Lamb slain from the foundation of the world" (Revelation 13:8) should have been killed on the day appointed for sacrificing the paschal lamb. The actual historical facts follow from the mythic and symbolic necessity and truth of the Incarnation and the Crucifixion.

The way of the cross, like all authentic spiritual paths, demands human sacrifice. When one is emptied of one's own self, one can be filled with God and become one with the Source. In the way of the cross, there is no place for egoistic ambitions and projects or personal salvation based on a wish for some cheap grace in which Christ has made all the sacrifice and we can go on sinning. "Not everyone who calls me 'Lord, Lord' will enter the kingdom of Heaven, but only those who do the will of my heavenly Father" (Matthew 7:21).

 PPENDIX 4

### RESPONSES FROM K R SUNDARARAJAN

Professor K R Sundararajan kindly agreed to answer some questions related to the theme of this book. Extracts are included in chapter 7 but the full text is given here. The questions were:

1.  Do you think there is currently any serious dialogue or exchanges between Hindus and Christians about Christ or are most well known Hindu positions responses to colonialism / Christian mission in India / Hindu mission in the west etc and now out-dated or increasingly irrelevant?
2.  If there is meaningful contemporary encounter on this theme, what would you say is the primary Hindu incentive / focus / understanding?
3.  Does Hindu embrace of Christ as an avatar have any real significance for Christians?
4.  Does an avatar Christ really have any significance for Hindus?
5.  What for you would be the most important insight / message Hindu spirituality can offer / share with others at this time?

These are his responses.

GENERAL COMMENT

"It is true to say that the phase known as 'Modern Hinduism,' beginning from the Brahmo Samaj movement and continuing to the time of Gandhi, is a response to the impact of the West, including Christianity, positively and negatively. There was also a scholarly interest in finding a place for Christ within the framework of Hinduism and the concept of incarnation (*avatara*) is the broad rubric under which Christ was appropriated. But Christ represented a challenge with regard to questions of suffering, death, and resurrection. Can the incarnations suffer? Probably the story of Rama displays instances of suffering and, of course, all human incarnations 'die.' But theologically speaking, the divine incarnations cannot suffer and die. So a sort of 'docetist' understanding of Hindu *avataras* and Christ came to be stressed. But Vivekananda and Radhakrishnan represent a different phase of Modern Hinduism, when Hinduism in its 'essential and true form' was sought to be 'exported' to the West, a phase which is called 'counter attack from the East.' That phase continues with 'free-lance' swamis and gurus and their disciples, Indian and

Western, running ashrams in the West and serving the spiritual needs of primarily Western disciples."

RESPONSES TO YOUR QUESTIONS

"In contemporary India, missionary work is suspect. Various Christian de-nominations train priests and ministers so that they might serve the Christian community. Therefore, the focus of their mission is rather internal. This is also the primary intent of Hindu missions in the West, though both of them are 'open' to converts. I believe that Christ is not the primary subject of con-versation in inter-religious dialogues that take place in the West. The interest seems to be 'conceptual' and thematic. In all these cases, the Hindu scholars often rely very heavily on the source materials in their presentations. The 'revered' persons of early times such as Radhakrishnan and Vivekananda are not referred to frequently.

I believe that the main thrust of contemporary Hinduism is to understand itself, rather than to dialogue with other faith communities. From the Ph.D. disser-tations I get for evaluation, I see the focus as being on the exploration of the richness of the tradition, Brahmanical as well as regional. The fact that the universities in India now allow Ph.D. dissertations to be written in regional languages, instead of English as it used to be, often encourages the exploration of regional religious and cultural resources. The exploration of Western philo-sophical thought, however, is still very much with many Indian scholars.

It is interesting to see that these days traditional scholars who are experts in Sanskrit or a regional language play a prominent role in conferences, national and international. It is now stressed that the language skills are essential in order to claim expertise in a field, as it is assumed that translations into English are inadequate. There is a feeling that the Western scholarship of Hinduism is somewhat flawed. In the present mind-set of the Hindus, the tradition has everything one needs and there is nothing to learn from 'others.' I personally feel that the sound basis for inter-religious dialogue goes beyond mere curiosity, and should be motivated by what I would describe as 'the existential need' to learn from others and be conceptually broadened and spiritually benefited.

I believe that an inter-religious dialogue should be marked by a two-fold process of 'appropriation' and 'appreciation.' In the process of appropriation, a Hindu attempts, for instance, to appropriate Christ in categories that are indigenous to the Hindu tradition and therefore, could consider him as an avatar. To the question of whether this 'embrace of Christ as an avatar' has any real significance for Christians, my response is to say that I am not sure. One might suggest that the Hindu tolerance of Christians historically probably reflect this kind of understanding. Finally, the Hindu tolerance could be accounted for by the very fact that the tradition stresses that there are several ways of finding God and being united with Him. Yet what was considered by the Hindus as 'conversion by force' or 'economic incentives' has resulted in opposition to Christian missionary work in India.

'Does an avatar Christ really have any significance for Hindus?' is an interesting question. At the philosophical and religious level, as I have indicated in the beginning, it raised questions regarding the possibility of a 'suffering God.' The notion of God as loving, as one who steps out of his transcendent state to embrace the devotee out of love, is a common theme in the theistic traditions of India. At the level of popular piety, one may find themes of suffering in the story of Rama, and in the puranic episode of Siva drinking the poison when the ocean was churned by both the devas and asuras and became the blue-throated Siva (Nilakanta). Again at the level of popular piety, Hindus pray and worship in places considered to have spiritual powers of healing. Here, I may mention a Church in Velanganni in Southern India, where Hindus and Muslims pray and worship Mary, the Mother of Jesus. I believe that the Hindu tradition with its stress on diverse ways of experiencing God, makes it possible for a Hindu to attend Church services, if necessary, without serious discomfort."

WHAT IS HINDU SPIRITUALITY? "On the question of major insight of Hindu spirituality that could be shared with others, I am attaching a copy of my paper presented at the 2004 World Parliament of Religions."

"In his introduction to the volume on Hindu Spirituality, the editor, Dr. Sivaraman defines the Hindu spiritual journey as a process of 'turning round,' 'turning from what serves one's temporal ends toward growing insight into both reality and the resulting fullness of life which is variously called life eternal or life divine or more simply life of the spirit.' Such a life of spirit, according to Dr. Sivaraman, could be described as a life of 'worldlessness.' Worldlessness is not a 'life- and- world negation' but a disposition to live in the world differently from worldliness where one's world is generated and reared by one's ego where one is locked in the cave of isolated existence plunging into greater and greater spiritual darkness. Such an 'ego oriented life' has to be renounced. One's life is to be 'spirit-charged' instead of being 'ego-charged.' According to Dr. Sivaraman, 'The story of the spiritual wisdom of India is the story of concerted effort to contain the power and pretension of the egoistic or self-asserting will and this is accomplished by a discipline of mind and reason, through heart and love and through will and power.'

In the Hindu tradition, the spiritual core that lies deepest in the person and from where a person remains open to the transcendent dimension is *atman,* the true self. It is the experiencing of *atman* that enables one to be truly *situated* and *centered.* Such experiencing includes understanding its true relationship with *brahman,* the Supreme, the unconditional and the ultimate source of all existence on the one hand, and understanding the existential human conditions marked by *samsara* and *karma* on the other. One is not necessarily motivated to renounce the world after having experienced *atman* in the above manner, but is often inspired to live in the world in the spirit of 'worldlessness' as described by Sivaraman. Perhaps this is indeed the implication of the Vedantic notion of *jivanmukta* as stated in the Advaita of Sankara.

What I would describe as '*lila* spirituality,' developed in the theistic Vedanta of Ramanuja and in post-Ramanuja Sri Vaishnava schools of Southern India, supports this type of 'positive' approach to the world, as the goal of human life here is to participate with 'playful spirit' in the divinely created world thus adding a sense of joy to the 'worldlessness' described by Sivaraman. From a Vaishnava perspective, creation is divine play (*lila*) expressing spontaneity and joy as, in some sense, it is not required and in itself has no purpose; the true role of humans is to be participants in the divine play, sharing the same sense of freedom and joy as the 'creator.'

The very fact that the basic spiritual orientation of Hinduism is not necessarily towards world and life renunciation, but rather towards living one's life free of limitations of 'ego-centered life,' in my view, opens Hinduism to meaningful dialogues with other spiritual traditions. Perhaps this is one of the directions of 'world spirituality into the future.' I am not saying that inter-religious dialogues are not taking place. But I am sure that not much of a meaningful and serious dialogue has taken place between the Hindu and Chinese spiritual traditions. This lack of active interaction has not only characterized the past, but it is also true at the present time. No serious effort for the Hindu scholars to 'Journey East' or of Chinese scholars to 'travel West,' in a real or metaphorical sense, has thus far taken place at the level of scholarship. However this was not the case with regard to Buddhism. Buddhism entered China in the early Christian centuries, and since then a few Chinese pilgrims even visited India to gain a deeper understanding of Buddhism. Perhaps this should be one of the directions of 'spiritualities into the future.' To claim some sort of credit for myself in this 'futuristic context,' recently, I have begun to focus my interest in the study of Chinese spiritual traditions, especially the Confucian and the Daoist, and engage in comparative studies with my own academic training in Hinduism and grounding in the Vedanta of Ramanuja and Post-Ramanuja Sri Vaishnavism. These comparative studies, mostly in the realms of ideas and concepts, have in some way enabled me to gain a deeper understanding of the richness of the Hindu tradition and a greater appreciation of Chinese spiritual traditions. I am increasingly finding common grounds between the Hindu and the Confucian and Daoist spiritual traditions. I am convinced that one can undertake a serious study of a spiritual tradition even without the necessary textual and linguistic skills of a scholar working within that tradition. The enormous amount of literature and scholarly works that are currently available in each of the major religious traditions make such academic ventures possible. On the basis of the availability of sources in translations, I am suggesting that a fruitful and academically rewarding study of a tradition other than one's own is possible in the realm of ideas and concepts. Now no one needs to remain strictly an 'outsider,' I feel, as the insider's understanding is not totally outside of the reach of a serious seeker. However, this 'journey' to the 'inside' should be done with a great caution, recognizing the fact that there is a rich variety within the tradition itself in regards to the formulation and interpretation of texts and concepts.

On the question of World Spirituality into the future, I now like to consider the question whether Hindu spirituality could provide some insight into how to live our lives now and in the future. In fact all religions deal with this question how best to live given the 'realities' of human life and its predicaments. The Hindu answer or insight in terms of 'good life' would combine 'worldlessness' and 'play' (*lila*). The Worldlessness points to a life free of the constraints of ego-centered consciousness where the moral value of action is judged by the attitude which one performs any action rather than the action itself (*nishkama karma*). The notion of play (*lila*) interestingly adds a component of 'serious-ness' to such a life, since to participate in play requires that one should play to one's best. Hence *lila*, play, complements worldlessness; as life freed of the constrains of ego-centered consciousness becomes a source of joy as it makes it possible for one to give full expression to one's innate potential.

I want to stress here that Hindu spirituality, in common with Indian spirit-uality, is oriented towards serving the community, and this described as a process of 'returning' by Sivaraman. Thus the realization of one's innate potential includes an 'outward,' 'communal' direction. The great Hindu sages, regarded as model persons since early times, have sought to serve the needs of the larger community as teachers, spiritual guides and counselors. Such 'engaged persons' are seen in the Upanishads and the epics, and in the monastic centers (*maths*) established by Sankara in the 8th century A.D. The modern instance of 'engaged renunciants' are members of the Ramakrishna Order, though most of the religious establishments in our times could fit into this category as all of them have institutionalized activities that serve the community at large.

How would I relate the spiritual heritage of Hinduism to some of the issues that have become important in the contemporary world, issues which were non-issues or not important in the traditional society? I need to look into the religious resources of the Hindu tradition in order to find material that might provide meaningful responses to issues of modernity. The enormous diversity within the Hindu tradition, and its richness in terms of materials, scriptural or otherwise, are indeed great assets as I proceed with this investigation. In the past I have found materials that relate to issues such as 'global community,' 'the Global Village,' and 'human rights,' and I have written papers on these themes from the perspective of the Hindu tradition. For me the living quality of a religious and spiritual tradition lies in its open-endedness and in its capacity to respond to new situations and be meaningful even in a changing world. It is interesting to see that in the task of exploring the previously un-familiar areas in a tradition, one's understanding of the tradition also achieves depth and broadening.

However, often times the richness of a tradition also creates a situation where one could end up finding several equally valid and meaningful answers for a single issue; and in that case the researcher is required to make a case for the most appropriate answer or look for foundational principles that could unify the variety of responses. There is some kind of 'tentativeness' in situations like this, and one has to be fully aware that the responses he or she chooses to highlight are not final and definitive in nature. One could at best consider them as probable directions that the spiritual tradition could take in order to respond to the situation. Thus it carries with it an element of subjectivity as the choices are shaped by the researcher's own training and preferences. Assuming these limitations, let me take the theme of war and peace where the Hindu spiritual tradition has a message to humankind present and future.

How might Hindu spirituality address the issue of war and peace? In the first instance, this issue is not simply a contemporary issue; it is an issue which has also confronted traditional societies. At a broader level, the issue is an issue of violence and non-violence; under what conditions is violence justifiable? I believe that the moral precept of non-violence as not causing injury to any living being is part of Indian spirituality itself. This moral precept has become close to a categorical imperative in the Buddhist and Jaina traditions. In the Hindu tradition, however, its enforcement had remained 'selective,' possibly because violence of some sort is intrinsic to the human situation. To address the issue of war, we could look to the Hindu epics, the *Mahabharata* and the *Ramayana*. We could read the message of both *Mahabharata* and *Ramayana* on this issue as saying that war becomes unavoidable in certain situations, but it should be the last resort when all negotiations to defuse the conflict have failed. In the *Mahabharata*, Krishna is on a peace mission, negotiating for a peaceful resolution of the conflict between the Kauravas and Pandavas. In the Ramayana story, Rama would not have resorted to the declaration of war if Ravana had agreed to return Sita. There are several incidences in the story when Ravana has been urged to do this to avoid the conflict. In both stories war is the last resort when negotiations for conflict resolutions had failed. In addition, the moral of the epic, *Mahabharata*, can be read as saying that ultimately war is futile. In a war there is no final victory and there are no real winners. Winners lose and if we could take the final episode in the *Mahabharata* seriously, when all the Kaurava brothers remain in Heaven while Yuddhistra, the most noble one of the Panadava brothers, sees his own brothers suffering in hell, one could say also that losers win thus reinforcing our earlier statement that there are no real winners or losers in war. Hence the messages we could read here are very apt and meaningful to our times when questions of war and peace have become important issues."

# APPENDIX 5

## HINDU-CHRISTIAN POINT-COUNTERPOINT
From the Himalayan Academy
Founded in 1949 by Satguru Sivaya Subramuniyaswami

HINDUISM:

1) Hindus believe in one, all-pervasive Supreme Being who is both immanent and transcendent, both Creator and Unmanifest Reality.

2) Hindus believe in the divinity of the four Vedas, the world's most ancient scripture, and venerate the Agamas as equally revealed. These primordial hymns are God's word and the bedrock of Sanatana Dharma, the eternal religion.

3) Hindus believe that the universe undergoes endless cycles of creation, preservation and dissolution.

4) Hindus believe in karma, the law of cause and effect by which each individual creates his own destiny by his thoughts, words and deeds.

5) Hindus believe that the soul reincarnates, evolving through many births until all karmas have been resolved, and moksha, liberation from the cycle of rebirth, is attained. Not a single soul will be eternally deprived of this destiny.

6) Hindus believe that divine beings exist in unseen worlds and that temple worship, rituals, sacraments and personal devotionals create a communion with these devas and Gods.

7) Hindus believe that an enlightened master, or satguru, is essential to know the Transcendent Absolute, as are personal discipline, good conduct, purification, pilgrimage, self –inquiry, meditation and surrender in God.

8) Hindus believe that all life is sacred, to be loved and revered, and therefore practice ahimsa, non-injury, in thought, word and deed.

9) Hindus believe that no religion teaches the only way to salvation above all others, but that all genuine paths are facets of God's Light, deserving tolerance and understanding.

CHRISTIANITY:

1) Christians believe that the bible is the uniquely inspired and fully trust-worthy word of God. It is the final authority for Christians in matters of belief and practice, and though it was written long ago, it continues to speak to believers today.

2) Christians believe in one God in three persons. He is distinct from his creation, yet intimately involved with it as its sustainer and redeemer.

3) Christians believe that the world was created once by the divine will, was corrupted by sin, yet under God's providence moves toward final perfection.

4) Christians believe that, through God's grace and favor, lost sinners are rescued from the guilt, power and eternal consequences of their evil thoughts, words and deeds.

5) Christians believe that it is appointed for human beings to die once and after that face judgment. In Adam's sin, the human race was spiritually alienated from God, and that those who are called by God and respond to his grace will have eternal life. Those who persist in rebellion will be lost eternally.

6) Christians believe that spirit beings inhabit the universe, some good and some evil, but worship is due to God alone.

7) Christians believe that God has given us a clear revelation of Himself in Jesus and the sacred Scriptures. He has empowered by his Spirit prophets, apostles, evangelists, and pastors who are teachers charged to guide us into faith and holiness in accordance with his Word.

8) Christians believe that life is to be highly esteemed but that it must be subordinated in the service of Biblical love and justice.

9) Christians believe that Jesus is God incarnate and, therefore, the only sure path to salvation. Many religions may offer ethical and spiritual insights, but only Jesus is the Way, the Truth and the Life.

*http://www.himalayanacademy.com/basics/point/index.html*

# GLOSSARY

ABRAHAMIC RELIGIONS: Judaism, Islam and Christianity; sharing common root / link to the patriarch Abraham

ACHARYA: Teacher, preceptor, spiritual guide

ADVAITA VEDANTA: Philosophy of Non-Dualism, from Upanishads

AHIMSA: Non-violence; harmlessness to any being

ANUBHAVA: Personal experiences, impressions, understandings of reality

ANUGRAHA: Grace

ARATI / ARTI: Act of worship celebrating light; ritual of waving light from lamp before deity, then offering light to all present

ARJUNA: One of the 5 Pandava brothers, heroes in *The Mahabharata*; Krishna's dialogue partner in the Bhagavad Gita

ASHRAM: Spiritual community

ASURA: Evil, demonic being from lower planes of existence

ATMAN: Self (not self); our true reality

ATONEMENT: In Christianity, Christ's saving act upon the cross, taking human sins upon himself

AUM OR OM: Eternal sound / vibration, symbol of God; Logos; sound of God in creation

AVATAR: Divine incarnation come to earth with a special message for humanity

AVIDYA: Ignorance; what keeps us from knowing our true Self

BHAGAVAD GITA: 'Song of the Lord'; Holy scripture of Hinduism, part of the *Mahabharata* epic

BHAGAVAN: Name for the Lord, often Krishna; God

BHAVASAMADHI: Ecstatic bliss, union with God

BHAKTI / BHAKTA YOGI: Devotion / one who loves God

BRAHMA: God as creator; first of the Hindu Trinity: Brahma, Vishnu, Shiva

BRAHMACHARYA: Student, disciple, on the spiritual path, often celibate

BRAHMAN: The Real as itself, One without a second, totally non-dual

BRAHMINS: Priestly branch of the Hindu caste system

CHAITANYA: Great Vaishnava devotee of Lord Krishna, 1486-1533 CE

CHRISTOLOGY: Study of the nature, person and meaning of Christ

DARSHAN: Blessing received through being in the presence of holy person; realization of the ultimate truth

DAYA: Compassion

DHARMA: Righteousness, the Way, our specific duties

DIASPORA: Hindu communities around the world, outside of India

DIVALI: Festival of Light; often associated with Goddess Lakshmi at beginning of New Year (October / November, lunar calendar)

DIVINE MOTHER: God in the feminine form

DOCETISM: Belief that Christ's body was ethereal and not really, fully human; considered a heresy by the Christian Church

DWAITA: Duality

EKAM EVADVITYAM: There is only One

ESCHATOLOGY: Study of last days / final matters: death, judgment, afterlife

EXCLUSIVISM: In Christianity, belief that there is no salvation outside the Church

EXEGESIS: Critical study of texts, especially Biblical

GURU: Spiritual guide, much more than an ordinary teacher; one who dispels darkness

INCLUSIVISM: In Christianity, belief that all are anonymously saved by Christ's grace

INCULTURATION: Bringing someone / something into your own world-view, cultural mind-set

ISHTADEVATA: The form of God with which a person has a special relationship

JAGAD GURU: World teacher, spiritual preceptor

JANMASHTAMI: Commemoration of Lord Krishna's birth

JI: Sign of respect, added to name or title eg. Babaji, Swamiji

JIVA: Life, in individual sense

JNANA / JNANA YOGI: Wisdom, discrimination / one who knows Self through discriminative path

KAIROS: Pivotal moment when everything is ripe for new possibilities and change

KALAS: Special characteristics

KALI: Mother God, the 'black one, sometimes considered as 'fierce' goddess

KALKI AVATAR: Tenth incarnation of Vishnu, the avatar still to come at end of Kali Yuga, riding a white horse; avatar of a new age of spiritual renewal

KARANA JANMAS: Masters born with a purpose

KARMA: Actions, the result of personal actions; cause and effect

KAIVALYA: Oneness, unconditioned Aloneness

KENDRA: School, place of knowledge and understanding

KIRTAN: Chanting of God's name, especially in groups

KRISHNA: Name for God, incarnation of God

KRIYA YOGA: Special form of meditation; 'Union through a certain action or rite'

KSHAMA: Forgiveness

LILA: Divine play; life and creation understood as God's play

LOGOS / LOGOS CHRISTOLOGY: Word of God from John's Gospel; Christ understood as Logos with implication that 'Christ' could include more than historical Jesus

MADHAVA: Wandering Vaishnava, 12<sup>th</sup> century; founder of Dvaita Vedanta
MAHASAMADHI: 'Great' Samadhi; Yogi's final conscious exit from body; passing away
MANTRA: Special incantation for spiritual development, often given at initiations
MATH: Ascetic or monastic community
MAYA: Cosmic illusion, delusion, false appearance of reality
MENDICANT: Wandering monk
MOKSHA: Spiritual liberation, freedom from rebirth
NAGARJUNA: Critic of Vedas who became Buddhist philosopher of Sunyata ('emptiness')
NAMASTE: Hindu greeting, the God in me bows to the God in you
NEO-HINDUISM: Western view that Hindu reform movements influenced by external sources, particularly European
NIRBIKALPA SAMADHI: Complete union with God, beyond duality; highest spiritual state
ONTOLOGY: Study of the nature of divine incarnation
OUSIA, FOUSIA, HYPOSTASES: Aspects, components, of incarnations. Used in Christian theology to describe the nature of Christ as both fully human and fully divine
PARAMAHANSA: Supreme swan; Hindu spiritual Master
PARAMATMAN: Supreme Self
PARMARTHA: Supreme state of being, unity of being
PROSELYTIZATION: Mission, conversion, evangelism
PUJA: Worship rituals; ritual worship
PURANAS: Ancient Hindu stories and myths relating to religion and culture
PURNAVATAR: Full incarnate manifestation of God
PURUSHA-SHUKTA: Person, spirit, representing higher principles; individuals emanating from Cosmic Person
RAJA / RAJA YOGA: King / king of yogas, incorporating all others
RAMA: Divine incarnation; 7<sup>th</sup> incarnation of Vishnu; hero of *Ramayana* epic
RAMANUJA: Founder of Visisht Advaita philosophy of qualified non-dualism, 11-12<sup>th</sup> century CE
RASHTRA: State, nation
RAVIDAS: Hindu poet, 15<sup>th</sup> century CE
RELIGIOUS PLURALISM: Religious co-existence in place where many religious traditions are practiced; view that all religions are equal or worthy of respect; acknowledgement of religious diversity that can lead to inter-religious cooperation and understanding
RISHI: Sage, seer, wise person
RITA: Cosmological order
SABIKALPA SAMADHI: Spiritual ecstasy, in trance form
SADHAKA: Spiritual adept
SADHANA: Spiritual practices

SADHU: Hindu renunciant, holy person in search of God
SAKTAVESA-AVATAR: Person empowered to do God's will; God's missionary on earth
SAKTI: Power, energy; Siva's active energy permeating all existence
SAMADHI: State of bliss, ecstasy, wrapped in God
SAMADHANA: Reconciliation, mental balance
SAMANVAYA: Harmony of many visions, understanding
SAMKHYA: Dualistic philosophy, from Vedas
SAMPRADAYA: Particular sect, denomination, group; spiritual transmission
SANATAN DHARMA: Eternal Religion or Truth; Indian name for Hindu traditions
SANGHA: Community, often monastic
SANNYASIN: Hindu renunciant
SARVODAYA SAMBHAVA: Reverence for all religions
SAT, TAT, AUM: Truth, Absolute, Bliss. For some Hindus, equivalent to real understanding of Christian 'Father, Son, Holy Ghost'
SATCITANANDA: Knowledge-consciousness-bliss; Brahman; Absolute Reality
SATGURU: Spiritual preceptor of highest attainment
SATSANGA: Debate, discourse, questions and answers with spiritual teacher
SATYA: Truth
SATYAGRAHA/I: Philosophy of non-violence / one who practices non-violence; especially used by Gandhi
SATTWA: Purity, state of pure awareness, light; one of the three *gunas* or qualities, constituent principles of *prakriti* or primal nature. The other two are *rajas* or passion, energy, and *tamas* or inertia, darkness
SELF-REALIZATION: Realization of our reality, knowledge of the true Self
SEVA: Service
SHANKARA: Eminent Advaita Vedanta philosopher and monk, 788-820 CE
SHANKARACHARYA: Title given to four primary monastic religious authorities of Shankara's Advaita tradition in India
SHANTI: Peace
SHUDDI: Purification, cleansing
SIDDHIS: Yogic powers
SIVA: Supreme Being of the Saivite religion; 3$^{rd}$ person of the Hindu Trinity, destroyer of the universes
SOTERIOLOGY: In Christianity, study / doctrines of salvation
SRIMAD BHAGAVATUM: One of the Puranas; story of Lord Krishna
SRUTI: Directly heard truth, usually referring to the Vedas
SWAMI: One who renounces 'self'; a monastic religious and spiritual teacher
SWARAJ: Self-rule. Used by Gandhi for his independence movement
TATHAGATA: Enlightened being; one of titles for Buddha
TAT TVAM ASI: Thou art That; we are the undifferentiated Self
TATTVAS: Essential nature; building blocks of the universe

TRANSMIGRATION: Re-incarnation; cycle of rebirth
UNIVERSALIST: Embracing all, fit for all
UPANISHADS: Final part of Vedas; profound Hindu reflections on God, Self and the Cosmos
VAISHNAVA: Devotional tradition / devotee recognizing Krishna as the Ultimate Godhead
VEDAS: Ancient, authoritative texts for Hindus; Wisdom, 'that which is heard'
VEDANTA: Wisdom encapsulated in the Upanishads
VICARIOUS: Living, experiencing or imagining through another person's life; in Christianity, Jesus' sacrifice on cross saving others from effects of sin
VISHIST ADVAITA: Qualified non-dual philosophy as taught by Ramanuja
VISHNU: God; second Person in Hindu Trinity; Sustainer of the universes
VYAVAHARA: Worldly activity
YAJNA: Sacrifice
YOGA: Union; practices to bring human and divine consciousness into union
YOGI: One who practices yoga in one or more of its forms
YUGAS: Ages, aeons; four great passages of ascending and descending time with specific qualities and possibilities

*From ancient times the lotus, the national flower of India, has been a divine symbol for Hindus. Serenely beautiful yet arising from the mud it symbolizes our own spiritual possibilities.*

# BIBLIOGRAPHY

References to relevant books and journals
*Many books have multiple reprints*

ABHEDANANDA, Swami: *Complete Works of Swami Abhedananda*:
Ramakrishna Vedanta Centre: Calcutta: 1969.

ABISHIKTANANDA, Swami: *Hindu-Christian Meeting Point*: ISPCK:
Delhi: 1976.

ADAM, William: *A Lecture on the Life and Labours of Rammohun Roy*:
Sadharan Brahmo Samaj: Calcutta: 1879.

AKHILANANDA, Swami: *Hindu View of Christ*: Philosophical Library Inc:
New York: 1949.

ALEAZ, K P: *Harmony of Religions: The Relevance of Swami Vivekananda*:
Punthi-Pustak: Calcutta: 1993.

ARAI, Tosh, and ARIARAJAH, W: *Spirituality in Interfaith Dialogue*: World
Council of Churches: Geneva: 1989.

ARIARAJAH, W: *Hindus and Christians*: Eerdmans: USA: 1991.

ASESHANANDA, Swami: *Glimpses of a Great Soul: A Portrait of Swami
Saradananda*: Vedanta Press: Los Angeles: 1982.

*BACK TO GODHEAD*: Journal: 6 issues annually: Bhaktivedanta Book Trust:
USA.

BADRINATH, Chaturvedi: *Dharma, India and the World Order*: Saint
Andrew Press: Edinburgh: 1993.

BALU, Shakuntala: *Living Divinity*: Sawbridge: London: 1981.

BESS, Savitri L: *The Path of the Mother*: Ballantine Wellspring: USA: 2000.

BHAKTIPADA, Swami Kirtananda: *Christ and Krishna: The Path of Pure
Devotion*: Palace Publishing: Moundsville: 1987.

BRAYBROOKE, Marcus: *Together to the Truth*: CLS-ISPCK: Madras: 1971.

BRAYBROOKE, Marcus: *What We Can Learn from Hinduism*: O Books:
Hampshire: 2002.

BROWN, Judith: *Men and Gods in a Changing World*: SCM: London: 1980.

BRUCK, M Von: *The Unity of Reality*: Paulist Press: New York: 1991.

BURKE, Marie Louise: *Swami Vivekananda in America*: Advaita Ashrama: Calcutta: 1958.

BURKE, Marie Louise: *Swami Vivekananda: His Second Visit to the West: New Discoveries*: Advaita Ashrama: Calcutta: 1982.

CHATTERJEE, Abhas: *The Concept of Hindu Nation*: Voice of India: Delhi: 1995.

CHATTERJEE, Ramananda: *Rammohun Roy and Modern India*: Sadharan Brahmo Samaj: Calcutta: 1972.

CHATTERJI, Sati Kumar: *Behold The Man*: Navavidhan Trust: Calcutta: 1977.

CHATTERJI, Sati Kumar: *The Bharat Ashram*: Navavidhan Trust: Calcutta: 1979.

CHATTERJI, L, & MOOKERJI, S & CHATTERJI, S K: *Brahmananda K C Sen*: Navavidhan Publication Committee: Bombay: 1934.

CHATTERJI, Lalitmohan & MOOKERJI, Syamprasad & CHATTERJI, Sati Kumar: *Brahmananda Keshub Chunder Sen*: Sind Brahmo Sikhya Sameran: Bombay: 1934.

CHATTOPADHYAYA, D P: *On the Alleged Unity of Religions*: S Radhakrishnan Memorial Lecture: Indian Institute of Advanced Study Shimla, and Manohar Publications: Delhi: 1992.

CHOWDURY, B S: *The New Wine of Jesus: Christ Taught Vedanta*: Tapas Sankar Chowdury: Calcutta: 1982.

CHOWGULE, Ashok: *Shri Klaus Klostermaier on the Ethos and the Future of Hinduism*: Hindu Vivek Kendra: Mumbai: 1995.

COLLETT, Sophia Dobson: *The Life and Letters of Raja Rammohun Roy*: Sadharan Brahmo Samaj: Calcutta: 1962.

CORNELL, Judith: *Amma, A Living Saint*: Judy Piatkus: London: 2001.

COWARD, Harold G, Ed: *Modern Indian Responses to Religious Pluralism*: State University of New York Press: Albany: 1987.

COWARD, Harold: *Hindu-Christian Dialogue: Perspectives and Encounters*: Orbis: New York: 1990.

CRAGG, K: *The Christ and the Faiths*: SPCK: London: 1986.

CUERDON, Helen: *Sai Baba - A Christian's Story*: Global Services Publishing: India: 2001.

DAS, Rasamandala: *The Heart of Hinduism: A Comprehensive Guide for Teachers and Professionals*: ISKCON Educational Services: UK: 2002.

DAS, Sisir Kumar: *The Shadow of the Cross: Christianity and Hinduism in a Colonial Situation*: Munshiram Manoharlal Pubs Private Ltd: Delhi: 1974.

DAVID, M D, Ed: *Western Colonialism in Asia and Christianity*: Himalaya Publishing House: Bombay: 1988.

DAVIE, Ian: *Jesus Purusha*: Lindisfarne Press: New York: 1985.

DEVAMATA, Sister: *Days in an Indian Monastery*: Vedanta Centre: Massachusetts: 1975.

DEVARAJA, N K: *Hinduism and Christianity*: Asia Pub House: Bombay: 1969.

*DIALOGUE AND ALLIANCE*: Journal: Bi-annual: Inter-Religious Federation for World Peace: New York.

DIWAKAR, R R: *Satyagraha: The Power of Truth*: Henry Regnery Co: Illinois: 1948.

DUPOIS, Jacques: *Jesus Christ at the Encounter of World Religions*: Orbis: New York: 1991.

ELLSBERG, Robert, Ed: *Gandhi on Christianity*: Orbis: New York: 1991.

FARQHUHAR, J N: *Modern Religious Movements in India*: Macmillan: New York: 1915.

FRAWLEY, David: *How I Became a Hindu*: Voice of India: Delhi: 2000.

FRAWLEY, David: *Awaken Bharata*: Voice of India: Delhi: 1998.

FRAWLEY, David: *Hinduism: The Eternal Tradition*: Voice of India: New Delhi: 1995.

FRAWLEY, David and RAJARAM, Navaratna S: *Hindutva and the Nation*: Naimisha Research Foundation: Bangalore: 2001.

GANDHI, Arun: *M K Gandhi's Wit and Wisdom:* Gandhi Institute: 1998.

GANDHI, Arun: *Legacy of Love: My Education in the Path of Nonviolence*: North Bay Books: 2003.

GANDHI, Mohandas K: *An Autobiography: The Story of My Experiments with Truth*: Beacon Press: Boston: 1993.

GANDHI, M K: *The Collected Works*: Indian Government: 1968.

GANGULY, Adwaita P: *Vedanta Philosophy for the Unity of Mankind*: Vikas Publishing House: Delhi: 1995.

GHOSE, Sri Aurobindo: *Essays on the Gita*: Arya Pub House: Calcutta: 1926.

GHOSE, Sri Aurobindo: *Sri Aurobindo Birth Centenary Library*: Sri Aurobindo Ashram: Pondicherry: 1972.

GHOSE, Sri Aurobindo: *Complete Works of Sri Aurobindo*: Sri Aurobindo Ashram: 1998f.

GHOSE, Sri Aurobindo: *On Himself*: Sri Aurobindo Ashram Trust: Pondicherry: 1976.

GOEL, Sita Ram: *History of Hindu-Christian Encounters*: Voice of India: Delhi: 1989.

GOEL, Sita Ram: *Catholic Ashrams*: Voice of India: Delhi: 1988.

GOEL, Sita Ram: *How I Became a Hindu*: Voice of India: Delhi: 1982.

GOEL, Sita Ram: *Jesus Christ: An Artifice for Aggression*: Voice of India: Delhi: 1994.

GOEL, Sita Ram: *Hindu Society Under Siege*: Voice of India: Delhi: 1981.

GOEL, Sita Ram: *Defence of Hindu Society*: Voice of India: Delhi: 1983.

GOKAK, V K: *In Defence of Jesus Christ and Other Avatars*: M Gulab Singh & Sons: Lahore: 1979.

GOKULANANDA, Swami: *Our Holy Trinity*: Ramakrishna Mission: Delhi: 1991.

GOSH, Sananda Lal: *Mejda*: Self-Realization Fellowship: Los Angeles: 1980.

GOSWAMI, Satsvarupa dasa: *Srila Prabhupada-lilamrta Vol. 1: A Lifetime in Preparation*: Bhaktivedanta Book Trust: Los Angeles: 1980.

GOSWAMI, Satsvarupa dasa: *Srila Prabhupada-lilamrta Vol. 2: Planting the Seed*: Bhaktivedanta Book Trust: Los Angeles: 1981.

GOSWAMI, Satsvarupa dasa: *Srila Prabhupada-lilamrta Vol. 3: Only He Could Lead Them*: Bhaktivedanta Book Trust: Los Angeles: 1981.

GOSWAMI, Satsvarupa dasa: *Srila Prabhupada-lilamrta Vol. 4: In Every Town and Village*: Bhaktivedanta Book Trust: Los Angeles: 1982.

GOSWAMI, Satsvarupa dasa: *Srila Prabhupada-lilamrta Vol. 5: Let There be a Temple*: Bhaktivedanta Book Trust: Los Angeles: 1983.

GOSWAMI, Satsvarupa Dasa: *Prabhupada: He Built A House In Which The Whole World Can Live*: Bhaktivedanta Book Trust: Los Angeles: 1983.

GRAFE, H: 'Hindu Apologetics at the Beginning of the Protestant Mission Era in India': *Indian Church History Review*: June 1972.

GRIFFITHS, Bede: *A New Vision of Reality*: Collins: Glasgow: 1989.

GRIFFITHS, Paul J: *Christianity through Non-Christian Eyes*: Orbis: New York: 1990.

GYANAMATA, Sri: *God Alone: The Life and Letters of a Saint*: Self-Realization Fellowship: Los Angeles: 1984.

HARSHANANDA, Swami: *Hinduism through Questions and Answers*: Sri Ramakrishna Math: Mylapore: 1984.

HERMAN, A L: *A Brief Introduction to Hinduism*: Westview Press: San Francisco: 1991.

HEWLETT, Lee & NATARAJ, K, trans: *An Eastern View of Jesus Christ: Divine Discourses of Sathya Sai Baba*: Sai Publications: London: 1982.

*HINDUISM TODAY*: Journal: Quarterly: Himalayan Academy: Hawaii.

HISLOP, John S: *My Baba and I*: Birth Day Pub Co: San Diego: 1985.

HISLOP, John S: *Seeking Divinity*, Sri Sathya Sai Books and Publications Trust: Prashaanthi Nilayam: 1998.

HIXON, Lex: *Great Swan: Meetings with Ramakrishna*: Shambala Press Publications: London: 1992.

HOOKER, Roger: *Journey into Varanasi*: Church Missionary Society: UK: 1978.

ISHERWOOD, Christopher: *My Guru and His Disciple*: Eyre Methuen: London: 1980.

*ISKCON COMMUNICATIONS JOURNAL:* Bi-Annual: ISKCON: Oxford.

JOB, G V; CHENCHIAH P et al: *Rethinking Christianity in India*: A N Sundarisanam: Madras: 1938.

JONES, Stanley: *The Christ of the Indian Road*: Hodder and Stoughton: London: 1955.

JORDENS, J T F: *Dayananda Saraswati: His Life and Ideas*: Oxford University Press: Delhi: 1978.

*JOURNAL OF ECUMENICAL STUDIES*: Quarterly: Temple University: USA.

*JOURNAL OF HINDU-CHRISTIAN STUDIES*: Annual: Society for Hindu-Christian Studies: USA and India.

*JOURNAL OF INDIAN COUNCIL OF PHILOSOPHICAL RESEARCH*: Tri-Annual: Indian Council of Philosophical Research: Delhi.

KANU, Victor: *Sai Baba – God Incarnate*: Sawbridge Enterprises: London: 1981.

KASTURI, N: *Sathyam Sivam Sundaram*: Gulab Singh: New Delhi: 1974.

KLOSTERMAIER, Klaus K: *Kristavidya: A Sketch of an Indian Christology*: CISRS: Bangalore: 1967.

KLOSTERMAIER, K: *Hindu and Christian in Vrindaban*: SCM: London: 1969.

KLOSTERMAIER, K: *A Concise Encyclopedia of Hinduism*: Oneworld: Oxford: 1998.

KLOSTERMAIER, Klaus: *A Survey of Hinduism*: Munshiram Manoharlal Publishers Pvt Ltd: Delhi: 1990.

KNITTER, Paul F: *Jesus and the Other Names: Christian Mission and Global Responsibility*: Oneworld: Oxford: 1996.

KOPF, David: *The Brahmo Samaj and the Shaping of the Modern Indian Mind*: Archives Publishers PVT: Delhi: 1988.

KRISHNAMURTI, Mathoor: *Mathoor in Britain*: M P Birla Foundation: Bangalore: 2004.

KRISHNAMURTI, Mathoor: *Gandhi Upanishad*: M P Birla Foundation: Bangalore: 2004.

LAKHANI, Seeta: *Hinduism for Schools*: Vivekananda Centre London Ltd: Wembley: 2005.

LECOCQ, Rhoda P: *The Radical Thinkers*: Sri Aurobindo Ashram Press: Pondicherry: 1969.

LIPNER, Julius J: *Brahmabandhab Upadhyay: The Life and Thought of a Revolutionary*: Oxford University Press: Delhi: 1999.

LITTLE, Gwyneth, Ed: *Meeting Hindus*: Christians Aware: Leicester: 2001.

LOKESWARANANDA, Swami, Ed: *World Thinkers on Ramakrishna-Vivekananda*: Ramakrishna Mission: Calcutta: 1983.

LOKESWARANANDA, Swami: *Studies on Sri Ramakrishna*: Ramakrishna Mission Institute of Culture: Calcutta: 1988.

M: *The Gospel of Sri Ramakrishna*: Trans. Swami Nikhilananda: Ramakrishna-Vivekananda Centre: New York: 1973.

MAHARSHI, Ramana: *Spiritual Instruction*: Sri Ramanasramam: Tirvvannamarai: 1939.

MANICKAM, S: 'Hindu Reaction to Missionary Activities in the Negapatam and Trichinopoly Districts of the Methodists, 1870-1920': *Indian Church History Review*: December 1981.

MARSHALL, P J, Ed: *The British Discovery of Hinduism in the 18th Century*: Cambridge University Press: Cambridge: 1970.

MASON, Peggy & LAING, Ron: *The Embodiment of Love*: Sawbridge: London: 1982.

MATA, Sri Daya: *Finding the Joy within You*: Self-Realization Fellowship: Los Angeles: 1990.

MATA, Sri Daya: *Only Love*: Self-Realization Fellowship: Los Angeles: 1971.

MAZZOLENI, Don Mario: *A Catholic Priest Meets Sai Baba*: Leela Press: USA: 1994.

MONKS OF THE RAMAKRISHNA ORDER: *Meditation*: Ramakrishna Vedanta Centre: London: 1972.

MOOKERJEE, Nanda, Ed: *Sri Ramakrishna in the Eyes of Brahmo and Christian Admirers*: Firma KLM Private Ltd: Calcutta: 1976.

MOZOOMDAR, P C: *The Oriental Christ*: Geo Ellis: Boston: 1883.

MUNDARAN, A M & THEKKEDATH, J: *History of Christianity in India: Volumes I & II*: Church History Association of India: Bangalore: 1982/4.

MURPHET, H: *Man of Miracles*: Samuel Weiser: New York: 1971.

MURTY, K Satchidananda: *Philosophy in India*: Motilal Banarsidass: Delhi: 1991.

MY NEIGHBOUR'S FAITH – AND MINE: World Council of Churches: Geneva: 1986.

NANDA, B R: *Gandhi and Religion*: Gandhi Smriti and Darshan Samiti: New Delhi: 1990.

NIKHILANANDA, Swami: *The Mandukya Upanishad with Gaudapada's Karika*: Sri Ramakrishna Ashram: Mysore: 1974.

NIRLIPTANANDA, Swami: *Defining the Hindu Way of Life*: London Sevashram Sangha: 2006.

NIRODBARAN: *Talks With Sri Aurobindo*: Sri Aurobindo Society: Calcutta: 1985.

PANDEY, R K: *The Concept of Avatars*: BR Pub Corp: Delhi: 1979.

PANIKKAR, Raimon: *The Unknown Christ of Hinduism*: Orbis: New York: 1989.

PARAMANANDA, Swami: *Christ and Oriental Ideas*: Vedanta Centre: Boston: 1923.

PARRINDER, Geoffrey: *Avatar and Incarnation*: Oxford University Press: New York: 1982.

PRABHAVANANDA, Swami: *The Sermon on the Mount according to Vedanta*: Vedanta Press: Hollywood: 1963.

PRABHAVANANDA, Swami: *The Eternal Companion: Spiritual Teachings of Swami Brahmananda*: Sri Ramakrishna Math: Mylapore: 1978.

PRABHAVANANDA, Swami & ISHERWOOD, Christopher, Trans: *Bhagavad-Gita: Song of God*: Phoenix: London: 1947.

PRABHUPADA, Srila: *The Path of Perfection*: Bhaktivedanta Book Trust: Los Angeles: 1979.

PRABHUPADA, Srila: *Conversations with Srila Prabhupada*: Bhaktivedanta Book Trust: Los Angeles: 1991.

PRABHUPADA, Srila: *Letters from Srila Prabhupada*: The Vaisnava Institute: Los Angeles: 1987.

PRABHUPADHA, Srila: *The Science of Self-Realization*: Bhaktivedanta Book Trust: Los Angeles: 1977.

PRABHUPADA, Srila: *Srila Prabhupada Siksamrta* Vol. 2: Bhaktivedanta Book Trust: Los Angeles: 1992.

PRABHUPADA, Srila: *Raja-Vidya: The King of Knowledge*, Bhaktivedanta Book Trust: Culver City: 1973.

PRABHUPADA, Srila: *Bhagavad-Gita As It Is*: Bhaktivedanta Book Trust: Bombay: 1968.

PRESLEY, Priscilla; PRESLEY, Lisa-Marie; and other family members: *Elvis by the Presleys*: Ritz, David, Ed: Century: London: 2005.

PURANI, A B: *The Life of Sri Aurobindo*: Sri Aurobindo Ashram: Pondicherry: 1978.

RADHAKRISHNAN, S: *Eastern Religions and Western Thought*: Oxford University Press: Delhi / Oxford: 1939/1991.

RADHAKRISHNAN, S: *The Hindu View of Life*: Unwin Hyman: London: 1988.

RADHAKRISHNAN, Sarvapelli Gopal: *Radhakrishnan: A Biography*: Oxford University Press: Oxford: 1989.

RAJARAM, N S: *A Hindu View of the World: Essays in the Intellectual Kshatriya Tradition*: Voice of India: Delhi: 1998.

RAJARAM, N S: *Secularism: The New Mask of Fundamentalism: Religious Subversion of Secular Affairs*: Voice of India: Delhi: 1995.

RAMAKRISHNA, Paramahansa: *Sayings of Sri Ramakrishna*: Ramakrishna Math: Mylapore: 1971.

RAMAKRISHNA, Paramahansa: *The Vision of Sri Ramakrishna*: Sri Ramakrishna Math: Madras: Undated.

RAMAKRISHNA, Paramahansa: *Teachings of Sri Ramakrishna*: Advaita Ashram: Calcutta: 1981.

RAMAKRISHNA, Paramahansa: *Studies on Sri Ramakrishna*: Ramakrishna Mission Institute of Culture: Calcutta: 1988.

RAMAKRISHANANDA, Swami: *God and Divine Incarnations*: Sri Ramakrishna Math: Madras: 1947.

RANGANATHANANDA, Swami: *Eternal Values for a Changing Society*: Bharatiya Vidya Bhavan: Bombay: 1971.

RANGANATHANANDA, Swami: *The Christ We Adore*: Advaita Ashram: Mayavati: 1991.

RAO, K L Seshagiri: *Mahatma Gandhi and C F Andrews - A Study in Hindu-Christian Dialogue*: Punjabi University Press: Patiala: 1969.

RAO, K L Seshagiri: *Mahatma Gandhi and Comparative Religion*: Motilal Banarsidass: 1991.

RAVINDRA, Ravi: *The Yoga of the Christ: In the Gospel According to St John*: Element Books: Longmead: 1990.

RICHARDS, Glyn, Ed: *A Source Book of Modern Hinduism*: Curzon Press: London: 1985.

ROBINSON, Gnana, Ed: *Influence of Hinduism on Christianity*: Tamil Nadu Theological Seminary: Madras: 1980.

ROMAIN, Rolland: *The Life of Vivekananda and the Universal Gospel*: Advaita Ashrama: Calcutta: 1988.

ROMAIN, Rolland: *The Life of Ramakrishna*: Advaita Ashrama: Almora: 1954.

SAMARTHA, S J: *The Hindu Response to the Unbound Christ*: CLS: Madras: 1974.

SAMARTHA, S: *One Christ - Many Religions*: Orbis: New York: 1991.

*SANATHANA SARATHI*: Journal: Monthly: Sri Satya Sai Books and Publications Trust: Prasanthi Nilayam.

SARASWATI, Dayananda: S*atyarthaprakasha*: Arya Samaj: Delhi: 1975.

SARKAR, Chandra and SARKAR, H C: *Brahmo Dharma*: Brahmo Samaj Centenary Committee: Calcutta: 1928.

SARKAR, Chandra: *The Religion of the Brahmo Samaj*: Sadharan Brahmo Samaj: Calcutta: 1982.

SASTRI, Sivanath: *History of the Brahmo Samaj*: Sadharan Brahmo Samaj: Calcutta: 1974.

SASTRI, Sivanath: *The Mission of the Brahmo Samaj*: Brahmo Mission Press: Calcutta: 1952.

SASTRI, Sivanath: *Theistic Church of India*: Sadharan Brahmo Samaj: Calcutta: 1966.

SASTRI, Sivanath: *The Brahmo Samaj, Religious Principles and Brief History*: Sadharan Brahmo Samaj: Calcutta: 1915.

SATPRAKASHANANDA, Swami: *Hinduism and Christianity: Jesus Christ and His Teachings in the Light of Vedanta*: Vedanta Society of St Louis: 1975.

SCHWEITZER, Albert: *The Quest for the Historical Jesus*: A & C Black Ltd: London: 1906.

SEAL, Brajendranath: *Rammohun, The Universal Man*: S B Samaj: Calcutta: 1966.

*SELF-REALIZATION*: Journal: Quarterly: Self-Realization Fellowship: Los Angeles.

SEN, K C: *Keshub Speaks*: Navavidhan Trust: Calcutta: 1975.

SEN, K C: *Sadhusamagama*: Navavidhan Publishing Committee: Calcutta. Undated.

SEN, K C: *Keshub Chunder Sen in England: Diaries, Sermons, Addresses and Epistles*: Writers Workshop Greybird Book: Calcutta: 1980.

SEN, K C: *Selected Writings of Bramanand Keshav*: 150th Birth Anniversary Committee: Calcutta: 1990.

SEN, K C: *Spiritual Integration*: Navavidhan Pub Committee: Calcutta: Undated.

SEN, K C: *The New Samhita*: Brahmo Tract Society: Calcutta: 1915.

SEN, K C: *Why New Dispensation: Selections*: Navavidhan Press: Calcutta: 1929.

SEN, K C: *Jeevan Veda*: Nababidhan Trust: Calcutta: 1969.

SEN, K C: *True Faith*: Sadharan Brahmo Samaj: Calcutta: 1976.

*SEVASHRAM NEWS*: Newsletter: Quarterly: London Sevashram Sangha: London.

SHAH, Giriraj: *Gurus, Philosophers, Mystics and Saints of India*: Diamond Pocket Books: Delhi: 2002.

SHARMA, Ram Murti: *Encyclopaedia of Vedanta*: Eastern Book Linkers: Delhi: 1993.

SHARPE, Eric J: *Faith Meets Faith: Some Christian Attitudes to Hinduism in the 19th and 20th Centuries*: SCM: London: 1977.

SINGH, Balbir: *Hinduism and Western Thought*: Arnold Publishers: Delhi: 1991.

SINGH, Karan: *Mundaka Upanishad*: Bharatiya Vidya Bhavan: Bombay: 1987.

SINGH, Karan: *Autobiography*: OUP: India: 1995.

SINGHAL, D P: *India and World Civilizations*: Pan Macmillan Ltd: London: 1993.

SIVANANDA, Swami: *Life and Teachings of Lord Jesus*: Divine Life Society: Rishikesh: 1959.

SIVANANDA, Swami: *Lives of Saints*: Divine Life Society: Rishikesh: 1941.

SONTHEIMER, Gunther D & KULKE, Hermann: *Hinduism Reconsidered*: Manohar Publications: Delhi: 1991.

SPIRITUAL DIARY: Self-Realization Fellowship: Los Angeles: Annual publication.

SRIDURGANANDA, Swami: 'Sri Premananda's Incarnation: A Study': *Prabuddha Bharata*, Vol. 101: August 1996.

STAFFNER, Hans: *The Significance of Jesus Christ in Asia*: Gujurat Sahitya Prakash Anand: India: 1984.

STIEBER, Michael: *Theo-Monistic Mysticism: A Hindu-Christian Companion*: St Martin's Press: New York: 1994.

SUBRAHMANIAN, N: *Hinduism at the Crossroads of History*: Kanishka Publishing House: Delhi: 1993.

SUGITHARAJAH, R S: *Asian Faces of Jesus*: SCM Press: London: 1993.

SWARUP, Ram: *Ramakrishna Mission in Search of a New Identity*: Voice of India: 1986.

SWARUP, Ram: *Hinduism vis-à-vis Christianity and Islam*: Voice of India: Delhi: 1992.

SWARUP, Ram: *On Hinduism: Reviews and Reflections*: Voice of India: Delhi: 2000.

TAGORE, Rabindranath: *Rammohun Roy, The Inaugurator of the Modern Age in India*: Sri Birendra Kumar Roy: Calcutta: 1961.

TAGORE, Saumyendranath: *Raja Rammohun Roy*: Sahitya Akademi: Delhi: 1966.

TAKYI, H K and KHUBCHANDANI, Kishin J, Eds: *Words of Jesus and Sathya Sai Baba*: Prashanti Printers: Bombay: 1986.

TATTVABHUSHAN, Sitanath: *A Manual of Brahma Rituals and Devotions*: S B Samaj: Calcutta: 1924.

THOMAS, M M: *Salvation and Humanisation: Some Crucial issues of the Theology of Mission in Contemporary India*: CLS: Madras: 1971.

THOMAS, M M: *The Acknowledged Christ of the Indian Renaissance*: SCM: London: 1969.

TORWESTEN, Hans: *Ramakrishna and Christ or The Paradox of the Incarnation*: Ramakrishna Vedanta Centre: UK: 1997.

TOYNE, Marcus: *Involved in Mankind: The Life and Message of Vivekananda*: Ramakrishna Vedanta Centre: UK: 1983.

*UNITARIAN UNIVERSALIST CHRISTIAN*: Journal: Annual: Unitarian Universalist Christian Fellowship: USA.

*VEDANTA*: Journal: Bi-monthly: Ramakrishna Vedanta Centre: UK.

VIVEKANANDA, Swami: *Raja-Yoga*: Advaita Ashram: Calcutta: 1970.

VIVEKANANDA, Swami: *Inspired Talks*: Ramakrishna Math: Mylapore: 1969.

VIVEKANANDA, Swami: *Christ the Messenger*: Udbodhan Office: Calcutta: 1989.

VIVEKANANDA, Swami: *Collected Works of Swami Vivekananda*: Advaita Ashrama: Calcutta: 1969.

VIVEKANANDA, Swami: *Vedanta Philosophy*: Ramakrishna Math: Madras: 1969.

VIVEKANANDA, Swami: *Chicago Addresses*: Advaita Ashrama: Calcutta: 1974.

VIVEKANANDA, Swami: *The Yogas and Other Works*: Ramakrishna-Vivekananda Center: New York: 1953.

VIVEKANANDA, Swami: *The Universal Religion*: Ramakrishna Vedanta Centre: UK: 1993.

VIVEKANANDA, Swami: *The Complete Works of Swami Vivekananda*, Vol I-VIII: Advaita Ashrama: Calcutta: 1970.

WALKER, Ethan: *The Mystic Christ: About Christ and Amma*: Devi Press: USA: 2004.

WERNER, Karel: *A Popular Dictionary of Hinduism*: Henry Regnery: Richmond: 1994.

WESSELS, Anton: *Images of Jesus: How Jesus is Perceived and Portrayed in Non-European Cultures*: SCM Press: London: 1990.

*WORLD PARLIAMENT OF RELIGIONS* (Rishikesh 1953): Commemorative Volume: Yoga-Vedanta Forest University: Rishikesh: 1956.

*YOGA INTERNATIONAL*: Journal: Bi-monthly: Himalayan Institute: USA.

YOGANANDA, Paramahansa: *Autobiography of a Yogi*: Self-Realization Fellowship: Los Angeles: 1981.

YOGANANDA, Paramahansa: *Man's Eternal Quest*: Self-Realization Fellowship: Los Angeles: 1976.

YOGANANDA, Paramahansa: *The Divine Romance*: Self-Realization Fellowship: Los Angeles: 1986.

YOGANANDA, Paramahansa: *Journey to Self-Realization: Discovering the Gifts of the Soul*: Self-Realization Fellowship: Los Angeles: 1997.

YOGANANDA, Paramahansa: *Songs of the Soul*: Self-Realization Fellowship: Los Angeles: 1983.

YOGANANDA, Paramahansa: *The Science of Religion*: Self-Realization Fellowship: Los Angeles: 1953.

YOGANANDA, Paramahansa: *God Talks with Arjuna: The Bhagavad Gita: Royal Science of God-Realization*: Self-Realization Fellowship: Los Angeles: 1995.

YOGANANDA, Paramahansa: *The Second Coming of Christ: The Resurrection of the Christ Within You: A revelatory commentary on the original teachings of Jesus*: Self-Realization Fellowship: Los Angeles: 2005.

YOGANANDA, Paramahansa: *Paramahansa Yogananda In Memoriam*: Self-Realization Fellowship: Los Angeles: 1976.

YOGANANDA, Paramahansa: *Whispers from Eternity*: Self-Realization Fellowship: Los Angeles: 1949.

YOGESHANANDA, Swami: *The Vision of Sri Ramakrishna*: Sri Ramakrishna Math: Madras: Undated.

YOUNG, Richard Fox: *Resistant Hinduism: Sanskrit Sources on Anti-Christian Apologetics in Early Nineteenth-Century India*: De Nobili Research Library: Indological Institute, University of Vienna: Vienna: 1981.

YUKTESWAR, Sri: *The Holy Science*: Self-Realization Fellowship: Los Angeles: 1974.

ZIEGENBALG, B: *Thirty Four Conferences between the Danish Missionaries and Malabarian Brahmans (or Heathen Priests) in the East Indies*: Phillips, I B: H, Trans: H Clements, W Fleetwood, J Stephens: London: 1719.

## ONLINE BIBLIOGRAPHIC SOURCES

AGNIVESH, Swami: www.swamiagnivesh.com

AMMACHI: 'Awaken Children, Teachings of Ammachi': www.amma.org/eServices/eNews/

AMMACHI: On Mission: www.ammachi.org/amma/mission.html

ANAND, Swami Sai Sharan: 'Sai Baba and Jesus of Nazareth': www.indiangyan.com/books/otherbooks/sai_baba/sai_baba_and_jesus_of_naz areth.shtml

ANANTHANARAYANAN, N: 'Swami Sivananda, Personality of the Master': Yoga and Inner Peace, an affiliated yoga center with the Sivananda Yoga Vedanta Centers: www.yogapeace.com/personality_of_sivananda.htm

ATHAVALE, Sri: www.goodnewsindia.com/Pages/content/newsclip/swadhyayaPankajJain.html

ARYA, Rohit: 'Dayananada Saraswati – Great Shark of God': India Yogi: www.indiayogi.com/content/indsaints/dayanand.asp

BABA, Sri Satya Sai: Sathya Sai Speaks (SSS): Christmas Discourses: www.sssbpt.info/html/sss.html

CHIDANANDA, Swami: 'Yoga and Christianity': www.dlshq.org/religions/yogachristian.htm

CHIDANANDA, Swami: Guidelines to Illumination: Divine Life Society: 1976: www.rsl.ukans.edu/~pkanagar/divine

DAS, Shaunaka Rishi: 'Jesus through Hindu Eyes': BBC Religion and Ethics: www.bbc.co.uk/religion/religions/hinduism/features/hindu_eyes/index.shtml

DAYANANDA, Swami: Light of Truth: www.aryasamajjamnagar.org/chapterthirteen.htm

DICTIONARY OF THEOLOGY: www.carm.org/dictionary.htm

DIVINE LIFE SOCIETY OF SOUTH AFRICA: www.sivananda.dls.org.za

GHOSE, Sri Aurobindo: Online Resource: www.intyoga.online.fr

GIRI, Swami Krishnananda, 'My Tsunami Experience': www.yogananda-research-centre.org/html/News/NewsHome.html

HINDUISM TODAY: 'How They Prey on Hindus': January 2000: www.imb.org/resources/HPG.pdf

KRISHNANANDA, Swami: 'To Thine Own Self Be True': *Spiritual Import of Religious Festivals*: The Divine Life Society: Sivananda Ashram, Rishikesh: www.swami-krishnananda.org/fest/fest_apx3.html

NIRMALANANDA, Swami: 'The Christ of India': www.atmajyoti.org/spirwrit-the_christ_of_india.asp

RAMBACHAN, Anantanand: 'What Difference does Religious Plurality Make?' www.wcc-coe.org/wcc/what/interreligious/cd34-09.html

RAMBACHAN, Anantanand: 'Visions of Dialogue': www.oikoumene.org/Prof_Anantanand_Rambacha.1053+B6Jkw9.0.html?&MP=935-1037

RAMBACHAN, Anantanand: 'What does it mean to me to be at a college of the church?' www.uniyatra.com/hinduism/presskit/anantspeech.html

RAMBACHAN, Anantanand: 'Towards One World Family': www.wcc-coe.org/wcc/what/interreligious/cd31-04.html

RAVINDRA, Ravi: 'What calls You Pilgrim?': www.metanexus.net

SINGH, Karan: www.karansingh.com

SIVANANDA, Swami: Life and Teachings of Lord Jesus: Divine Life Society: 1959: www.rsl.ukans.edu/~pkanagar/divine/

SIVANANDA, Swami: 'Lord Jesus' and 'Jesus in India': www.dlshq.org/saints/jesus.htm#india

SIVANANDA, Swami: Lives of Saints: Divine Life Society: 1941: www.dlshq.org/saints/jesus.htm

SIVANANDA, Swami: Christianity: www.dlshq.org/religions/christianity.htm#jesus

SIVANANDA, Swami: 'All Religions Are One', Inspiring Talks of Swami Sivananda, 21st September 1948: www.divinelifesociety.org/html/misc/ITGS/september.shtm

SIVANANDA, Swami: 'Jesus and the Modern Man': www.dlshq.org/religions/christianity.htm#man

SUNDARARAJAN, K R: The Hindu Models of Inter-Religious Dialogue: www.interfaithstudies.org/interfaith/hindumodelsdialogue.html

TEMPLETON PRIZE FOR PROGRESS IN RELIGION: www.templetonprize.org/bios_recent.html

# RESOURCES

Links to people and organizations connected to this book

AMERICAN INSTITUTE OF VEDIC STUDIES (David Frawley): PO Box 8357, Santa Fe, NM 87504-8357, USA. www.vedanet.com

ARYA SAMAJ (branches world-wide): www.aryasamaj.com

AUROVILLE: Pondicherry, India. www.auroville.org

BHAKTIVEDANTA BOOK TRUST: PO Box 34074, Los Angeles, CA 90034, USA. www.bbti.org and www.krishna.com

BHARATIYA VIDYA BHAVAN, LONDON: 4a Castletown Road, West Kensington, London W14 9HE, UK. www.bhavan.net

BHARATIYA VIDYA BHAVAN, BANGALORE: 43, Race Course Road, Bangalore - 560 001, India. http://bhavankarnataka.com

BRAHMO SAMAJ (branches world-wide): www.thebrahmosamaj.org

DIVINE LIFE SOCIETY: P.O. Shivanandanagar, Pin Code 249 192, District Tehri-Garhwal, Uttaranchal, India. www.divinelifesociety.org

ENCYCLOPEDIA OF HINDUISM: 937 Assembly Street, #1018 Columbia, SC 29208, USA. www.eh.sc.edu

GLOBAL PEACE INITIATIVE OF WOMEN: 301 East 57 Street, 3rd Floor, New York, NY 10022, USA. www.gpiw.org

HIMALAYAN ACADEMY AND HINDUISM TODAY: 107 Kaholalele Road, Kapaa, HI 96746-9304, USA. www.himalayanacademy.com; www.hinduismtoday.com

INTERNATIONAL SOCIETY FOR KRISHNA CONSCIOUSNESS (ISKCON) (branches round the world): www.iskcon.com

KARAN SINGH: "Mansarovar" 3, Nyaya Marg, Chanakyapuri, New Delhi 110 003, India. www.karansingh.com

LONDON SEVASHRAM SANGHA: 99A Devonport Road, London W12 8PB, UK.

MAHATMA GANDHI ONLINE INFORMATION: Bombay Sarvodaya Mandal, 299, Tardeo Road, Nana Chowk, Bombay 400, India. www.mkgandhi.org

MATA AMRITANANDAMAYI MATH (Ammachi): Amritapuri P.O. Kollam Dt., Kerala, India 690 525. www.amritapuri.org; www.ammachi.org

M K GANDHI INSTITUTE OF NON-VIOLENCE: 650 East Parkway South, Memphis, Tennessee 38104, USA. www.gandhiinstitute.org

OXFORD CENTRE FOR HINDU STUDIES: 15 Magdalen Street, Oxford OX1 3AE, UK. www.ochs.org.uk

PARAMAHANSA YOGANANDA RESEARCH CENTRE: 70, Jatog, Shimla 171 008, India. www.yogananda-research-centre.org

RAMAKRISHNA MATH: Chennai 600 004, India. www.sriramakrishnamath.org

RAMAKRISHNA VEDANTA CENTRE, UK: Blind Lane, Bourne End, Buckinghamshire SL8 5LG, UK. www.vedantauk.com

RELIGIOUS FREEDOM YOUNG ADULT NETWORK: International Association for Religious Freedom, 2 Market Street, Oxford OX1 3EF, UK. www.iarf.net

SARVAPELLI RADHAKRISHNAN: www.cs.memphis.edu/~ramamurt/srk_phil.html

SATYA SAI BABA: Prasanthi Nilayam, Puttaparthi, Anantapur District, Andhra Pradesh State, India. www.sathyasai.org

SELF-REALIZATION FELLOWSHIP: 3880 San Rafael Avenue, Los Angeles, CA 90065-3298, USA. www.yogananda-srf.org

SOCIETY FOR HINDU CHRISTIAN STUDIES: 232 Malloy Hall, University of Notre Dame, Notre Dame, IN 46556, USA and c/o Anand Amaladass, Institute of Philosophy and Culture, 81, Lattice Bridge Road, Thiruvanmiyur, Madras, India 600 041. www.ucalgary.ca/~shcs/

SRI AUROBINDO SOCIETY: Pondicherry, India. www.sriaurobindosociety.org.in

SWAMI AGNIVESH: Banfhua Mukti Morcha, 7 Jantar Mantar Road, New Delhi 110001, India. www.swamiagnivesh.com

VIVEKANANDA CENTRE LONDON: 6 Lea Gardens, Wembley, Middlesex HA9 7SE, UK. www.vivekananda.co.uk

VOICE OF INDIA: 2/18 Ansari Road, New Delhi 110 002, India.

YOGODA SATSANGA SOCIETY OF INDIA: Paramahansa Yogananda Path, Ranchi – 834001, Jharkhand, India. www.yssofindia.org

*Sunset on the Ganges*

# INDEX

## A

Abhedananda, Swami, 48
Adam, William, 13
Advaita, 97, 147, 155
Agnivesh, Swami, 20, 21
ahimsa, 31-34, 41, 186
Akhilananda, Swami, 56, 116
Al Khoi Shia Mosque, 131
Alfassa, Mirra, 26
Ambedkar, Babasheb, 159
Ammachi, 99-101, 144
Amrita Bazar Patrika, 74
Amritandamayi, Mata.
    See Ammachi
anonymous Christians, 8
anonymous Vaishnavas, 88
Anti-Conversion Bill, 109
anugraha, See: grace.
Arya Samaj, 18-21, 162
Athavale, Pandurang Shastri, 144, 145
Atman, 43, 96, 144
atonement, 10, 13, 29, 55, 104
Aurobindo, Sri, 25-31, 39, 48, 79, 139, 140, 147, 156
Auroville, 27, 30
avidya, 117, 149
Ayodha Movement, 162

## B

Babaji, Mahavatar, 65, 66, 69, 71, 77
Barnes, Derek, 128
bhadraloka, 125, 159

Bhagavad Gita, 2, 28, 36, 43, 57, 59, 70, 71, 74, 79, 81, 93, 113, 128, 138, 176
Bhagtani, Hiten, 109
Bhakti, 49, 144, 163
bhaktiferi, 145
Bhaktisiddhanta Saraswati Thakur, 89
Bhaktivinode Thakura, Srila, 133
Bharat, Jael and Sandy, 151
Bharatiya Janata Party, 139
Bharatiya Vidya Bhavan, 62, 113, 128, 143, 158
Bible, 19, 27, 43, 71, 73, 74, 85, 98, 103, 121, 126, 158, 161, 174
Blake, William, 175
Bowe, Peter, 98
Brahma, 12, 19, 22, 87
Brahman, 49, 81, 83, 92, 144, 169, 177
Brahmins, 8, 9, 14
Brahmo Samaj, 12-18, 179
Brihadaranyaka Upanishad, 123, 176
Brother Lawrence, 62
Brown, Judith, 141, 174
Bua, Swami, 152
Buddha, Buddhism, 3, 20, 27-29, 31, 39, 41, 42, 45, 48, 51, 52, 54, 62, 71, 82, 105, 114, 121, 122, 128, 140, 155, 157, 158, 160, 163, 166, 168, 182
Bultmann, Rudolf, 107, 108

## C

Cantwell Smith, Wilfred, 172
Carey, William, 9
Carpenter, J Eslin, 17

caste system, 18, 20, 35, 94, 109, 110, 125, 133, 139, 156, 159, 167
Chaitanya, 16, 84, 88, 155
Chandogya Upanishad, 123, 175
Chidananda, Swami, 43, 44
Chowgule, Ashok, 148
Christ Consciousness, 66-68, 71-73, 77, 169
Christian Testament, 6, 24, 56, 71, 72, 87, 96, 105, 107, 124, 143, 173
Christmas, 42, 52, 66, 69, 77, 95, 97, 100, 109, 110, 132, 138, 143
Christology, 1, 87, 92, 126, 141, 145, 147, 161, 164, 167-170
Clooney, Francis, 50, 51
communalism, 102, 133, 139, 183
Confucianism, 182
conversion, 5, 8, 10, 14, 32, 51, 118, 127, 129, 133-139, 181
Cosmic Christ, 96, 170
Council of Chalcedon, 141
Council of Clermont, 38
Cox, Harvey, 80
Cracknell, Kenneth, 90, 91
Cragg, Kenneth, 146, 168

## D

Da Vinci Code, 72
darshan, 30, 31, 99, 169, 171
Das Gupta, Manoj, 27, 30
Dasgupta, Kalyansri, 17
Day, Atreyee, 110, 111

## A Global Guide to Interfaith: Reflections from around the world
Sandy and Jael Bharat

The media always present the negative aspects of conflicts in which religions are implicated. There are other stories waiting to be told, of dedicated and inspired women and men, working for peace across religious divides.

This book introduces the 'when, why, who, how and what' of interfaith. It is illustrated with personal reflections and photos from more than one hundred interfaith activists and academics from around the world. Topics include the origins of interfaith activity, reasons for and types of, how to organize events, central issues, thoughts about the future, and resources. Many inspiring stories and quotes are included and a broad variety of perspectives are given, providing local, regional and international dimensions.

1-905047-97-5 352pp £19.99 $34.95

---

[This] amazing book will give a wonderful picture of the variety and excitement of this journey of discovery. It tells us something about the world religions, about interfaith history and organizations, how to plan an interfaith meeting and much more – mostly through the words of practitioners. …. There is a Chinese saying, 'Change the world and begin with me.' This book is encouraging evidence that many people have been changed and spiritually enriched by sharing with people of other faiths.
*From the Foreword by Marcus Braybrooke*

It is particularly important that such work can be shared publicly with others so we can celebrate and learn from one another and strengthen the bonds between individuals and communities whilst respecting one another's differences and diversity.
*Judith Lempriere, Head of Cohesion and Faiths Unit, Home Office*

I am so impressed by the wide-ranging people and opinions. This is a great piece of work.
*Madeleine Harman, Trustee, International Interfaith Centre*

# O-BOOKS WORLD RELIGIONS / INTERFAITH

### A Heart for the World: The Interfaith Alternative
Marcus Braybrooke

This book is really needed. This is the blueprint. It has to be cherished. Faith in Jesus is not about creeds or homilies. It is a willingness to imitate Christ - as the Hindu guru Gandhi did so well. A must book to buy. *Peacelinks, IFOR*

1905047436 168pp £12.99 $24.95

### Bringing God Back to Earth
John Hunt

Knowledgeable in theology, philosophy, science and history, time and again it is remarkable how he brings the important issues into relation with one another... thought provoking in almost every sentence, difficult to put down. *Faith and Freedom*

1903816815 320pp £9.99 $14.95

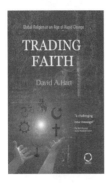

### Trading Faith: Global Religion in an Age of Rapid Change
David Hart

Argues boldly that the metaphor of trading provides the most useful model for religious exchanges in a world of rapid change. It is the inspiring biography of an intensely spiritual man with a great sense of humour who has chosen an unusual and courageous religious path. *Dr Anna King, Lecturer in Hinduism, University of Winchester*

1905047967 260pp £10.99 $24.95

### Transcending Terror: A history of our spiritual quest and the challenge of the new millennium
Ian Hackett

A return to the core values of all our faiths, putting aside partisanship and the desire to dominate is the only sure way forward, in order to "allow both our human and spiritual quests to continue as one family sharing one world." *Westminster Interfaith*

190381674 320pp £12.99 $19.95

# OTHER BOOKS BY SANDY AND JAEL BHARAT

**Touched by Truth: A Contemporary Hindu Anthology**
Sandy and Jael Bharat (Compiled/Edited by)
Sessions of York September 2006

Here are very personal reflections on ways in which so many
have found, within the Hindu umbrella, spiritual enlightenment,
help on the journey and answers to questions and heart
longings. Gurus, teachers and sacred books within Hinduism
today still provide a rich fountain of wisdom on which to draw
for those who yearn to be 'Touched by Truth.' Inspirational.
*Gwyneth Little, Editor of Meeting Hindus.*

1-85072-355-9 176pp £8 $14

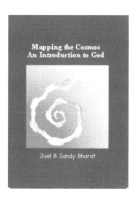

**Mapping the Cosmos: An Introduction to God**
Jael and Sandy Bharat
Sessions of York January 2006.

A stimulating read, providing much food for thought, both
for the newcomer to the reading of spiritual literature and
even for the jaded pallet of one who has read many books on
spiritual life. *Vedanta*

It's inspiring, thought provoking, hope-filled and an
important book for anybody concerned about the future of
humanity. *Yoga Chicago.*

1-85072-341-9 45pp £4 $6

*For more information: www.spiritualityfordailylife.com*

# O

is a symbol of the world,
of oneness and unity. O Books
explores the many paths of whole-
ness and spiritual understanding which
different traditions have developed down
the ages. It aims to bring this knowledge in
accessible form, to a general readership, providing practical spirituality to today's seekers.

For the full list of over 200 titles covering:
ACADEMIC/THEOLOGY • ANGELS • ASTROLOGY/
NUMEROLOGY • BIOGRAPHY/AUTOBIOGRAPHY
• BUDDHISM/ENLIGHTENMENT • BUSINESS/LEADERSHIP/
WISDOM • CELTIC/DRUID/PAGAN • CHANNELLING
• CHRISTIANITY; EARLY • CHRISTIANITY; TRADITIONAL
• CHRISTIANITY; PROGRESSIVE • CHRISTIANITY;
DEVOTIONAL • CHILDREN'S SPIRITUALITY • CHILDREN'S
BIBLE STORIES • CHILDREN'S BOARD/NOVELTY • CREATIVE
SPIRITUALITY • CURRENT AFFAIRS/RELIGIOUS • ECONOMY/
POLITICS/SUSTAINABILITY • ENVIRONMENT/EARTH
• FICTION • GODDESS/FEMININE • HEALTH/FITNESS
• HEALING/REIKI • HINDUISM/ADVAITA/VEDANTA
• HISTORY/ARCHAEOLOGY • HOLISTIC SPIRITUALITY
• INTERFAITH/ECUMENICAL • ISLAM/SUFISM
• JUDAISM/CHRISTIANITY • MEDITATION/PRAYER
• MYSTERY/PARANORMAL • MYSTICISM • MYTHS
• POETRY • RELATIONSHIPS/LOVE • RELIGION/
PHILOSOPHY • SCHOOL TITLES • SCIENCE/
RELIGION • SELF-HELP/PSYCHOLOGY
• SPIRITUAL SEARCH • WORLD
RELIGIONS/SCRIPTURES • YOGA

Please visit our website,
www.O-books.net